Live to Inspire

How to achieve your goals in life and reach your full potential!

DAVID COLEMAN

Website: www.davidcolemangb.co.uk

Enquiries: david.coleman@olympian.org

ISBN: 978-1-5272-4554-9

Instagram: @davecoleman24

First published 2019

Acknowledgements

Thank you to my parents for supporting me over the years and not questioning my decisions too much.

To everyone that told me I couldn't do this. Enjoy reading.

All my training partners from T69; Andy, Jade, Chris, Simon.

My team mates from Bobsleigh; Ben, Will, Jim, Henry, Lamin, Brad, Keith, Andy, Lee, Chris, John, Bruce, Stu, Jacko, Joel, Craig (sorry/not sorry about your back).

For the students who I have taught over the years, past present and future. You will forever be part of my legacy and I thank you for the challenges that you present me daily.

Thanks to Brett for always being there when the Ulcerative Colitis got the better of us.

To Blake for supporting me in my transition from a lifestyle of an elite athlete to applying my skills in day to day life. It has been a tough journey and long may it continue.

Finally, thank you to you for buying my book and being interested in what I have to say. I genuinely hope that my journey and experiences will provide some comfort and guidance to you as to how you can live your dreams, reach your goals and be the best version of yourself.

Preface

The main purpose of this book is to inspire people to reach their full potential in life. This is through the culmination of lessons and skills I have learnt throughout my life, both as an elite athlete in two different sports and my professional career as a teacher.

I have educated myself through different mediums then applied the skills and mindset that has allowed me to build as an individual and live my life to my full potential, whilst also inspiring others. I will explain these life lessons and how I learned then adapted them to my day to day life. I will divulge personal strategies that you can apply to your life and the goals that you desire.

Please note that there are no quick fixes.

As humans, we are always looking for a simple and easy solution. You know the "15-minute meals" which take 30 minutes to prepare or "8 weeks to a 6 pack" plan that will take you 12 weeks to get into a position to be able to undertake the 8-week plan. So, do not expect immediate results, but more how to make changes that will last for a long time, and how small changes can not only help you but also those around you.

Some actions that you can apply to your life will give you some instant gratification. However in order to create greater longevity that will require you to delay gratification. There has been a lot of research done on this are and that I will explain later in the book.

The advice and strategies are ones that I have developed and applied so I would advise that you do the same. This will be interspersed with quotes and summary points to help with motivation and making a change in whatever aspect you desire or simply the day to day life that you lead. Put simply, giving you a kick up the bum and empowering you to hold yourself accountable and your happiness before others, but not exclusively.

Some methods are based around physical actions that you can apply every day, which you will need to read on to find out. These are actions that I personally live by and I can assure you that they do work. The actions become significantly effective when combined with a positive mindset. This is the part that requires delayed gratification and personal accountability. Both factors take time and practice to not only develop and learn but also to become ingrained in your daily routine. Throughout my career as an athlete, coach, and teacher I have supported the growth and development of clients to achieve their desired goals.

During my career as an international athlete, I have learnt and applied a wide range of knowledge around performance and motivation. Having personally been through everything that I deliver, I know what it takes. Time is our most precious commodity. Making training sessions and decisions as effective as possible, on a daily basis, and without having to make huge sacrifices, is key.

Personal Sporting Achievements & Qualifications

Summer Olympic Trials - Discus 2008, 2012, 2016

Team GB Winter Olympian - Bobsleigh 2014, World Championships 2013, Winter Olympic Trails 2018

PGCE, MSc Sport and Exercise Science, BSc Science in Health Exercise and Sport

My story and how it's taught me the best way to help people

During my early school years, I was always bigger than most of the other kids and was never of great academic potential. So I found my escape from studious life and stress through the medium of sport. Whilst at primary school I was allowed to play a wide range of sports, as one does, from football, rugby and badminton in the winter through to cricket, athletics and golf – all of which I was able to excel at, and quickly too.

During one lunchtime training session, my teacher who was taking the session said to me that if I threw the javelin 20 meters then I could be selected for the county school competition, the biggest athletics competition on the school calendar.

This was my very first exposure to a "challenge" or a goal and I made sure that I did whatever it took for me to throw that magical 20 meters. It was during a PE lesson that I achieved the selection distance and ultimately was selected to represent the school at an athletics competition. The self-gratification of having accomplished the target set for me with nothing other than my tenacity to prove to my teacher that I could surpass the distance.

However, at the competition, I was a long distance away from other athletes and did not place. This was devastating for me and at the time I was not sure how to deal with the frustration and huge disappointment of not achieving my intention and also letting others down - my parents, my school and my friends. This was my first failure.

Upon returning to school the following year I continued to throw the javelin as it was something that I enjoyed and made me happy. As with most things in life, if it makes you happy then you shouldn't at any point feel bad about doing it. I will go into happiness later on in the book. As I had begun to specialise as a thrower within athletics, chiefly for the reasons that I was shocking at running anything more than 30 meters and could throw things quite a long way, I played to my strengths.

I watched some older students throwing a discus during a lesson and I went to the same PE teacher to ask if I could have a go at the discus. It was at this point, I believe that changed my training and sporting outlook for the rest of my career. He said to me "You are only allowed to throw the discus in year 7, you can't do it now."

I found this response most perplexing as I had some credibility as a thrower for the school already, and it was strange that I wasn't allowed to. Even more strange was that it was ok for me to throw a spear but not allowed to throw a plate? As humans, we learn by asking questions and finding out answers to problems. The answer that I received did not help me in any way to develop and learn. So it was at this point I took myself down to my local athletics club, picked up a discus, took myself into the cage and started to throw with no idea about technique or specifics related to the event. Some coaches encouraged me to be part of the track squad and I diligently did my stint for a few sessions, again highlighting that running was not for me.

For the next few years, my parents drove me to the athletics track three times a week and I stubbornly kept throwing to prove to my teacher that I could throw the discus and I would be damn good at it. Ultimately I coached myself to a bronze medal at my first national schools' championships where I represented my county. The rest is history.....

Thought...How does anyone else know what you are capable of? You know your limits and what you want to achieve

What I learnt from this experience is that people will always tell you that you can't do something or that you aren't allowed to do what you want.

Even if you don't know what your limits are, do not be afraid to find them. From experience, you will be able to do more than you originally thought you can.

When responding to individuals who are not supportive of you and your desires to achieve your goals, is this: find a way that will best fit your lifestyle that will contribute to reaching your goal. As long as you have a goal and a direction to work towards you can take steps towards it by achieving 1% every day. Cumulative all these 1%s will add up, if you do 1% a day then at the end of a week you will be 7% closer to what you desire. This generates a greater rate of adherence towards the end goal as opposed to trying to 10% in a day and falling short then feeling like you aren't making progress.

I was always told that I couldn't do something or I wasn't allowed to because I was too young. This only fuelled my fire to be the best possible version of myself.

It has always been my dream to get to an Olympic games and represent my country at the highest level in sport. The seed for this was planted when I was 6 years old during the 1992 Barcelona Olympics, you can work out how old I am now. My parents had a shop in London that was next to an off-license and I always spent most of my summer holidays playing in the office and getting treats from next door. One day I went to the off-license to get a can of coke and the man gave me a Barcelona 1992 Olympic pin badge, I still have it to this day and it is by my bed.

I can vividly remember watching Linford Christie, Steve Backley and Sally Gunnell and the euphoria they displayed when they had competed and achieved. I told myself that I needed some of that in my life and I had thought for at least 15 years that discus was the answer.

Having developed as an athlete I had made significant progress in strength, speed, and power in order to see me get to a career high of top 200 in the world for discus around the time of London 2012. I found more people noticed me from the local press and the crazy things I was doing in my gym at home. One gentleman spoke to me and said that he used to throw the discus and that we should do a session together. If I'm honest I was a little sceptical about this so went home and googled the man. It turns out he competed at the Olympics, World, European and Commonwealth championships for Great Britain and between him and his brother had one multiple National titles for both shot putt and discus.

As if this wasn't enough he was also the strongest man in Britain in 1986, the year which I was born. As I continued to read about this amazing athlete it mentioned that he had also competed in Bobsleigh.

I followed the links to the British Bobsleigh website and found that they had a Talent ID section. Being confident in my abilities I emailed the performance director and told him that I could do all of the tests. Much to my surprise I had an immediate response which I was asked, not in as many words, to prove it. So I sent a link to my national discus rankings and all of my performances from years gone by. The reply I received was a formal invitation to attend trials for the Great Britain Bobsleigh team. This was in 2012 after the London Olympic trails.

Upon arriving at the event I bumped into an old university friend from my undergraduate degree. To both of our surprise, we had both been invited to try out. This friendship is still strong to this day and we regularly help others with training and coaching.

As I stated to the director originally I passed all of the tests along with 3 others and in a final meeting where we were told the next stages of selection and requirements. He mentioned to us that he "genuinely believe that you can go all the way". This gave me motivation and encouragement to chase the dream of being a Team GB Winter Olympian - Bobsleigh 2014.

This was the "easy part". As with most things in life, we are thrown curve balls and challenges and we develop resilience along with mental toughness and tenacity in order to overcome them.

For me, I was dealt a curveball in the form of ulcerative colitis, an inflammatory bowel condition with no known cure. Symptoms can include chronic fatigue, the rapid loss of weight, food allergies, loss of blood, stomach cramps. Symptoms can be exacerbated during times of stress, however, it is worth noting that for people who suffer from the condition can have different triggers and symptoms vary significantly.

This challenge was "given" to me 6 months before the Winter Olympic selections.

I had to prove myself throughout the upcoming season as the Winter Olympics are the last race of the bobsleigh season. I was prescribed some catabolic steroids in order to reduce the inflammation of the ulcers which have from along the whole length of my colon. One issue with catabolic steroids and being an athlete representing your country is the doping tests. I had to acquire medical clearance/approval from multiple international governing bodies so that it was ok for me to take the medication.

During the first round of selections for the Olympics, I was unsuccessful. I was going to appeal the decision as I was one of the only athletes who had fulfilled all of the selection criteria. However, this incurred a cost which was insurmountable at the time. I returned home with a similar mindset to that I had experienced as a child throwing the javelin - frustration and huge disappointment of not achieving my potential and also letting others down who had supported me in all aspects of my life.

Fortunately, this set back allowed me to attend my sister's wedding and evaluate the decisions I had made. During this week I had a text from my old university friend who had been selected in the first round and he told me to "stay light and stay fit". I subsequently found out that one of the team had become injured and was unable to compete at the games so they needed a replacement spare. That evening I received a message from the director to call him on a Russian phone number. However, he had omitted the last digit and I ended up calling a lot of random Russian people. When I eventually got through he asked me "Would you like to come to the Olympics?" I said yes and then he told me that I would be on a plane in the morning.

One of the conditions of attending the games as a spare was that I had to be able to fit into either the GB1 or GB2 bobsleigh. So I had to lose over a stone or 7kg in 12 days. I made sure that I did this and it was through the incurable condition that I now live with every day that I was able to do this.

Please do not try to do this amount of weight loss, it is extremely dangerous and I lost a lot of strength and blood in the process.

As an athlete, you want to be the best version of yourself and show that to people through the medium of your chosen sport. I have been lucky enough to do this at very high levels in two sports over many years. However, with age comes more challenges and the body takes longer to adapt and recover from training.

Being impatient, with some aspects of my life, individual and someone who refuses to live a mundane life. We all need a goal, purpose, direction or challenge to work towards. For me, this came from a conversation I had with one of my bobsleigh teammates post Winter Olympics. We discussed a range of topics including happiness and where we both saw ourselves in the future, some people like to call it a 5 year plan but I will discuss this in another chapter.

Refuse to let others set their limitations on you and your abilities. To those that do push their own limits on you, prove them wrong.

Initially, you may feel that this will come across as arrogant and self-centred. That is fine. The difference between arrogance and confidence is that you are able to back up your "arrogance" with evidence. Time is precious and the most valuable commodity that you possess.

Invest your time in yourself

I decided to look through the Guinness World Records website and see if there were any records that I might be able to attempt, gym-related of course, as it makes sense to work to your strengths – literally. For many years I trained on my own and learnt as much as I could from books, magazines, videos and asking for advice from others. While watching others I regularly wondered how?! Through endless practice and at times two or even three sessions a day.

Upon the first review, I came across a 24 hour individual squat world record. For many years I have squatted and so thought I could have an attempt at it. Initially, you have to apply to Guinness to attempt the record which they will either accept or decline. I got approval to attempt the 24hour squat record which proceeded with an extensive list of very detailed specific criteria and rules which have to be followed for the attempt to be valid. Which in itself is more complex than the actual attempt itself.

I reviewed footage of the current attempt on YouTube and checked with my local gym along with friends and family to see if they were able to support me. As it turns out there was an overwhelming number of people who came to support and even donated towards fundraising for prostate cancer and Crohn's and Colitis UK. Before the attempt, I had sat down with my computer and calculated weight, sets, reps, rest, timings for each hour. I was confident in my ability to have a solid attempt at breaking the record and doing something that nobody else in the world has ever done, while also seeing what I can get my body to do. This was my motivation.

There were several factors that I had MASSIVELY underestimated along with the current record not following the exact rules. The result of which, at the time of writing this is still under review of the evidence, I was unsuccessful in my attempt at the 24 hour record. Upon review of the attempt and what I had lifted, I made a decision to still submit all of my evidence for review and apply for the 12 hour World Record. I lifted, with my legs, 137542kg in 9 hours. This is very nearly the same as an unladen Boeing 747. During the 9 hours and 1604 repetitions I did, I ended up in a very dark place mentally as well as physically. For example some of the physical pain I can distinctly remember two points during the attempt when I thought that my heart was going to stop I was in that much pain. I suffered from severe cramps in both quads, hamstrings, and calves to give some context as to the extent to which I push my boundaries. I was unable to drive, use the toilet, any stairs up or down were a no go. Plus walking took me at least 4 days before I could do more than a "shuffle".

Mentally I started excited, limited and full of determination, but by the 9th hour, I still had the same mindset. Excited to prove to people what I could do. Motivated to help other people around me achieve their own goals. Determined to set a record, determined to do something that no one else in the whole world has done before. Determined to find my boundaries.

The mental tenacity, resilience, and toughness I learnt about myself was crazy because it goes to show that no matter what you want in life, no matter how hard it is. If you truly want something, deep down you will find a way of getting it and doing whatever you have to do. As always, whether you believe it or not, it will be your body that lets you down far earlier than your mind will.

It was from this attempt that my friend whom I had discussed the "5 year plan" with got in touch as he and a team had plans to attempt the 24 hour team deadlift, a deadlift is where you put weight on to a bar and pick it up from the floor to mid-thigh and then put it down, world record. He invited me into the team!

Once again this gave me a new focus in the gym and my life while also allowing me to focus on something that is outside of work and life. Giving me a distraction from the day to day living. As with my individual attempt, there is an extensive list of rules and guidelines that must be adhered to for the attempt to be approved. Just for reference if you do attempt a World Record and want someone from Guinness to come to check everything they do charge you a lot of money! The team of 12 will be attempting the record on the 4th of May. Around 10 days before when my year 11 students start their Science GCSE exams.

Preparation for both of these attempts, squat and deadlift, took many months and years of hard work in the gym and outside of the gym. Nutrition, lifestyle, medical challenges, recovery. This list can go on as well as the famous, blood sweat and tears.

The mindset that I developed for the attempts was one based around the single limiting factor that we all have in our lives. YOU. It does not make any difference in the time, temperature, conditions, mood, etc. The sole factor that can determine if you want to be successful at something is you and your mind. As I mentioned before other people will always set their limitations on you because they know that they can't do it themselves so therefore you mustn't be able to do it either. Personally, this irritates me, how do you know what I am or am not capable of. Let me show you and let me find out what the boundaries, NOT limitations, are because then you can surpass them and achieve things that YOU didn't think you could do.

Control the controllables.

Do everything in your power that will ensure that when it comes down to the moment/goal you know that whatever the outcome is. You have done everything you can do to make sure you can deliver the best possible outcome that is a reflection of your tenacity and hard work. If at the end of the moment you do not get the results that you had anticipated then you can still hold your head high in the knowledge that there is nothing else you could have done.

If you think that there is more then you will need to reflect on areas for development. Areas that maybe we're not as strong or good as others. NOTE - not weakness or bad bits. Areas that can be improved.

Contents

Success means doing the best we can with what we have. Success is a personal standard that we strive to achieve and become the best possible version of ourselves.

CHAPTER 1 - HAPPINESS

Over the years, I've spent many many hours of my life trying to work out how to be happy and what makes me happy. This has resulted in the usual examples of purchasing nice things, having relationships and achievements within sport and or at work. However, this is not always entirely the case or a solution.

There is an age old cliché where you only know when you're at the top when you're on the way down and you know when you've got to the bottom when you are on the way up. But at no point in time do you know the highs and the lows that you are currently at.

What's your definition of happiness? Research in the field of positive psychology and happiness often define a happy person as someone who experiences frequent positive emotions, such as joy, interest, and pride, and infrequent (though not absent) negative emotions, such as sadness, anxiety, and anger (Lyubomirsky et al., 2005). Happiness has also been said to relate to life satisfaction, appreciation of life, moments of pleasure, but overall it has to do with the positive experience of emotions.

The key to these definitions is that positive emotions do not indicate the absence of negative emotions. A "happy person" experience the spectrum of emotions just like anybody else, but the frequency with which they experience the negative ones may differ. It could be that a happy person doesn't experience as many negative emotions because they process it differently or they may find meaning in a way others have not.

Using the phrase happy person is probably incorrect because it assumes that they are naturally happy or that positive things happen to them more often than it does to others. Nobody is immune to life's stressors, but the question is whether you see those stressors as moments of opposition or moments of opportunity. How do see a glass half full or half empty? A happy person is one who will see the same glass but view it as still having the opportunity to have a drink.

22

Regardless of where you are on the happiness spectrum, each person has their way of defining happiness. Philosophers, actors, politicians, and everybody in between have all weighed in on their view of happiness.

As an individual who likes to get shit done and doesn't wait for people to tell them what you can and can't do - finding happiness and being happy within oneself I found by undertaking multiple challenges at the same time. This allowed me to challenge not only myself my abilities but also to prove people wrong.

Example being a job and looking for promotion my new job title what increasing pay many times people will tell you that it will come next year or next month and with more experience there is justification. However, do not let people sit these limitations upon you. There are a lot of people that will set their limitations on you because they feel that they were unable to do what you are able to do. I truly believe if you feel you are capable of doing something and achieving something then you should do it. No questions asked and with no time wasted, take action and do it. No matter what happens at the end of the day, if you're taking action in a quest to find happiness whether the outcome is positive or not you will have achieved and you will have found the answer to the question that you originally thought or told what not able to do.

In my journey as an athlete to the highest stage the athlete ever dreams of competing, I was diagnosed with an incurable condition. This goes without saying that it was a physical limitation and came with a few mental limitations as well. Having come so far within my sports career I was not prepared to be limited or have limitations placed upon me so close to the dream. I took various steps to ensure that all available resources to me teammates from coaches doctors the Medication and to the clearance from National governing body international governing body and the Olympic Association to take the medication for my condition.

Having been through many selection processes, in both my professional and sporting career, I'm very aware of the hard work and tenacity that everybody goes through to get where they want. At the point in time when a decision is made about your abilities characteristics suitability for a position, this is one of a subjective nature and has factors that are out of your control.

Taking steps to find answers about why decisions were made can sometimes be very destructive and unfulfilling as you will never find the true answers. When speaking to other people about decisions are made all my abilities I was told someone's mantra. This is the first mantra I'd ever heard, being naïve and never having heard of water mantra is or was is stay with me I will do forever.

The mentoring question I apply to everyday life, be it personal or professional sporting, is control the controllables. It is very easy to blame others for being unhappy or decision has not gone your way. When this happens if you have control over the factors that would influence the outcome can you have every right to be unhappy with the outcome? When you have no control over these factors there is nothing you can do about it and therefore cannot blame or pursue unhappiness as a result.

This led me to develop the concept of happiness and what it is to be happy. Being happy is very subjective and different people become happy in different ways. Upon undertaking more research into happiness delivery to find that there are four hormones associated with happiness. Serotonin, oxytocin, dopamine, and endorphins.

Serotonin is a hormone that is more sensitive to die at any other neurotransmitter and helps to stabilise one's mood. Serotonin is most commonly believed to be a neurotransmitter, although some consider it to be a hormone. It is produced in the intestines and the brain. It is also present in the blood platelets and the central nervous system (CNS).

As it occurs widely throughout the body, it is believed to influence a variety of body and psychological functions. Serotonin cannot cross the blood-brain barrier, so any serotonin that is used inside the brain must be produced inside the brain.

Depression has been linked to low levels of serotonin, but whether this contributes to depression or results from it remains unclear. Low levels of serotonin have been linked with poor memory and low mood. You may also lead to the following symptoms: craving for sweet or starchy foods, difficulty sleeping, low self-esteem, anxiety, aggression. These are common symptoms of depression, but there appears to be little evidence linking them directly to low serotonin levels.

However, endorphins work as painkillers these can be incredibly addictive and the majority of athletes and gym goers will experience this after they have been to training or completed some exercise. The body's response to endorphins feeds the addiction and buzz the gym goers receive from completing work out and so continue to exercise harder and longer.

Both serotonin and endorphins are chemicals are produced by your body one on an individual basis, these require no external input from other people or situations.

Oxytocin is a chemical that your body will release during sex childbirth and lactation it is known as the Love hormone and can also be very addictive. The final chemical that your body will release is dopamine this is known as the reward chemical which is released during pleasurable situations, for example, physical contact or having a hug.

Depression has been linked to low levels of serotonin, but whether this contributes to depression or results from it remains unclear. Low levels of serotonin have been linked with poor memory and low mood. You may also lead to the following symptoms: craving for sweet or starchy foods, difficulty sleeping, low self-esteem, anxiety, aggression. These are common symptoms of depression, but there appears to be little evidence linking them directly to low serotonin levels.

Serotonin is most commonly believed to be a neurotransmitter, although some consider it to be a hormone. It is produced in the intestines and the brain. It is also present in the blood platelets and the central nervous system (CNS). As it occurs widely throughout the body, it is believed to influence a variety of body and psychological functions. Serotonin cannot cross the blood-brain barrier, so any serotonin that is used inside the brain must be produced inside the brain.

The last two chemicals oxytocin and dopamine are released as a result of interaction with other people. We can all produce dopamine more effectively than serotonin or endorphins. The simple act of picking up someone's wallet handing it back to them, doing a good deed, will produce dopamine for both the person returning the wallet and also anyone else who witnesses the act. Another example is in team sports whether you win or lose is a team every person Will release more dopamine and oxytocin. Because you are part of a team you've helped each other and losing can produce a greater amount of chemicals within your body that produces more happiness and bind the team together more. You only have to look at football teams and the fans to see how they respond to win or loss after a match.

From me, this poses another question as to why people a lot more helpful and caring towards each other as we all receive happiness and a reward from these acts.

This also tells me that everyone can be happy regardless of the situation.

Happiness is your ability to solve problems.

If it was a situation in your professional career that you do not like and makes you unhappy. Once resolved the problem you'll feel as though you have accomplished and achieved, resulting in a state of happiness.

In a sporting situation if you're losing the game the match or even a training session is going well you all know but to resolve the unhappy status you will have to solve the problem. This can be through; talking to your coach, changing your diet, seeing the doctor, changing the program or even simply changing the playlist that you listen to during your session.

On the face of having multiple problems to solve any one time, it can be a daunting and scary concept as we are very resistant to change. However, having these multiple challenges can be a very positive learning and life changing experience and one that will develop your mindset and self-belief that you are powerful beyond measure and you can achieve anything that you want. Happiness is a state of mind that is the result of solving problems.

When you see other people around you as "happier", discussed further in the next chapter. I would always stop before assuming that they are in a constant state of euphoria and ask them "Are you happy?" This is a very eye opening question as often if someone has made their millions or "has everything" they may still feel empty and incomplete. Hence referring back to my original thought of, happiness is a result of your ability to solve problems.

Key learning points.

- **Winning or losing as part of a team can make you happy**
- **It is important to help others**
- **Reward yourself**
- **Do what makes you happy**
- **Solving problems can lead to happiness**

You have to see the big picture. Its not about winning or losing. Its about everyday hard work and thriving on a challenge. Don't be afraid of the challenge.

CHAPTER 2 - OVERCOMING NEGATIVITY

What is negativity?

Do you see the glass as half empty? Are you around people at work or friendship circles that always seem to find fault? How often do you hear others moan about something that is out of their control? Do you start to notice others body language, defensive, short and abrupt response, passive aggressive, controlling?

What is a negative person and why are they negative? Here is a definition of negativity from the web dictionary:

"Negativity is a tendency to be downbeat, disagreeable, and sceptical. It's a pessimistic attitude that always expects the worst. Negative outcomes are bad outcomes like losing a game, getting a disease, suffering an injury, or getting something stolen."

This description of negativity sounds very much like sadness, irritability, hopelessness and catastrophic thinking that is part of depression or anxiety. Depression and anxiety are often intertwined in the same person.

I can understand avoiding "toxic" people such as bullies, sociopaths, conflict instigators and destroyers of the good. The medical recommendation in many cases is to do just that – walk away, don't look back and hang up the phone if you answer it. However, "negative" people, unlike "toxic" people, maybe more about vulnerability and less about vice. The label seems unfair if there is underlying frailty. So negativity is not necessarily about ingrained disposition. It could be a derailment.

A person might be positive but have been ransacked. An optimistic, more naturally cheery person can be thwacked by circumstances, chronic or acute, and appear to be an Eeyore when they are a Pooh. We have all been there. A breakup, homesickness, illness, betrayal, job loss, a biological illness or a lifetime of little assaults/empathic flaws on the part of caregivers take a toll.

It is very difficult to smile when you want to cry and it is a great relief when you can tell someone what is going on. All this to say that the "negative" person may be suffering, and could use reach-out rather than stay-away. If their despair shows up in the form of irritability or even hostility, it may be worth trying to perceive the deeper issue. It might help them personally, enhance the interpersonal dynamic and improve their environment. Pessimistic leanings do exist but even this is not necessarily a negative. These people are good preparers, critical thinkers and serious planners.

Negativity is all around us all the time and with continued exposure to it can impact our lives and how we live each day. When asked, can you name 1 thing that you like about yourself? I often ask this question to my students, most of them find it quite challenging. The reason for this is that nobody wants to come across as arrogant or cocky.

There is a line between confidence and arrogance and that is simply down to your ability to back up or evidence your "arrogance" and thus turning it into confidence. A simple strategy that I use to give myself confidence is to look in the mirror. Sounds strange but if you are happy with who and what you see in the mirror then that is a good way to start your happy. This being said if you are not happy with who and what you see in the mirror than as Michael Jackson said in his sounds "Man in the mirror" – make a change. You have the ability and the power to make a decision and change whatever it is that you don't like in the mirror.

Be proud of who you are and what you stand for

Every morning when you wake up, look in the mirror and be thankful that you are you. There is only one of you in the world and no one can take that away from you. Embrace the self-confidence and what it is that you stand for, what it is that you believe in.

For example, during my teacher training, we discussed good or nice classes and the same for students. What they would look like, how they would work. I am fairly sure that you would come up with the same ideologies that we did: polite, punctual, tenacious, committed, creative, well mannered, inquisitive, respectful. While the class would also reflect these values and personality traits. Students regularly asking for support or even more work if the content was too easy. These are all the positives and can also be reflected in the way a professional may approach a task or even situation.

As individuals, our perceptions and predicted outcomes of a situation are governed by prior experiences and learning. So when you wake up feeling positive and you tell yourself that it is going to be a good day with multiple success and achievements you have already set your outlook to that of a positive one.

This is where the but or however comes in. If you know that a situation may result in a negative outcome for yourself or potentially others it may skew your predicted outcomes and even your approach towards how you will deal with this situation.

As trainee teachers, we discussed the possibility of a challenging student and or class. For instance the last lesson on a Friday, you are tired, the class is tired, it's a nice warm sunny day, the weekend is an hour away.

What would you do? Will the work rate be high as always? Students asking for more challenging work? Students supporting others? Or would it be the complete opposite with the teacher in fear of how the class is going to behave? If you can face your biggest fear than the smaller worries and fears will fall away and seem insignificant. Changing your mindset to that of a positive one initially can be difficult for many. It is no more complicated than waking up and looking at yourself in the mirror. If you pre-empt a situation in your life, profession, sport then the chances are that you will have already set that limitation on the outcome.

Preconceptions and being positive, even if it is forced, can still result in positive outcomes. As with any situation if you provide yourself and at times others, an opportunity to be a success and positive. Why wouldn't you? Why would you inhibit your progress as a result of other people or a situation? You always can make a decision regardless of how bad or thought things can be. You can decide as opposed to just merely accepting the inevitable outcome that you have predicted.

Our inherited negativity bias is an outdated tendency that kept early humans and human ancestors alerted to potential threats in the environment. Negativity is the tendency to see what's bad versus what's good.

Our bodies tend to react more intensely to negative stimuli than to positive experience, and even reinforce it. The brain is like Velcro for negative experiences but Teflon for positive ones.

Positive experiences not only feels good but also help to shape our brains. Being happy can accelerate personal growth and human evolution by installing and transforming temporary positive states into lasting neural traits. While negative experience or mood disrupt our capacity to recognise, recall, or reinforce neural connections, positive events and exposure make us more attentive and productive. While many of us may presuppose that our thoughts are random and unmanageable, we can decide which thoughts to keep, reinforce or "install" and which to emphasis, minimise, or neutralise. Circulating happy, optimistic thoughts reduces cortisol and increases dopamine and serotonin (and the reverse is true too). This helps your brain to function at peak capacity, supporting more mental alertness, creative problem-solving, and an overall sense of well-being.

Awareness is key to rebalancing this predisposition to a negative experience that can distort reality and undermine the quality of life. Research has shown us that simply labelling with a single word a negative state of mind; pain, anxiety, irritation, causes activity in the brain. And, by intentionally and repeatedly registering beneficial experience, we can slant our brains and thoughts in a new direction.

Five steps to shifting negative thoughts:

1. Remind yourself of the plain existence of human negativity bias and the extent to which your brain is wired toward fear and anxiety.

2. Notice the inputs coming in from your various environments— mind, body, family, colleagues, community, and the world and how they might be affecting you internally. It can be helpful to simply notice that the feelings you have aren't synonymous with your identity—there's some separation.

3. To the extent possible, engage in and savor joyful, beneficial experiences in ways that allow them to take up residence in your body and mind.

4. When do you begin to ruminate or become bogged down by negative thoughts or commentary, ask yourself: Is it true? Is it kind? Is it necessary? Is it helpful?

5. Then, gently reframe any harmful thoughts and shift gears in your mind to positive thoughts, memories, or affirmations.

There are 100 billion neurons in the average human brain, and each makes 5,000 synaptic connections with other neurons. Learning occurs when these neurons begin to associate with one another.

Awareness of both our inherited negativity bias, as well as our capacity to absorb positive experiences simply by staying with them longer, has the potential to shore up your power. Remember, neurons that fire together wire together, and our thoughts are a choice. What we think, do, and say matters. You can retrain your brain to install, absorb, and harness the positive in your life for more joy and less suffering. With repeated practice, we can gradually alter our brains to the good. Finding what's right about what's wrong simply feels better.

Where does negativity come from

Common methods and expectations within society that require us to conform.

Doing what is socially acceptable and if you don't then people will be afraid of you and unsure as to why you have made that decision.

Do not feel that you have to be more like.....or that you have to do the same things as that person. Only to be accepted as "successful".

Success is different for everyone as I mention in chapter 3, marginal gains.

If I was to ask you to name 10 things that you don't like about yourself. The chances are you would find this quite an easy task. Whereas if you were to ask yourself 3 things that you do like about yourself it becomes more of a challenge. This is because society tells us not to come across as arrogant. My advice is to fully embrace what you have and what you like about yourself. Do you care what other people think? Does their opinion matter? We have all heard of FOMO, Fear of Missing Out, but what about FOPO. Fuck Other Peoples Opinion.

Social media influences

For example in the health and fitness industry some models have a very low percentage of body fat. One would be forgiven that if your body fat was not in single figures, this is dangerously low for a variety of physiological reasons. That you are not attractive or even simply that you are leading an unhealthy lifestyle by making poor fitness choices, food choices, drink and sleep patterns.

Peer pressure

The desire to conform to peers and how others live their lives. This is not to say that how anyone else leads their life is wrong. It could be that it is not the optimum strategy for you and how you want to achieve your goals. Personally, the concept of a 9-5 job and being sedentary is not one the appeals to me. Many benefits can be had from increasing productivity and the time you have available. Explained further in chapter 4.

Comparing yourself to others

How does one measure "success"? Very often when I have conversations with people they will tell me that I am successful and have achieved a lot in my life. Others have even used the words "hyper successful." I am not entirely sure as to what this is and how I would fit into that category. My point is, is that everyone has different views on success and you must know what yours are. How do you know when you have achieved? Ensure that you don't compare your success to that of others.

People around us being viewed as "happier"

More often than not people will only show you or let you see what they want you to see. That is to say that you will only see the results of continuous hard work. Chances are that to get an insight into the bad days. Yes, we all have them, I like to call mine "the dark place" because I would rather be able to light up the darkness than stay there for an extended period.

Desired lifestyles

Not everyone wants to be rich and famous but the majority of people want the lifestyle. A wise man once said to me that there you have an abundance of either two things. More time or more money. Will discuss the use of time in chapter 4. For the time being, however, think about would you want more time or more money. If you have more money then the chances are you will have compromised the amount of time that you have to spend it. Whereas if you have more time to do the things you want to; travel, family, house, sport, hobbies, etc. Then you may find it hard as you will not have a huge amount of disposable income to put towards it. You have to make a decision. If after some time the decision that you have made turns out to be the wrong one then you should reflect on this and learn from why and also the journey that you have been on throughout your decision.

What do you want your legacy to be??

During my secondary school years, I wasn't a hugely academic student no matter how hard I tried. However, I was able to excel in PE and sport which led me to be picked for quite a few teams to represent the school and then on to County sports level. This included badminton trials which were a whole day with around 100 other players and they went on to pick 1 definite and 2 maybes. It was a very tough day physically and mentally.

I then went on to athletics and throwing events and as outlined in the preface, is where I excelled.

However, the other side of the story is how I was picked on by my "friends" because I was good at sport. In my mind, I didn't understand it. Why would they pick on me because I was better than them at one subject? Nothing was ever mentioned about those who excelled in other subjects? So why me? Why sport? I truly believe it came down to the fact that others couldn't accept being beaten. As a result, they took to other methods to beat me.

As I was a little larger than the large majority of my peers some began to bully me at school because I was different. All associated with the negatives that were around me at the time and I wasn't able to focus on the positives that were I was County standard in around 8 different sports.

I especially recall a 400m race in one PE lesson. The track was grass and had some very suspect starting lines on the bend as well as being on the side of a hill. So the straights were flat and bends were down and uphill respectively. The 100m straight was also partly covered by trees so some of the roots made for an undulating last straight.

If you were to ask high level 400m runners they will tell you that it is a sprint event. When you considered world class times are around 50seconds, that works out at 12.5 seconds per 100m. Some of the fastest times in history for the 100m are less than 10seconds. So to run a 400m race in a PE lesson on the grass across the side of a hill was more about tactics. The best tactic was to pace yourself so that you had some energy to get up the hill, from 200 meters to 300 meters, while also keeping a little extra for a sprint finish or as the athletes call it "kick".

I had planned my race in my head and we were racing to see who would get to do it on sports day. As the teacher fired the gun 8 of us set off down the hill and along the back straight. The other chaps were doing the same as me and just keeping a steady pace ready for the hill. Once at the top of the hill, it was all very close so I knew I had to time when I made my kick for the line. With 80 meters left to run over the tree roots, I made my kick. To my surprise, I heard one of the other chaps in the race say to the others "NOW" to let them know when I kicked and so for them to start their sprint finish at the same time. At the end of the race, having beaten the other 7 lads, I was still amazed that they had all come together to create their plan and tactics to beat me.

It left a lasting mark on me and I still remember it clear as day. It allowed me to learn that people will always attack what is different from them as they are unsure of it and will feel threatened. So for most people who are threatened by someone or something and as sad as it is to say, the best form of defense is attack.

The gym, training and the pain that comes from pushing myself is one that allows me to escape the pain of everyday struggles of work and life and gives me a sense of personal achievement and motivation. To prove people wrong, not to judge me, not to set their limitations on me, not to assume what I am capable of. I have said it before and will say it again. You have two options when things get tough. They will get tough. The easy option will Always be there, sit back, so nothing, wait for it to pass, let someone else do it. All the usual excuses will come out.

My advice to you is to take action.

Celebrate the 1%s and small wins in everyday life.

If you want to go to the Olympics then do it, equally if your dream is to lose weight or even get a job. Take action and do it.

You are the only version of yourself in the whole world and every day you are presented with another opportunity to do/achieve/be successful/ build an empire. Regardless of whatever it is that you are focusing on it is part of your legacy and how people will remember you.

When your time on this planet, what do you want people to say? "They were fairly normal, went to work and had a house" for some people that is amazing. However, I truly and passionately believe that everyone has more to offer and a way of living to inspire every single day that we are alive.

Don't be limited by fear because everyone else is. Chances are that anything you want or have been dreaming about being on the other side of fear. Much like myself writing this book, it has been on my "to do list" for years but always found a reason to put it off. As it turns out all the reasons are just figments of my imagination and were never really worthy of my time or stress levels that I gave them.

- What if people don't like it?
- How will others receive my content?
- Will I lose money?
- Maybe I'm rubbish at writing as I've never written a book before?

- How long will it take?

- Maybe I will expose myself and my weaknesses/areas for development to others.

- How will I know if I have inspired one person to go out and take action on their goals and dreams? Surely I can reach 1 person?

- I can't do it on my own so why bother?

- Writing a book is tricky and I don't have a clue how to get it published?

The reality is that now I have allowed myself to inspire and motivate you reading this to do the same. Light up the darkness, don't be afraid.

Key learning points.

- **You have the power to make a decision NOT a sacrifice.**

- **Our brains will always go into self-preservation mode and put up barriers to what we desire.**

- **Retrain your brain to have happy Velcro thoughts and a Teflon negative.**

If you ever feel like you are being rubbish. <u>STOP</u> being rubbish and start being awesome again.

CHAPTER 3
- MARGINAL
GAINS

In the build-up to the 2012 Olympics professional cyclists in Great Britain had endured nearly one hundred years of mediocrity. Since 1908, British riders had won just a single gold medal at the Olympic Games and they had fared even worse in the Tour de France. In 110 years, no British cyclist had ever won the event. The performance of British riders had been so underwhelming that one of the top bike manufacturers in Europe refused to sell bikes to the team because they were afraid that it would hurt sales if other professionals saw the Brits using their gear.

The new performance director was relentless in his commitment to a strategy that he referred to as "the aggregation of marginal gains," which was the philosophy of searching for a tiny margin of improvement in everything you do. David Brailsford said, "the whole principle came from the idea that if you broke down everything you could think of that goes into riding a bike and then improve it by 1 percent, you will get a significant increase when you put them all together."

What are marginal gains?

Sir David Brailsford is well known for coining the term 'marginal gains'. This is a concept by which you strip back everything you can think of for a specific output, to continuously improve each element by a marginal percentage.

This will then subsequently improve the overall effectiveness of a specific output by combining these increments, through this "always on" philosophy of testing. This means that for those of us who are working towards a large output or objective, teams or individuals need to work collectively to identify all of the smaller components which comprise this larger output, and assess which of these smaller components could be improved. All of the improvements we can make to these smaller components, resulting in overall improved output. Simple, right?

Here is a quote from Brailsford explaining this:

"The whole principle of marginal gains came from the idea that if you broke down everything that could impact on a cycling performance — absolutely everything you could think of — and then you improved everything little thing by 1%, when you clump it all together, you're going to get quite a significant increase in performance. So we set about looking at everything we could."

An example of this can be found when Team Sky considered the beds the Tour de France cyclists were sleeping in. They had identified that during the tour a cyclist could potentially sleep in 21 different hotel beds, and potentially 21 different postures through the make and quality of the bed. Though 1 night's sleep on 1 bed wouldn't necessarily influence someone winning or not winning the Tour de France over the whole event, he identified that cyclists should be able to sleep in consistent beds. To overcome this they set up a process by which Team Sky cyclists would have the same bed setup for them at each of the hotels, meaning that their sleeping posture was consistent across the whole event.

What do marginal gain mean for you?

If we had to list our three main takeaways from Brailsford's approach, and what this could mean for you or even a business, we'd break it down to these:

Optimisation mindset – everyone working in your team needs to have the mindset that if we want to work to improve the performance of a given goal, we need to not just be accepting of, but strongly encouraging a culture of testing, optimisation, and continuous experimentation.

Every little helps – Brailsford acknowledges that he doesn't coach his athletes, he manages a group of specialists who carry out their coaching exercises to an expert level. He trusts that each of these coaches, no matter their area, are delivering a small improvement which will contribute to the overall goal. Sometimes it doesn't matter how small the testing focus is – I have seen small changes generate greater results than redesigning entire programs.

Identify key performance indicators – by breaking down his overall target into smaller, realistic goals, Brailsford was able to achieve a result which many hadn't thought possible. We all should have an overall goal which we must achieve to ensure the direction and purpose of our existence, this goal is then broken into smaller 'focus' goals. This might consist of breaking down a large goal, for example, purchasing a product, delaying gratification, making your bed.

During my training sessions for bobsleigh, we were told to focus on the 1%s. This is hugely significant in a sport of high speeds and very small margins for error. For example, at the Olympics, the race was contested over 2 days with each team taking 2 runs down the track on both days. There is a saying widely used within bobsleigh "where you start is where you finish". If you have the fastest start time you will probably have the fastest time down the track. Start times vary depending on the track and various other factors but it can be as close as 5.00seconds to 5.01seconds. This is for the first 50 meters of the track. So when we have a focus of shaving off 0.01seconds, this is 1%.

The significance of this was proved in the 2018 Winter Olympics in both the 2 man and 4 man events. At the Olympics teams, complete 4 runs down the track over 2 days. There is a large number of external variables that can impact on the race least of which is the weather and also the temperature of the ice. So a difference in 1% at the start of each run becomes hugely significant. In the 2 man race, the winning time was 3:16.86. This time was the same for the Canadian and German teams who shared the gold medal. While in the 4 man event time of 3:16.38 was achieved by both the German and South Korean teams who shared the silver medal.

Having worked consistently towards the marginal gains on the start myself and the team applied this to our training and then all aspects of our lives.

To be successful and develop adherence to change and moving forward you can also apply the 1% rule. It is much easier to change one aspect by 1% or work towards your goal by 1%. If you were to make a drastic change in a short space of time, such as 10%, the progress is huge however you are likely to not continue with the progress as it is not sustainable and lacks rewards. In a week if you were to improve by 1% a day as well as reward yourself for the achievement then at the end of the week you are now 7% closer towards the goal and are more likely to repeat your success the following week and further.

You should reward your successes or mini wins and tell people about it. As we let our light shine we unconsciously permit other people to do the same. This will further empower you as you have allowed other people to feel that it is a good thing to be positive and share positive experiences.

Make your bed at the start of every day.

If you want to achieve things in your day and catch as many of the 1 %s or marginal gains as possible. I strongly advise you to start every day by making your bed. Now I don't mean fresh sheets and a full turn down. All you need to do is put the pillows back in place and make sure your duvet is covering the mattress. This may sound like a silly thing to do every morning but let me explain.

By making your bed every day you will have started the day by accomplishing a goal. This is a small goal or even a 1% (marginal gain). You are effectively setting up your brain and mindset for the day that is to be successful and find small wins. As always there is a but, however, in this case, there isn't.

47

Regardless of whether you have had an amazing day or a day that can be improved on. Note not using negative terminology like "I've had a bad day". The fact of the matter is simple, you will always come home to a made bed. A bed that you made at the start of the day. You will then go and get into bed and feel happy that you have a nice made bed. Going to sleep feeling like a winner. Waking up feeling like a winner and thus changing the mindset from a simple little task like making your bed.

The day to day applications of marginal gains are vast and there is a 1% to be found almost everywhere in your daily routine. Such as waking up 1 minute earlier, this will allow you more time in your day in which to be successful. Leaving for work earlier Will allow you more time to be productive when you get to work this is a marginal gain. If you get to work earlier you may be able to park closer to the building and so saving time on your commute and allowing you more time in which to be successful. However, if your mindset or goal is to be healthier or more active you may be able to walk to work by parking further away or even making extra time at the end of the day as you have been successful and productive all day. This will then allow you to go for a walk or exercise during the additional time you have created in the evening.

Resilience linked to marginal gains

Whilst training in the gym and lifting some weights I decided to make a change and take on a new challenge. In doing so I went home, made some dinner, had a shower and then set about doing my homework around the new challenge.

Sir Ranulph Fiennes, the world's greatest living explorer and highly celebrated fundraiser on JustGiving, said during a seminar "never let anyone know your next move". I initially thought that this was a strange thing to say however he went on to explain that by letting others know what you are about to enter into there are some individuals who may try and beat you to it. He was talking about setting exploration world records for circumnavigating the globe.

During my research, it became apparent that I would need some support and guidance with the challenge. It is ok to ask for help!!! Don't ever let fear or failure limit the path that you have chosen to be successful. If you do then you will never achieve anything. Get out of your comfort zone and try something, try the marginal gains principle. No matter how big or how small your goals are.

One of the ways in which I developed some of my achievements is through being held accountable.

Accountability is a hidden secret to success.

Being held accountable is defined by the Cambridge dictionary as "Someone who is accountable is completely responsible for what they do and must be able to give a satisfactory reason for it". As far as my life experiences have allowed me to learn, accountability can be best utilised by two methods. Personal and social.

Social accountability is telling others what you are going to do and when you are going to complete it by. This is very common on social media platforms where individuals will document their journey from start to finish. Taking the form of "checking in" with their followers at a specified time.

Social accountability can also be done by making use of a coach. Not specifically a sports coach but similar in the role which they take. A coach will keep you on track while also providing you with support and guidance and even a plan that can be weekly, monthly or annually. Coach or social accountability is very strong in keeping on track to your end goals. Weekly check ins can be done by applying the 1% or marginal gains theory with rewards from your coach to ensure acknowledgment on your success.

Personal or self-accountability once learned and applied to become a habit can ensure regular success with virtually any outcome you desire. I find the use of a mini notice board in my room where I write goals and even letters I need to action. One strategy you may want to adopt could even be a few post it notes with weekly targets on is key to keeping you on track towards your goals. You may want to try something similar with pictures of the desired outcome you are working towards.

Key learning points.

- **Don't try to make a big change immediately.**
- **Celebrate small wins as this will help you with adherence to your goals.**
- **Start every day by making your bed.**

.

Yesterday is history, tomorrow is a mystery, today is called the present. That is why it is a gift.

CHAPTER 4 - VALUING YOUR TIME

Time is all we have. This moment, right now.

There's only one thing in our lives that we are never able to reacquire once it has gone and I'm not talking about money I'm not talking about material items I'm talking about time. And it is such a unique concept you are unique idea because when utilised correctly it contains ingredients to success the success and happiness to growth prosperity all of the things we want but the very same time if neglected it leaves us very little. Because the truth is that every morning when you wake up you were living minutes you will never get back.

You are breathing air will never take in again. It is your one opportunity to embrace this gift. Every second sees a little of it slip away. My point is that there is no moment more important, more perfect and than right now. Not in a week not after your promotion not in 30 years when you plan to retire and relax. We have this mentality that the future is going to somehow mean more than the present that if we suffer now or if we're unhappy and now that will save the best in life for "some other time."

The reality is we don't get younger; yes, we should be working hard absolutely success comes from effort, hard work, dedication, persistence. But the key is to allocate your precious time to the work, to the things that make you feel like today is powerful.

Today is when you take the first step towards the things that you want. When you become who you want to become. No one is ever or will ever keep you from that other than yourself. There is no ceiling, there are no limitations, there is no special requirement. There is you and what you allow yourself to accomplish. You are the gatekeeper, you have your foot on the drive pedal. It is very easy to point at others and the environment in order to blame things on everything but our own decision. Our decision to stick to what we want because believe it or not it is that simple. You are where you are because of that where you've decided to be along with your acceptance that this place is ok.

However, if you want to change and you don't like the place you are in then you have to manufacture a change. Make a plan to move forward and action it so that you can begin your transformation.

If you think about how lucky we are to be alive in this day and age, in this world at this time with access to all the information we could ever dream of. What is the reason for you not to be the best possible version of yourself? Is there something that you could do as a concurrent activity to make the best use of your time? During 2012, following an unsuccessful application to get onto a teacher training course. I made a decision to undertake a master degree at the University of Brighton. While doing this; I was also working 3 days a week to help fund the course, coaching young athletes 3 evenings a week, training 6 days a week and had a part time job as a security guard. Don't allow yourself to fall into a position where you haven't made the best use of the time and resources that you have available to you. The easy way is always there, do nothing, sleep, stay in bed, just exist. I truly believe that every single individual on this planet is unique and we can all learn from each other and add value to become the best possible version of ourselves.

We have the freedom to pursue any path that we desire and for whatever our reasons. Anything we could ever want is right in front of us and yet we choose not to embrace it, why?

Nothing is more important in life than to live our lives, nothing makes us feel more energised, more free, happier. Than following the path that we were meant to take and have the courage to step over the obstacles, to face the challenges, to be uncomfortable.

I promise you that there will be a few on your way. If the outcome or goals were not worth the effort then nothing in life would be worth having. You will learn more from the journey towards your goal than when you actually get there. The bigger the goal, the longer the journey, the more time committed towards it, the bigger the reward at the end.

The concept of time that we have in our small existence on this planet and the greatest gift a human being can receive. You, by default, have it and don't ever let it be in vain. The future isn't when happiness "someday" occurs it is a continuation of you making a decision to live every moment that you have been given to the fullest from now until your last.

Never allow yourself to find blame or an excuse to blame a moment of sunshine, clouds or rain to deprive you of your gift. Be the best version of yourself that you can be and add value to others' lives. Live to inspire.

There is saying that "if you want something to be done ask a busy person to do it". Being busy allows your mind to be active and engaged. If you are sitting true and have an underactive brain then it will start a cycle of decline. It is important to keep your brain active as well as challenged. This can be achieved through marginal gains. Four examples at weekends there are the usual Jobs that need to be done such as taking out the rubbish, cleaning and washing clothes. These are all jobs is that not many people really enjoy however when they are completed it brings satisfaction and ultimately increase your productivity.

If you apply the same principle of waking up earlier by one minute then you will have more time available during the day to do what you want. Time is one of our most precious and valuable commodities however in this day and age it is valued less than that of money and health. Time is something that we will never get back, it is a free asset to every single human on this planet. So if you want to achieve your goals and become more successful make the best use of your time through the application of the marginal gains principal. Which we discussed in the previous chapter.

Now while money is significant and will facilitate you to do certain things in your life such as purchasing your house, a car, going out for meals and drinks with friends. The materialistic things that we desire can always be replaced however time cannot.

I ask you the question of how much do you value your time over money?

Once I passed my driving test when I was 18 I purchased my first car, it was a Fiat Punto. It cost me £1500 and it gave me a huge sense of freedom and new-found independence during my late teenage years. I spent many hours tinkering with the engine the radio Windows cleaning the car inside and out and I took great pride and care of my car. Unfortunately being a young man with the car I crashed it not only once but twice.

The second time I crashed I was on my way to work, there was a parked car on the road and a tractor coming the opposite way. I decided to hedge my bets and slam my brakes on as driving headfirst into it moving tractor was a bad idea. I subsequently hit the parked car and the car was written off. This was a valuable life lesson for me as with all the pride and care I took of my car I ultimately had to have it scrapped. That this is not to say those nice things do not bring you happiness however making best use of your time to acquire the materialistic objects that you desire is more important. As the materialistic object may end up broken.

I am reminded of the film home alone. The young man says to the neighbour that he asked for a pair of roller skates for Christmas. He was so overjoyed with the roller skates that he never wore them because he was worried that he might break them all damage them. The young man goes on to say but when he did eventually go to try them on and the roller skates did not fit. So what are you desired he never got to use.

So should you desire a nice car, a big house, nice watch, or other materialistic objects, my advice to you would be to make best use of the time that you have with it if you spend all your time working and earning money to pay for the object you may be at risk of not having use of it.

During my time at university, from all three of my degrees that I completed at Brighton and Cardiff Metropolitan. I was also training intensely to be at my peak for throwing the discus with the aim of representing England at the 2010 commonwealth games and further onto representing team GB at London 2012. Made a decision not to sacrifice one day to cut out alcohol. At University the hangover the following day seriously impacted on my mood what time management my health and my ability to train along with study.

One morning was nursing one of the more severe hang hangovers. My housemate came in to see me to discuss the previous night antics. As is the way with a hangover memory and ability to recall information can be seriously limited. When asked questions about what had happened and where we went I was most confused as to how the night unfolded. The conversation quickly turned into breakfast and then onto plans for the day which involved training. It was on this day that my coach had arranged for the British record holder for the men's discus to come down and to train/coach the throwing squad that I was part of. At this point being terribly hung over my housemate reminded me that this was taking place. He said to me are you going to go and train today? I cannot remember the exact response I go to my housemate but in short, it was along the lines of "not a chance mate!" To which his response to me and is one that will stay with me for the rest of my life. Something that I apply to myself when things become difficult. When I have to talk to myself and give myself a kick up the backside to make sure I get on with things. Was this. "it's okay mate, I'm sure all the other discus throwers in the country are having a day off as well. There is no reason why you should go and train either!"

I think we can appreciate that this role of reverse psychology, at the time, was very clever and I thank him for giving me that kick up the bum.

Please do not take this as a lesson in don't drink and don't be hungover because if that is what makes you happy then I have no right to tell you what to do or not to do. However, it is my belief and personal experiences that have allowed me to learn these lessons in being productive and successful through the best use of the time and resources that I have available to me.

It is okay to have a chat about the situation or scenario that you are facing in the oncoming day. Or even to reflect on something that hat that has happened in the previous day so that you can learn from it and develop your skill set mental resilience.

Routine and time

It can sound counter-intuitive but developing a daily routine can help us to feel more in control of everything, and help us to make room for all that's important. Routine can aid our mental health. It can help us to cope with change, to form healthy habits, and to reduce our stress levels.

Routine can be an anchor. No matter what's going on in our day, knowing that we will be having our evening meal around 6 pm, and going to bed around 10 pm, can be a real comfort. The certainty of our routine can help us to manage the uncertainty that life can throw up. Coping with unpredictable periods of time can feel more doable when we have a little structure in place to look to.

Having a daily routine can help to reduce our stress levels. Trying to remember things can be really stressful and can fill our brains up with everything on our 'to do' list; which can be incredibly overwhelming. When we have a routine, a lot of the things we do day-to-day slot in, and we don't have to think about them anymore. For example, when we're well we don't have to remember to clean our teeth, because we know from habit that teeth-cleaning comes after breakfast every day.

Routine can take the guesswork and uncertainty out of bits of our day, which can allow us to feel more in control and less stressed.

Having a routine can help us to cultivate positive daily habits and to prioritise self-care. Organising our time gives us the opportunity to build in blocks of time for things that are important to us. This can allow us to build in daily habits that help us with our mental health. It could include things like time to relax, or a regular bedtime. When they're part of our routine, it can make it easier to keep up with them because we have the time to do them and they become our 'new normal'.

One of the things that having a regular routine can really help with, is sleep. Sleep is really important for our mental health because going to bed and waking up at a similar time most days allows our body gets used to our sleep-wake cycle and sets our sleep-wake clock accordingly. This means that by having a regular sleep routine, especially if we build in some time to wind down before we go to bed each day, we should begin to find that we find it easier to get to sleep and sleep better once we are asleep.

Creating a routine allows us to build in time for the important things. This includes time to rest, relax, and have fun. It's not perfect, there are always going to be days when something overruns, a job takes three times as long as we expect it to take, or someone pops in unexpectedly. But structuring our time to include some downtime increases the likelihood that we'll manage to have that time most days. We all value different things, for some of us it might be reading with the kids, others might want some time each day to play with their cat, some of us might enjoy sitting and reading for a little while. For many of us, it will be something else entirely, but that's why our daily routines are individual to us.

The 6 biggest time wasters

1 – Watching TV

2 – Procrastination, simply prioritising tasks, not just putting them off.

3 – Saying yes to everything.

4 - Perfectionism

5 - Multitasking

6 – Worrying

Conscious And Subconscious Thought Processes

The function of your subconscious mind is to store and retrieve data. Its job is to ensure that you respond exactly the way you are programmed. Your subconscious mind makes everything you say and do fit a pattern consistent with your self concept. This is why repeating positive affirmations, see chapter 9, is so effective you can actually reprogram your thought patterns by slipping in positive and success-oriented sound bites.

This is why motivational activities, such as reading inspirational quotes, such as at the start of every chapter in this book, are so impactful for people committed to positive thinking. By focusing your thoughts on uplifting ideas, your subconscious will begin to implement a positive pattern in your way of thinking and your outlook on life.

Your subconscious mind is subjective. It does not think or reason independently; it merely obeys the commands it receives from your conscious mind. Just as your conscious mind can be thought of as the gardener, planting seeds, your subconscious mind can be thought of as the garden, or fertile soil, in which the seeds germinate and grow. This is another reason why harnessing the power of positive thinking is important to the foundation of your entire thought process.

Your conscious mind commands and your subconscious mind obeys. For example, what is your tongue doing right now?

A subconscious thought can become a conscious thought very quickly and also stay there for a long period. Your subconscious mind is an unquestioning servant that works day and night to make your behaviour fit a pattern consistent with your emotionalised thoughts, hopes, and desires. Your subconscious mind grows either flowers or weeds in the garden of your life, whichever you plant by the mental equivalents you create.

Your subconscious mind has what is called a homeostatic impulse. It keeps your body temperature at 37 degrees Celsius, just as it keeps you breathing regularly and keeps your heart beating at a certain rate. It maintains a balance among the hundreds of chemicals in your billions of cells so that your entire physical machine functions in complete harmony most of the time.

Your subconscious mind also practices homeostasis in your mental realm, by keeping you thinking and acting in a manner consistent with what you have done and said in the past.

All your habits of thinking and acting are stored in your subconscious mind. It has memorised all your comfort zones and it works to keep you in them. This is why it's so important to make writing SMART goals a regular habit, see chapter 7. After a time, staying productive and focusing on all of your goals will become part of your comfort zone. Your subconscious mind causes you to feel emotionally and physically uncomfortable whenever you attempt to do anything new or different or to change any of your established patterns of behaviour. The sense of fear and discomfort are psychological signs that your subconscious has been activated. But it's been working to establish those behaviour patterns in the background long before you'll ever notice such feelings.

The tendency to commit to these patterns is one reason why habits can be so hard to break. However, when you learn to purposefully create such patterns, you can harness the power of habit and purposefully instil new comfort zones to which your subconscious will adapt.

You can feel your subconscious pulling you back toward your comfort zone each time you try something new. Even thinking about doing something different from what you're accustomed to will make you feel tense and uneasy.

This is why time management tips may be tougher to implement at first, but once they become habit or routine they will stay in your comfort zone. In doing so, you've reprogrammed your subconscious to work in your favour.

Superior men and women are always stretching themselves, pushing themselves out of their comfort zones. They are very aware of how quickly the comfort zone, in any area, becomes a rut. They know that complacency is the great enemy of creativity and future possibilities.

For you to grow, to get out of your comfort zone, you have to be willing to feel awkward and uncomfortable doing new things the first few times. If it's worth doing well, it's worth doing poorly until you get a feel for it, until you develop a new comfort zone at a new, higher level of competence.

For those looking to expand their realm of comfort zones, I highly recommend considering the habits of successful people as they are the patterns commonly adopted by the minds of great leaders and thinkers. Unlocking the power of these behaviours will put you one step closer to being able to make the same things happen in your life.

Learning techniques to reprogram your subconscious mind will help you believe in yourself because your confidence will no longer be challenged by fear of the unknown. But more importantly, doing so will train your brain to be in line with your true desires, dreams, and life goals.

The more in tune with your subconscious you become, the closer you will be to breaking through to success. I had an idea for a book that had been at the bottom of my to do list for years. With the right level of confidence, I took the next step in learning how to write a book, rather than clinging to the dream, but never acting. One reason why I never took the first step was that the course that I had signed up to, multiple times and never went to, was because the course was free. I didn't have to pay for it I merely had to get myself there. That is why if someone was to write a training programme to teach you Science at school you wouldn't value it because have not had to invest anything to give it value. So you may take it for granted. This further reinforces accountability whether it is public, self or financial. Imagine if you tell someone that you will do something and then never actually do it? Chances are the negative social repercussions of this will make you do it. Therefore you are more likely to stick to and even complete the goal if you have invested in it.

Key learning points.

- The most important thing to you? Money health or time?
- How can you increase the time that you have it every day?
- Wasting time is a time that you will never get back.
- Carpe diem – seize the day.
- Make the best possible use of every opportunity and time that you have.
- Taking immediate action on your ideas is a powerful key to success.

No matter if you see the glass as half full or half empty. You will still have something to drink

CHAPTER 5 - MAINTAINING POSITIVITY

Emotional intelligence refers to the ability to identify and manage one's own emotions, as well as the emotions of others.

Emotional intelligence is generally said to include at least three skills: emotional awareness, or the ability to identify and name one's own emotions; the ability to harness those emotions and apply them to tasks like thinking and problem solving; and the ability to manage emotions, which includes both regulating one's own emotions when necessary and helping others to do the same.

There is no validated psychometric test or scale for emotional intelligence as there is for general intelligence and many argue that emotional intelligence is therefore not an actual theory, but a way of describing interpersonal skills that go by other names.

Emotional intelligence or emotional quotient "EQ" as its sometimes known has wide appeal among the general public. In recent years, some employers have even incorporated emotional intelligence tests into their application or interview processes, on the theory that someone high in emotional intelligence would make a better leader or co-worker.

While some studies have found a link between emotional intelligence and job performance, others have shown no correlation, and the lack of a scientifically-valid scale makes it difficult to truly measure or predict someone's emotional intelligence on the job.

Even if you love your job, there are times when things get a bit negative. You may get bogged down by an angry customer or a feeling of lacking in productivity. While it's easy to fall into a slump based off one negative experience, it can be just as easy to redirect your mind and, instead, focus on the more positive experiences. In general, having a positive attitude means being optimistic about situations, interactions, and yourself. People with positive attitudes can remain hopeful and see the best even in difficult situations. In contrast, those with negative attitudes may be more pessimistic and disagreeable, and typically expect the worst possible outcome in tough situations.

While having a positive attitude doesn't necessarily make you less stressed, it can equip you with the tools you need to cope with stress more healthily. Those individuals may not fear stress as something physically deprecating and dangerous, but as a means to a greater end. Other benefits include creating actionable goals based on dreams, making and maintaining more positive relationships, and even give your immune system a well-needed boost.

Having a positive attitude is pleasing, yet it may seem easier said than done. However, by adopting some of the following tips, you can maintain a positive attitude through highs and lows and improve your work ethic.

10 Creative Ways to Keep a Positive Attitude

Start a gratitude diary.

There's so much for which to be grateful in life, so why not remind yourself of that on a daily basis?

A gratitude diary is a wonderful way to stay positive every day with little to no effort. Once a day, you can jot down at least three aspects of your day for which you feel thankful for. They can be as small as seeing a cute dog on your way to work or as large as getting an offer from your dream job. Also, they can be something that happened to you on that specific day. Such as getting yourself a large latte or something that exists in your life always for example as having a family who loves you.

Whatever you want to write is up to you. All that matters is that you're remembering to feel grateful every day. By retraining your mind to think about all the good things in your life, you can develop a more positive outlook.

Treat yourself to some self-care every day.

It's always important to take care of both your physical and mental health. It can feel overwhelming when you're working a full time job that requires you to constantly interact with people whether they be students, co-workers, team mates or managers.

To keep moving forward with a positive attitude, it's essential that you take a step back sometimes and treat yourself to something special. Self-care doesn't always have to involve a night time soak in the bath with a glass of wine.

Consider the ways you can unwind, de-stress, and have some "you" time. Some examples are watching a movie, baking, calling a friend, getting a takeaway, or even just saying "no" to plans and, instead, staying in. No matter what it is, you should get into the habit of practicing something every day. By allowing yourself these moments of pure bliss and rest, you can ensure a more positive attitude when you're on the work grind.

Start every morning strong.

It's easier to maintain a positive attitude all day if you implement it right when you open your eyes. That dreaded moment when the alarm goes off can often lead to irritation, which sets you on the path to have a negative attitude all day.

Instead, think about some ways to make your morning the best part of your day, especially if you're not a morning person. Consider waking up a half hour or an hour earlier than usual. This means getting into bed earlier too! Give yourself time to do the things you love but may not always have time for; go for a run, a hot shower, have a cup of coffee, and actually make breakfast. Put on your favourite music or even whip out a book, and start your morning doing something you love while enjoying your home cooked meal.

If you want to be successful then start every day by making your bed. Now, this may appear very military however by simply putting the covers back and the pillows in the correct place you will have started your day by accomplishing a task. This will then perpetuate into more success. Furthermore, regardless of if you have a good day or a bad day, you will always be coming home to a made bed. A bed that you made. So the chances are that you will feel a sense of relief and happiness to come home to something as simple as a made bed. When your morning is more productive and less rushed, you'll be sure to head to work in higher spirits. That morning glow will spread throughout your day, and then the cycle can repeat.

Avoid spreading gossip.

It can be hard to avoid gossip, but simply refuse to get involved. If someone tries to reveal to you a dramatic story about a coworker, simply decline and tell them you'd rather not participate. While that may feel odd to do, you'll actually find that you feel lighter when not carrying the weight of secrets. And, when you're not talking about other people, you can feel more confident that others are keeping their lips zipped about you and that's a reason to feel optimistic.

Crack more jokes.

Humour truly is the best medicine. Laughter has great short term results on your mindset and body. According to the research, laughter can increase endorphins, relieve stress, and release tension.

In the long term, laughter and the positive thoughts associated with laughter can release neuropeptides, which fight stress and other serious illnesses. It can also help you cope with difficult situations and generally make you feel happier. By cracking more jokes, you can make humour out of potentially negative situations at work, and at the same time prepare your body and mind for a more positive outlook.

Take real breaks.

Throughout a busy day, it can sometimes be difficult to find time for a serious break. That means leaving the workspace, having a meal, and putting away all work related information. You are legally allowed to have a break, and you should never feel like that rest period is jeopardised.

Working for eight hours straight can make you feel sluggish and irritated. A break for 30 minutes can re-energise you and make you more motivated to continue your work for that day. Give yourself time to refuel your positivity, and you'll be sure to end the day on a better note.

Have something to look forward to after work.

You may be tired after a long day of work, but having something planned after 5 p.m. can make the day look a little brighter. Whether it be with your co-workers, family, or friends, a night of fun can make the day go by a lot faster.

Your plans don't always have to involve going out for drinks or dinner. Even planning a wine night with friends or a Netflix marathon can put a silver lining on your workday. The point is to craft your days to be more than just "work." By pencilling in some fun time several days a week, you can find a healthy way to balance your personal and professional life.

Practice meditation.

Practicing meditation can do a lot to decrease stress and anxiety, as well as improve mental and spiritual health. A study published in 2003 in the journal of psychosomatic medicine compared the brains of those who practiced mindfulness meditation, a style of meditation, and those who didn't. The results showed that those who practiced meditation showed changes in brain activity in areas focused on optimism and positive thinking.

Another from the journal of stress management, 2005, showed that meditation was able to decrease anxiety in health care professionals. This means that proper meditation may help decrease workplace anxiety for those in other high-pressure work environments, such as in customer support or service.

Even five minutes a day is a great start to a meditation routine. Practice deep breathing and clearing your mind. Simple methods like this are effortless and will help you find balance in your life, as well as let go of negativity and stress that you may experience daily.

Focus on the long-term instead of short-term.

When a conflict arises either with a co-worker, a friend or partner your immediate reaction might be to jump to the defence. You want to protect yourself and garner respect, which is a good thing. However, the more conflicts in which you partake, the more negativity will surround your life.

Instead, take a second to step back and view the situation from a third party perspective. Will participating in this conflict be beneficial in the long run? Or, will it simply cause unnecessary stress and negativity at the moment? Often, someone is simply having a bad day or is stressed. Rather than snapping back, you can practice empathy. This might help you get to the root of the problem and end the conversation on a positive, lighter note.

Listen to music that matches your mood.

It seems ironic, but sad music may help boost your mood. According to research in 2014 many people tune into sad songs as a form of mood enhancement. Many consider sad music to be "beautiful," which helps people feel better. Also, sad songs can invoke memories, distract from negative situations, and carry strong messages. However different research states that sad music might evoke positive moods because sadness somehow feels satisfying and cheerful when experienced through art. So, listening to sad music might just lift your mood during or after a long, tough workday. Cue up some Adele, and let your negative mood disappear.

These are just some ideas that can help to set yourself on a path to a positive, refreshing attitude on life. And maybe, just maybe, this will help you find more happiness in your work life.

Personal situation

Following from my highest porting accolade of being part of Team GB in Sochi 2014 returned home to find myself trying to build a professional career. I made applications for all sorts of roles with a wide range of salaries and locations.

Unsure of what I wanted to do.

What was the correct career for me?

From working with a range of individuals it has become very clear to me that not everyone knows what they want to do. As previously mentioned we are usually governed by social conformity and what is deemed "the right thing to do". There several individuals who achieved their dream at a late age. Please note I am not using the word success as that is very subjective.

- Samuel L. Jackson. Believe it or not, as much of a Hollywood staple as Jackson has become over the past two decades, he didn't get his big break until he appeared in Jungle Fever in 1991 at the age of 43.

- Vera Wang had dreams of becoming an Olympic figure skater. After her dream was crushed when she failed to make the team, she entered the fashion industry at the age of 40, later becoming one of the world's most respected names in fashion.

- Momofuku Ando invented instant ramen noodles way back in 1958 just before the age of 50.

- Ray Kroc as the legendary McDonald's founder didn't purchase the burger and shake franchise until he was 52.

- Colonel Sanders, the founder of KFC. He franchised the company back in 1952 at the age of 62 and would later sell the company for several million dollars.

You have time to do what you want. Age is just a number.

I tried lots of various part time job roles from coaching in primary schools and local sports clubs. Most of these were voluntary positions that allowed me to gain experience and establish a portfolio of credibility. Working as a security guard at various nightclubs being paid not very much to work long unsociable hours and dealing with all manner of society. Personal training both at the gym and privately, which is an incredibly challenging field to build a reputation in as so many students with a BSc Sport and Exercise Science degree feel that they can provide high level "coaching" to clients in return for a large chunk of money. The health and fitness profession is saturated with supplement companies, clothing brands, a wide range of unique gyms popping up all over the place, 1000s of online personal trainers. The list goes on. None of the roles provided me with a regular salary nor did I have the time or money to invest in starting up a business regardless of having a niche of being an Olympian.

It was suggested to me to speak to the Dame Kelly Holmes Trust who work with young people aged 16-25 years on a range of projects in the local community as well as supporting businesses and entrepreneurs to help establish themselves. The trust "employ" current and former elite athletes to deliver sessions to the clients and local communities. I was successfully recruited and was given a series of opportunities to support the clients on their journey to find their "why" and continue to build through inspiration and motivational strategies'. This was a turning point for me, the work was inconsistent in terms of when the placements would come up and the finances didn't match up with the time not working.

As I mentioned it was the turning point. It gave me joy and happiness to work with young people and to be put in pressure environments such as public speaking. It also allowed me an opportunity to share my experiences with others and motivate them. This provided me with a means of coping with the aftermath of the Olympics and elite sport lifestyle.

There are some processes that you will perform in your day to day life that will be autonomous. This is action from your subconscious brain and doesn't require a huge amount of thought. If you can work efficiently and potentially even monetise these skills that may be the value that you are looking for.

Emotional intelligence

Emotional intelligence refers to the ability to identify and manage one's own emotions, as well as the emotions of others.

Emotional intelligence is generally said to include at least three skills: emotional awareness, or the ability to identify and name one's own emotions; the ability to harness those emotions and apply them to tasks like thinking and problem solving; and the ability to manage emotions, which includes both regulating one's own emotions when necessary and helping others to do the same.

Daniel Goleman, an American psychologist, developed a framework of five elements that define emotional intelligence:

Self-awareness

People with high emotional intelligence understand their emotions and they don't let their feelings rule them. They know their strengths and weaknesses, and they work on these areas so they can perform better.

Self-regulation

This is the ability to control emotions and impulses. People who self-regulate typically don't allow themselves to become too angry or jealous, and they don't make impulsive, careless decisions. They think before they act.

Motivation

People with a high emotional intelligence are willing to defer immediate results for long-term success. They are highly productive, love a challenge, and are effective in whatever they do.

Empathy

This is the ability to identify with and understand the wants, needs, and viewpoints of those around you. Empathetic people avoid stereotyping and judging too quickly, and they live their lives in an open, honest way.

Social skills

People with strong social skills are typically team players. Rather than focus on their success, they help others to develop and shine. They can manage disputes, are excellent communicators, and are masters at building and maintaining relationships.

Along with developing a high level of emotional intelligence there has been research that looks at a growth and fixed mindset. If you are in the process of developing your emotional intelligence and are struggling. It might be worth taking a step back and working out if you have a fixed or growth mindset.

Growth Mindset vs Fixed Mindset

A positive mindset is the difference between simply giving up because they're "not an achieving person" and a productive struggle that yields growth. But a growth mindset isn't just about effort. Dweck, 2015, wrote that "In the fixed mindset, everything is about the outcome.'

If you fail or if you're not the best it's all been wasted. The growth mindset allows people to value what they're doing regardless of the outcome. They're tackling problems, charting new courses, working on important issues. Maybe they haven't found the cure for cancer, but the search was deeply meaningful. I would challenge you to develop a more growth mindset, find the positives in situations and also outcomes. What did you learn? Was it worth getting emotional over? Link it back to emotional intelligence as previously mentioned.

Carol Dweck, a psychologist from Stanford University researched the fixed and growth mindset. As a professional in the education system we are encouraged to develop students mindset, how they think about what they can learn and also their abilities. While working in a variety of professions in order to fund my training and Olympic dreams it became apparent to me that I had been inadvertently been making use of the growth mindset.

Dweck came up with the following definitions in 2015 about both fixed and growth mindsets of individuals. Take note of what they are and what your current mindset is.

Fixed Mindset:

In a fixed mindset, people believe their basic qualities, like their intelligence or talent, are simply fixed traits. They spend their time documenting their intelligence or talent instead of developing them. They also believe that talent alone creates success—without effort.

Growth Mindset:

In a growth mindset, people believe that their most basic abilities can be developed through dedication and hard work. Brains and talent are just the starting point. This view creates a love of learning and a resilience that is essential for great accomplishment.

Whether you are a student, professional, young person or an adult it is important to figure out your mindset. Knowing if you hold a fixed mindset or a growth mindset can significantly impact the learning experience from primary school through to secondary and even onto university. Individuals that hold a fixed mindset give up when they can't solve a problem and admit defeat. This can be detrimental to students' future efforts and leads to limited student growth. With a growth mindset you will continually work to improve your skills, leading to greater growth and ultimately, success. The key is to train yourself into that growth mindset.

Key learning points.

- **Learn to develop a growth mindset**
- **Make more jokes**
- **Establish a high level of emotional intelligence**

Veni Vidi Vici

CHAPTER 6 - "YOU CAN'T DO THAT!"

Go back to when you were young, and somebody told you, you couldn't throw discus. It's important people believe they can challenge the norm and what society expects them to do and say. If they challenge constructively, they can achieve greater success.

How many times has someone or society told you that you can't do something? Or that its not the right/best thing for you to do?

On one hand you may take these bits of advice as supportive, if you look at it from a positive mindset. Where someone who you trust or you have perceived credibility from has advised you and given you possible outcomes. This advice or behaviour towards your new goals is more advice based and can be helpful.

More often than not society and others around you will say these phrases to you. Some of the subconscious reasons for this can include, but not limited to, that people are afraid of what they can or can not do. So subsequently impose their limitations on you.

I find this very frustrating and patronising for the reasons of. How do other people know what I am capable of? What gives others the right to form a judgement on something that I want to achieve? Just because someone has given themselves a limitation is no reason for you to set it on yourself.

As a young child I recall my journey into athletics. As outlined in the preface I threw the discus for at least 15 years and competed at 3 Olympic Trials. There is a part of me that thinks I wouldn't have continued to go this far with the sport had it not been for one of my teachers in primary school.

I played football for my school and scored many goals in rapid succession during a fixture. The teacher who was looking after us told me that they were going to speak to the head of sport and see if I could move up to play for the 1st rugby team, 2 years above my age group. I was strong and big for my age so this made sense, but the powers that be thought better of it and said no. As I continued to develop my athleticism it became apparent that I was better at throwing things rather than running long distance. I excelled quickly with throwing the javelin when I was 10 years old.

I was selected for the county championships and finished 6th. Upon return to school I asked if I could have a go at throwing the discus and the head of sport said that I was only allowed to throw the discus when I was 11 years old. As you can imagine I was slightly disgruntled by this decisions as I felt I had proven myself capable of throwing things. Subsequently I took myself down to my local athletics club, picked up a shot put and a discus and started to throw them. With little to no coaching and reading books about the event and techniques I trained myself to the English Schools Athletics Championships.

I anticipated finishing last, which would have allowed me to say that there were 19 other lads who could throw further than me in the whole country. As it turns out I placed 3rd. Proving that even on an individual level you can set your limitations on your abilities and you can achieve more than you think.

As we let our light shine, we unconsciously give other people permission to do the same.

Do not be limited by fear or ambition.

Were you ever told by a teacher or adult that you were not allowed to go and play with your friends? Climb a tree? Or even as an adult when you read signs that say "Do NOT push the red button!!"

There are some psychological connotations to this which I made use of in both my discus and bobsleigh sporting careers as well as my professional career.

Once you become more aware of something you notice it more. Much like when you are going to buy a house, new clothes, new car. The more you are looking at them, the more likely you are to notice it around you.

When you read "Do NOT push the red button!!" what is it that you see in your head? A big red button with white writing on? In the split second that the image has appeared in your mind what do you also think about? Pushing the button to see what happens? The reason for this is because the command "push the red button" is written and your brain will pick up on this. If you take this psychology into the world we live in you will notice it all around you. For example, Nike's slogan is "Just do it". The more you think about something the harder it will become. Weather it be in life, profession, sport or even purchasing some sporting clothes. Just do it, don't think about it.

Making use of your subconscious brain as opposed to your conscious. Subconscious thoughts and actions are ones that are performed by your body with a level of autonomy. For example your heart beating and breathing. Where are your conscious brain requires active thought and decision making based on past experiences as well as generating plausible future outcomes. Applying the same principle of the more you think about something the harder it becomes or the more aware you are. It can be very easy to change a thought from subconscious to conscious but challenging to reverse the process.

The best example is if I ask you "what is your tongue doing right now?"

Were you thinking about your tongue before the question? Even by the time you finish this chapter you may still be thinking about it.

Take this principle and apply it to a decision you are thinking about. Or even when setting your goals albeit short, medium or long term. Take action, write them down so you can see them and are reminded of them every day. Tell your friends and family what you are working towards as they may also inadvertently hold you accountable by bringing it up in a conversation.

Don't be limited by what others think.

You may be familiar with the phrase FOMO, Fear Of Missing Out, to some this is very apt and missing out of a particular social event can be disastrous. I was exposed to a development of this which was simply FOPO, Fuck Other People's Opinions. If there is something that you are deeply passionate about or enjoy doing and it brings you happiness. Then why should it matter what other people think. Yes it is human nature for us to care about others and to ensure that no harm falls to anyone close. If your goals and happiness allow to create more opportunities for yourself and in turn inspiring others to go out and do something that they have always wanted to then why wouldn't you do it?

The most important factor in a successful person's life is gratification.

Several psychological studies have been completed around delayed rewards and gratification. A study that used hundreds of children between the ages of four or five were used to reveal a trade that is known to be one of the most important factors that determine success in a person's life gratification. This experiment is famously referred to as the marshmallow test.

The experiment involved introducing every child into a private chamber with a single marshmallow.

At this stage the researcher struck a deal with the child and informed them that he would be gone from the chamber for a while and that if you she/he didn't eat the marshmallow they would reward them with an additional marshmallow apart from the one on the table. However if they did eat the marshmallow placed on the table in front of them it wouldn't be rewarded with another. It was clear one marshmallow immediately or two marshmallows later. The researcher would walk out of the chamber and return 15 minutes later, predictably some children ate the marshmallow in front of them as soon as the restructure walked out of the room.

However, others tried hard to restrain themselves by diverging their attention. Many of these children successfully resisted due to the increased temptation and eventually their patience was rewarded. 1 in four children waited until the very end without leaving the marshmallow. The study was published in 1972, commonly known as the marshmallow experiment however it doesn't then there.

The real twist is what followed several years later. Researchers undertook a follow-up study to track the children from the initial experiment. They studied several areas of the person's life and were surprised by what they discovered.

Those children who delayed gratification for higher rewards are waited until the end were reported to have significantly higher grades, in all instances substance abuse was not reported, lowered chances of obesity and better stress coping abilities. The research was known as a ground breaking study and gratification.

Becoming a teacher after sport and the transition to "normal" life.

After graduating from the University of Wales Institute of Cardiff with a BSc Honours in Science in Health Exercise and Sport I was faced with the decision that every graduate has. What to do with the degree I now have?

As I was unsure as to how best to apply the knowledge and skills I had acquired from university I took up many different occupations including; bouncer, bar man, close protection, mentor, business development, accountability coach, sports coach, primary school sports cover and I even applied to be a holiday rep. Im sure you can imagine that none of these careers worked for me and made the best use of my skill set.

This is something that I would actively encourage you to think about, even go as far as to write down. What are you good at, what are you areas for improvement, what do you enjoy etc. If you are unsure as to what you enjoy most or how you spend your time. There are several apps on phones that will tell you information about your screen time and sleep patterns. Failing that, have a look at your bank statements to see where you spend your money and what you spend it on. It will be a strong indicator as to some of the answers to the questions.

I found that I could mix my training with coaching and helping young athletes to start the journey to reach their potential. This was a concurrent activity for me, unbeknown at the time, but one which provided a subconscious answer to my why. It lead me to working in a local mixed comprehensive, now known as non selective, school, taking up the role as a teaching assistant. Supporting a range of students with varying learning and physical barriers to their learning. Seeing students make progress and be able to recall information and skills that I had passed on to them was immensely rewarding and the other good thing about it was that someone was paying me to do it!

When the role of a cover teacher became available I jumped at the opportunity as it was more responsibility and allowed me to develop myself along with having a greater impact within the school. I was successful in my application and maintained the position for a few years growing in my skills and understanding of the role of a teacher. Other staff noticed this and combined with my sporting background they allowed me my classes within PE. This planted the seed for me and sparked my ambition to become a PE teacher. This became a huge personal battle for me as I was fiercely passionate about becoming qualified and very determined. Which I will now explain to you why the chapter is called "You can't do that".

- Applied for internal training position at the school I was working at – unsuccessful

- Applied to PE PGCE courses at multiple universities – unsuccessful

- Took up a Masters degree at an institution to gain more knowledge and meet course leaders

- Applied to PGCE course 3 more times, consecutive years, shortlisted. – unsuccessful, due to international student application who pay the university 3 times the amount in fees.

- Interviews were all day long, including multiple sports activities, dance, swimming, English and maths tests, paired interviews.

- Left the education system to pursue Olympic dream – successful

- Pre Olympic selection, applied for trainee PE teacher at the school I worked at, invited to interview, flew back from Austria for the interview, was not shortlisted, flew back to Switzerland the same day.

- Post Olympics – applied for trainee Science teacher at the school I worked at – successful. However during the interview process I was asked. "Once you are qualified what's to say that you won't change subjects and teach PE?" It was at this point that in my head I said to myself, "Really, can you do that?"

To this day I am still teaching Science and have had a positive impact on over 1000 students increasing their life chances in succeeding to gain, employment, further education or work experience. I now regularly get asked by fellow staff if they can observe my lessons as well as having visits from the CEO who delivers positive feedback on my lessons. There rarely goes a day when I don't have students come and talk to me asking for advice on topics that range from; Science specific through to problems at home, friendships and even health related. Please rest assured that I do tell them that I am not a qualified doctor and that they should go and seek advice from a trained medical professional.

There are several points to be taken from this 5 year section of my life.

I am extremely tenacious, when I know what I want and I know I am good at something I fail to see how anyone can form a judgement on me in 5 minutes.

It pisses me off when someone tells me that I'm not allowed to do something or that I am not ready for the job/level/race/competition. As a direct result of this I set about processes to prove people wrong. Vinnie Jones said in the film Lock stock and two smoking barrels "Assumptions are the mother of all fuck ups".

Now as much as all of this is how I became a Science teacher and am building a career. It is very easy to apply this to yourself and events that happen in your life. Refer back to the start of this chapter and think about the questions that I and others have asked or even told you.

Please do not let others tell you what you are capable of. If you want something or believe you can do something. Go out and do it. If you believe you can do it then you can do it! Maybe not straight away but you will be able to.

Sports companies marketing slogans are spot on when it comes to the mental toughness and call to action, simply put "Just do it" and "Impossible is nothing".

Key learning points.

- **Delaying gratification can result in better success and adherence to goals.**
- **Never let others set their limitations on you.**

We only die once.
We live every day.

CHAPTER 7 –
PRE-PLANNING
FOR SUCCESS

There is a saying, "dreams without goals are just dreams."

Have you ever heard the phrase "Prior preparation prevents piss poor performance" or "Fail to plan and you plan to fail". The harsh reality of these phrases is that they are entirely true.

Goal setting is an essential part of life. We all need goals to help keep us focused on the journey to achieving our dreams. They help to invoke a more tangible and actionable path to what we desire in life. When we write out goals, they become more real. They help us to visually embrace what we want out of life, enabling us to provide some measurable metrics to the progress that we make along the way.

Having goals are very important to life, which is why we all need to set them the right way. And, what's clear is that we all have goals in life, but we don't all set those goals the right way. We tend to leave those goals as obscure targets in our mind, never actually putting pen to paper to write them out and see them in front of our eyes.

Why Are Goals So Important?

Many people go about their lives lost, like a puppy without a home. They go from day to day, week to week, month to month, and even year to year without a real concrete direction for their lives. They fail to steer their lives in the right direction, because without goals that are set the right way, they're not even clear on what that direction is. In order to make a gal more visceral to the mind and more clear, you have to be able to quantify that goal. Without specifics, there's no real target, just some obscure direction. When the goal is obscure, it allows the psychology of your mind to override your goals. You succumb to things like emotion-numbing activities, to easily avoid doing something that wasn't that concrete in the first place.

Goals are an important aspect of life, not just dreams and ambitions but what those goals mean to us. We don't just want things for the sake of wanting them – when that's the case, we're unable to achieve what we set out to achieve. We can't just say that we want something because we think it's "cool" or will make us look good in front of others. If the things that we don't want to have a more profound meaning beyond the superficial, when the going gets tough, we will often get going.

So, goals are important. They help to pour a concrete solid foundation to our hopes and dreams, and the things that we want. They help to steer the ship of our lives through stormy and choppy waters, across the channels of struggle, and onto the shores of accomplishment. We need goals in our lives, just as much as a captain needs a compass to navigate the high seas.

S.M.A.R.T.E.R. Goal Setting

A simple starting point to help you set goals and is commonly used around the world are SMART(ER) and/or FITT acronyms to ensure that any planning is done correctly.

This is a mnemonic acronym that can be applied to goals in a way that makes them easier to tackle. This originally dates back to a November 1981 publication in an issue of *Management Review*, penned by George T. Doran, which addressed SMART goal setting when referring to businesses management's objectives. SMART goals are goals that are specific, meaningful, achievable, relevant, and time-bound. As you can see, the acronym, SMART is also a play on words.

But, SMARTER goal setting takes this two steps further, forcing you to evaluate and readjust your approach. This added sense of measurement and readjustment is critical to the achievement of anything in life. All too often, we tend to set our goals, but not put any type of measurement to them. When we don't measure and track something, it becomes far easier for the mind to trick us into either putting things off or thinking that we've come further along than we have.

As you look at the acronym for SMARTER. goals, it's clear to see that there are seven steps since there are 7 letters in the word.

S – Specific

The first step in setting SMARTER goals is to be specific – very specific. The more specific you are about your goals, the better and more able you'll be to accomplish them no matter what method you use. This means that you don't just say you want to make more money or lose more weight, you have to say exactly how much money you want to make or how much weight you want to lose. You have to put a real and exact figure on it. Make it specific.

A personal favourite that was taught to me is simply change *try* to *will* this change in word holds you accountable and detracts from any lateral thinking and excuses that you allow your mind to generate.

Specifics are the fuel in the engine of your goals. You have to provide specifics if you're going to achieve anything at all. When you write out your goals, be as specific as possible. And never be afraid to be too specific. This can also link in with yourself affirmation, which is explained in chapter 9.

M – Meaningful

The second step in setting SMARTER goals is to set goals that are both measurable and meaningful enough to you that you'll get out there and do whatever it takes to achieve them. This is you "why".

When your goals have a deep enough meaning to you, you'll do whatever it takes to achieve them. This doesn't have to do with vanity or superficial reasons, but more profound and life-altering reasons why you want to achieve something.

People don't want more money because they want more paper with deceased notables on them. No, they want more money because of what that money will bring them: time, freedom, family, security, contribution, and so on. You have to attribute a strong enough meaning to your goals, beyond just being specific about them. So, next to your specific goal, write out what that goal means to you and make sure that it's something important.

A – Achievable

The third step in setting SMARTER goals is to set achievable goals. Now, there's certainly a school of thought out there that says that you can accomplish whatever you want, whenever you want it. But, when you're setting goals, especially when they're short-term goals (i.e. within 1 year), make sure that they're achievable. This doesn't mean that you can't shoot for the stars in your long-term plans, such as 5 years down the road or even 10 years down the road. It just means that you have to pick goals that you can achieve in the short term.

For example, if you've never made more than £100,000 a year, don't say that you're going to be a millionaire in one year. Indecently if you did want to make £1,000,000 in a year you would have to average a daily earning over £2700.

Set goals that you can achieve so that you build on your momentum, reward yourself with the small wins, as mentioned in chapter 3 – Marginal Gains. Your short-term goals should be something within your reach, but not so easily attainable that they won't take much work or effort on your part. This will also help you to build that all-important momentum. Once you achieve your year-long goals, you can broaden those into much greater hopes and dreams down the road.

R – Relevant

The fourth step in setting SMARTER goals is to set goals that are realistic and relevant to your life. This means that the goals should be in line with and in harmony with what you want out of life; they should match up with your core values. If your core values are contradicting your goals, then you'll find yourself merely getting frustrated and giving up.

When you set goals that are relevant, you have to dig deep down inside yourself and truly understand what you want out of life.

Sometimes I often use the question "How do you want to be remembered?" as a self-motivation tool. If one of your core values is freedom, then setting goals that have you bound to a desk most of the year won't help you to live a fulfilled life. Remember, your goals shouldn't be designed with the notion of succeeding to be happy, but rather, with happily succeeding. Set goals that are relevant and in line with what you truly want out of life.

T – Time-Bound

The fifth step in setting SMARTER goals is to ensure that they're time-bound goals. You have to set an exact date on when you plan to achieve these goals. Focus on goals that are in 3-month intervals. If you plan to achieve a 2 stone weight loss in one year, then break that down into 3-month intervals. That's 1 kilo every month, which fits in with the marginal gains rule.

When your goals are time-bound, measurable, and you should hold yourself accountable by measuring those goals on a daily, weekly, and monthly basis. How close are you to achieving your goals? How much further did you get from achieving your goals? Without making your goals time-bound and measurable, you won't be able to see your progress.

E – Evaluate

The sixth step in setting goals using the SMARTER method is to ensure that your goals are evaluated. By evaluating your goals every single day, you'll be much more likely to achieve them. Why is that? Well, long-term goals (and also goals that are 3 months or 6 months out), can easily be ignored if they aren't evaluated every single day.

Make sure that you setup a system for evaluating your goals and you make the evaluation of your goals habitual. Don't ignore this all-important step. Your mind has a very clever way of allowing you to ignore your goals by pushing you into emotion-numbing behaviours when those goals aren't closely evaluated.

R – Readjust

The final step in setting goals with the SMARTER method is to re-adjust your approach. If, for example, you find yourself pursuing a goal but continuously hitting a brick wall, readjust your method and techniques. For example, when a plane has a goal of flying from London to Sheffield, it has to constantly evaluate its progress and readjust its approach to ensure that it reaches its target. The plane constantly evaluates and readjusts until it arrives in Sheffield. You should be doing the same for your goals.

Readjust doesn't mean that you have to throw your goals out and start all over. What it means is that you have to try different approaches until you find yourself getting closer and closer to your goals. That's why constant evaluation on a daily basis is so important. If you don't evaluate you can't measure your progress.

New Year's Syndrome

Setting goals is important. We all need to set goals in our lives and set them the right way. When we don't set goals the right way, we suffer through uncertainty, frustration, and a generally unfulfilled state-of-mind. However, what's even worse is that, not only do we set goals the wrong way, we tend to only set them once a year. And, this, of course, happens on New Year's Eve.

We get stricken with something called New Year's Syndrome, which sees us setting those goals once per year, and essentially forgetting about them.

In fact, according to a University of Scranton study in 2014;

- 64% stick it out past one month
- 46% past 6 months
- 8% of people who set out to achieve their New Year's goals, actually achieve them.

If you're tired of not setting goals the right way or only setting them once a year, then there's something missing from the recipe. If all the ingredients aren't there and the proper steps aren't taken, how can we profess to saying we want something, yet continually not doing what it takes to achieve it?

FITT Goal Setting

The FITT Principle (or formula) is another mnemonic acronym that can be applied to setting your goals. It is also a great way of monitoring any goals and or exercise that you do and have and can be easily interchanged, for this purpose I will relate it to exercise

FITT outlines the key components, or training guidelines, for an effective exercise program, and the initials F, I, T, T, stand for: Frequency, Intensity, Time and Type.

Frequency: refers to the frequency of exercise undertaken or how often you exercise.

Intensity: refers to the intensity of exercise undertaken or how hard you exercise.

Time: refers to the time you spend exercising or how long you exercise for.

Type: refers to the type of exercise undertaken or what kind of exercise you do.

F – Frequency

Frequency is a key component of the FITT Principle. Remember that it's important to know why you're exercising and what you want to achieve before rushing into any exercise program or goal setting.

Adjust the number of times you exercise per day/week/month to reflect: your current fitness level; the time you realistically have available; your other commitments like family and work; and the goals you've set for yourself.

I – Intensity

This is an extremely important aspect of the FITT Principle and is probably the hardest factor to monitor. The best way to gauge the intensity of your exercise is to monitor your heart rate.

There are a couple of ways to monitor your heart rate but the best way by far is to purchase an exercise heart rate monitor. They consist of an elastic belt that fits around your chest and a wrist watch that displays your exercise heart rate in beats per minute. Failing purchasing a belt there several apps and also smart watches that can also do this for you but may not be quite so accurate.

T – Time

The time you spend exercising and working towards your goals is also an important part of the FITT Principle. The time dedicated to exercise usually depends on the type of exercise undertaken. It is also important to ensure that you have an appropriate balance in terms of time spent working towards your goals and also exercising. If you spent all day every day exercising then you would be unable to do anything the next day. Trust me on this one, having completed a team deadlift world record for most weight lifted in 24hours. I was unable to walk much further than to the toilet the following 3 days.

If you spend excessive time working on your goals then you may come across a similar situation where you are unable to make any progress the following days. So ensure that you have a plan that allocates an appropriate amount of time.

T – Type

The type of exercise and or goals you choose or set will have a big effect on both when how often you achieve the results you set out to. That's why it's important to know what you want to gain from your efforts.

Personal

With reference to the previously mentioned new years syndrome I for one have fallen fowl of these statistics and never managed to keep to my resolutions for much more than 4 weeks. I believe that this is partly due to lack of understanding as to what my why is or even was at the time. Along with allowing myself to make full use of the word try.

I have come to realise and learn that through my profession and sporting tribulations that for me the bigger picture is the one that counts. Please note that this is personal to me, my lifestyle, goals, dreams, ambitions and mental capabilities. It is never an easy task to work out your why, it takes time. Some of you may already have it, if you do then please do act on it and strive to achieve it. It will empower others by sharing what you are doing.

Indirectly I reflected and readjusted my goals at the start of 2019. I had come close to getting to my second Winter Olympics and was able to compete for a spot in my 5th Olympic trials, not too shabby when I was 32 at the time. However it is worth noting that at this point I struggled to relight the fire that had always existed inside me. This is continually relit when people tell me I can't do something, chapter 6.

Through challenging myself and supporting others on their journey it allowed me to rebuild mine. I worked with personal training clients, entrepreneurs, old school friends, retired athletes and even mentored students at work. Along with the help of one of my close friends and bobsleigh team mates we discussed setting a world record and that rapidly developed into multiple world records, for added credibility and challenge. So on my return home I went on to the Guinness world records website, set up an account, feeling very audacious. Set about finding current world records that I thought I could have a go at and break. To then achieve something that no one else in the history of the world has ever been able to achieve. Needless to say I found a few and this then helped me to set goals, SMARTER goals and FITT goals for the attempts.

In order to keep myself accountable to these I purchased a small cork and white board from the local pound shop and wrote on the board what the records are and that was a constant reminder of what I was working towards.

Along with a few other targets, setting goals just for the gym is very narrow and wouldn't contribute entirely to me being the best version of myself in 2019. I wrote on my white board the following goals, some of these may sound silly to you....

- Get a mortgage
- Get a partner
- Promotion at work
- At least 1 World record

At the time of writing this I have ticked off 3 out of 4 of these goals for the year. Note I did not wipe them off, they are dreams and goals that I have achieved myself this year and it is important to remind yourself of what you have done, what you have achieved and how far you have come.

If the journey wasn't challenging the goals wouldn't be rewarding.

Key learning points.

- Set goals using the SMART principal
- Targets should include both long and short term
- Reward yourself when you have achieved and then evaluate
- Enjoy the journey and the process of working towards your goals
- Avoid big or sudden changes.

When you want to succeed
as bad as you want to
breathe, then you'll be
successful.

CHAPTER 8
- GRABBING
OPPORTUNITIES

The dictionary defines an opportunity as a situation in which it is possible for you to do something that you want to do. You need to be aware of burnout by saying yes to everything that comes your way. It is important to have an awareness of managing your own time and health.

Opportunities to achieve what you want in life are coming to you more often than you realise. The reason those opportunities don't always turn into the experiences you hoped for often has to do with whether or not you are ready for them. Most people live ready for what they expect in life, not what they want. You might want a better job or a new relationship but if you don't expect to get one, then, likely, you won't put forth the effort to make it happen. For example, if you want a great partner but never expect to meet anyone, then chances are that half the time when you leave the house, you never think twice about what you look like.

If, however, you expected to meet your great new partner any moment, you would probably pay more attention to your appearance even when just going out for a pint of milk. If you felt great about yourself every time you leave the house, you would be more likely to give off great energy and also more likely to talk to others, which would greatly increase the chances of meeting someone. Expectations leads to action, which creates experience. I've said it before and it is one of my favourite quotes.

As we let our light shine we unconsciously give other people permission to do the same.

People often make the mistake of believing that if the good things in their lives would just show up, then they could be happy, and everything would change. "If I had a job, I would have a reason to stop watching TV all day." The problem with this line of thinking is that if you are sitting on the couch all day, the job you want will never show up. We get things in life that we "match up" with. While there are always exceptions to the rule, most people who have great jobs showed up ready for the job. It is likely he/she worked hard, identified the skills that were needed, gained experience, build their resumes, polished their interview skills, paid careful attention to how they were being perceived, and gave the potential employer exactly what they were looking for. It didn't just happen; they weren't just lucky. They wanted it and were ready for the opportunity when it arrived.

So how can you learn to be more prepared for the opportunities that are coming your way?

Be clear about what you want.

When you don't know what you want, it is hard to know when an opportunity for something better has arrived. Clarity gives you focus and direction, vagueness is like driving around in a dark cloud with no idea where you are going. Finding your clarity starts with tuning in to your emotions. A lack of clarity often comes from not trusting your feelings. When you are weighing various options in your mind, ask yourself how one option compares to the other in terms of your emotions. If an option feels interesting and exciting then do some homework and find out more about it, as you gather information about that option see if your enthusiasm grows or diminishes.

If you are stuck sometimes it helps to first identify what you don't want in a certain situation. For example, if you don't know what type of job you are interested in looking for, it can be helpful to fold a sheet of paper in half lengthwise and then write down everything you don't want in a job on one side. Then open the paper and next to every item you don't want, write down what it is you would like instead. If you don't want to work a rigid 9-5 M-F work schedule, perhaps what you want is a job with a lot of flexibility. Once you are done with writing out the inverse of what it is you don't want, you should have a nice long list of what it is you do want on the subject. Use this to begin to build clarity. What kind of jobs might fit these criteria? If the answer is not many, then identify which areas you are willing to be flexible on and which areas are absolute must haves. When you are clear about what you are looking for, it creates a selective filter that causes you to see more opportunities that match and to disregard other opportunities that are just distractions.

Know what steps are necessary to achieve it.

This step is often a stumbling block for many people. They know what they want but they don't know what to do to achieve it, so they don't try. Identifying the necessary steps is a key part of the process that may require investigating, studying, and learning lots of new information. Luckily, we live in an age where information is readily accessible, we just have to be willing to put forth the effort to figure it out. Google is your best friend when you don't know how to do something. If you are stuck, start there.

Look for books, websites, classes, organisations, or people who might be able to provide you with information. If you'd like to start a new business, there are many groups and organisations that support first time entrepreneurs. They often offer mentorship to help guide newcomers through the process. The knowledge is out there but you have to be willing to look for it and ask for help. Doing this creates opportunities by engaging with others, and it increases your positive expectations about your ability to achieve what you want because you have the knowledge to create an action plan.

Behave as if what you want is about to show up.

Now that you know what you want and how to accomplish it, the most important part is to act as if what you want is coming at any moment. There are two huge benefits to living ready for what you want. First, when you live as if what you want is coming, your belief that it will occur starts to grow very rapidly and you start to engage in more and more actions likely to make it happen. This leads to the second benefit, which is that when an opportunity shows up, because you have been in action mode, you are ready to take advantage of it.

To start this process, take your list from step number two and just start doing. If you want to start a business but are worried about not having any customers, you can't wait until you have customers to get started. You have to build the business and create the services that you will be ready to deliver on when your first customers show up.

The thought that trips many people up on this step is. What if it's not worth the effort? To conserve energy and resources people are inherently programmed to not want to take action unless there is some return on the investment. What if I build my business and no customers show up? What if I fail? Won't that be a total waste of my time, money, and energy? Worrying about what you don't want can stop you from taking action toward what you do want. Instead, focus your energy on how to make what you want happen. Know that if it doesn't work out, you don't have to globalise the failure to mean that you will never succeed, or personalise it to mean that you don't deserve to succeed. By taking the action you create the opportunity to learn something new and isn't that the most important opportunity you can take advantage of?

There is a story about a young man who wanted to make a lot of money, and so he went to a guru to seek advice. The conversation went as follows.

"I want to be on the same level that you're on" so the guru said, "If you want to be on the same level that I'm on, I'll meet you tomorrow at the beach at 4 am." The man thought, The beach. I said I want to make money, I don't want to swim. But the young man got there at 4 am, all ready to rock and roll. The old guru grabbed his head. "How bad do you want to be successful?" The young man replied "Real Bad." So the guru said, "Walk on out into the water." So he walks out into the water,

about waist deep. He said to himself, This man's crazy. I want to make money, he's got me out here swimming. I didn't ask to be a lifeguard. I want to make money.

The guru said "Come out a little further." So he did. He was at the shoulder area. He thought, this old guru is crazy. He's making money, but he's crazy. The guru said, "Come out a little further". He came out a little further. The water was at his mouth. The young man was like, "I'm about to go back in. This man's out of his mind."

But the guru shouted, "I thought you wanted to be successful!"

He said, "I do!"

The guru said, "Walk a little further..." The guru dropped his head in the water. He Held him down, and was holding him under. The young man was scratching, clawing, fighting to get up. The guru kept him down under water. And just before the young man was about to pass out the guru raised him up.

The Guru said, "I got a question for you. When you were under water, what was the only thing you wanted to do? More than anything?"

He said, "I wanted to breathe." The guru said, "When you want to succeed as bad as you want to breathe, then you'll be successful.

If there are no opportunities then you have every ability to make new opportunities. As I mentioned at the beginning does not let people set their limitations on you. If you want something, go and get it and prove to people what you are capable of. Everyone has the opportunity every single day to make your dreams become a reality.

There is a chain of thought that says if you go to sleep you might miss the opportunity to be successful. Opportunities can appear at any time and if you are not around to take action on them then they will pass you by. Arnold Schwarzenegger has a series of rules for success and one these pieces of wisdom he mentions is about sleep.

Most people will sleep for around 8 hours, 8 hours out of a 24 hour day leaves you with 16 hours in which to take and make opportunities. With the growth mindset you would be encouraged to make best use of your time and maybe even created more time, not too sure how this is possible. However Arnold's advice is to sleep faster. So if you can get your 8 hours' worth of sleep done in 6 hours then that will give you more time, 18 hours, in which to be successful. I will let you formulate your own opinions on this.

Every single person has multiple opportunities; opportunity to travel, to live, to succeed, promotion at work, go on dates, try new food, have new experiences. The challenge for most is to overcome the fear of "what if?" that so often comes into our heads. The fizzy drink known as "*Dr Pepper*" has a famous marketing line based around "What's the worst that could happen?" Have you ever tried eating Marmite, some people say they do not like it but yet have never tried it. How can you form a judgement on something or even someone if you don't know anything about it?

During 2017 I applied this principle to my bobsleigh and Olympic journey. I wanted to attempt to go to my second winter Olympics as I had unfinished business from the 2014 games. To give myself the best possible opportunity to be selected for the World cup squad and then be in with an opportunity of being in the mix for Olympic team selection. I again relocated myself to Bath, as I did in 2013, to ensure that I was in the best possible environment and around coaches.

The basic principle of setting myself up to win with the goal that I had in mind. After a few weeks of training with my friends who were in the team it motivated me more and I wanted to be able to train officially with the world cup squad. Not all the athletes in the set up knew who I was and as I previously mentioned majority of people are afraid or threatened by what they don't know and can't control. As a result of several athletes were talking about me, asking why I was around and what I was doing. When I spoke to one of my friends who had supported me after the 2014 games he said to me "Why don't you just ask if you can train with them?"

I subsequently asked one of the head coaches for a meeting to ask if it would be possible to train with the squad. He replied with no. Now on face value, as much as this rejection and negative outcome highly irritated me. As I was a current Olympian at the time. I changed my mindset to find a more positive outcome from his comment. He had denied me the opportunity so it gave me motivation to train harder. I spoke with my old team mates and they were all confused by the decision so they took it upon themselves to help, support and even invite me to sessions.

This one question taught me a lot about the world of sport, people and life is that you should not be afraid to ask.

When you ask a question, do not be afraid of what the outcome will be. For me it was more destructive to my training and mental health to not know if I was allowed to train with the squad. The outcome of the question provided me with a black and white answer to all possible scenarios I had gone through in my head. I knew the outcome and was able to train and work more effectively afterwards.

If you think about a time when maybe you wanted to ask someone out on a date, go to see a particular country, try a new food, go exploring. If you don't ask or even take actions towards doing it then you will never know.

Decisions and sacrifice

During my time with the GB Bobsleigh team I had a conversation with one of the coaches about how best to get to the Olympics and also what I needed to do in order to learn to drive a bobsleigh. He told them that as an athlete you should only ever make decisions, never a sacrifice.

It took me a while to process this statement as I felt like I was talking to Yoda. The coach had been a competitive athlete in the sport for over 20 years and had competed for Great Britain at 3 Winter Olympics. So I naturally figured they knew what they were talking about. It struck me that I use the word sacrifice too much.

I tell myself that I sacrifice my evenings and weekends for all sorts; work, emails, training, helping others when I should be saying that I had made a decision to work after hours so that I can get the best out of my training, be more efficient at work, create more opportunities for myself.

Or I tell myself that I sacrifice my social life and hobbies for my sport and health, when I should be saying that I decide to prioritise my own needs as the opportunities that I had created and also asked for may only appear once in my life time.

The problem with using the word sacrifice is that you can very easily become a victim and can fall into the trap of begrudging all the small and simple things that are around you and may be able to help you.

But when I started to use the word decision, I became empowered as I know that I have made choices and they are good choices that match my personal and professional values.

What about you, do you make sacrifices, or decisions?

The reasoning behind decisions over sacrifice is that if you are going to sacrifice something then you are completely removing that aspect from your life. Whereas making a decision to not focus as much on it will allow you to come back to it, should you need it. Also you are always able to learn from decisions. They can be both good and bad but either way you will still be able to learn from them and evaluate the outcome along with the journey. This also links to the growth versus fixed mindset and maintaining positivity.

Try to Will

When you ask someone to do something, one of two answers are usually heard: "I'll try" or "I will." At first glance, these two responses sound a lot alike. After all, aren't we taught to always try, or try real hard or try our best? Yes, it seems pretty easy to answer most questions with the words, "I'll try."

When you think about it, "I'll try" is a slick and convenient response to just about anything that presents a challenge. When we say those two words, what we're really saying is: "I'll put some effort into this... but I think I'll hedge my bets too. I may succeed, or maybe I won't, but don't hold me accountable."

The best part about the words, "I'll try" is if you use them, you'll never fail. If you succeed in whatever you're *trying* to do, good for you! If you are unsuccessful, it's not a big deal; at least you tried. In fact, "I'll try" is almost like our own personal, "Get out of Jail Free Card." You can use that phrase every time you're not fully committed to succeeding. Of course, the problem with this particular "Get out of Jail Free Card" is that, unlike the game of Monopoly, where you can only use it once, you can just keep using the card over and over again. Each time you use it, the card becomes easier and easier to use. And failing will be easier and easier to accept, too.

"I will." Why are we so worried about using those words? I believe it's because when we use those words, we make ourselves 100% accountable for our actions and it scares us. When we say "I will," there is no "Get out of Jail Free Card." There is no place to hide. There is just the knowledge that we have to do our very best to succeed. But even though we try our hardest, we may not succeed, we might fail. But is that such a terrible thing?

Failure is not a death sentence, and it's certainly something we can rebound from. Isn't failure one of the keys to success? Read any success story you choose, and I can almost guarantee you that you will find a story of failure woven into the fabric of that success. Failure is often what paves the way to accomplishment.

In the end, the words "I'll try" are *almost* the right words. Mark Twain once wrote, "The difference between the right word and the almost right word is the difference between lightning and the lightning bug." The next time you are challenged to take on a task, whether by another individual or by yourself, use the right words: I will. What's the worst thing that will happen? Failure? You'll be that much closer to success and sooner or later, you *will* succeed.

Key learning points.

- **Only ever make a decision never a sacrifice**
- **If opportunities don't exist, make them**
- **Change try to will and hold yourself accountable**
- **Create a self affirmation to read every morning and start your day strong**

I didn't come this far, to only come this far.

CHAPTER 9 - MIND THE GAP

Psychologically speaking, a goal can give us a powerful sense of direction and order. It satisfies the natural desire for something to do, and we can feel good as we progress and check off milestones.

But perhaps more importantly, goals can affect our overall sense of connection and purpose. We assign positive attributes, such as intelligence, perseverance, curiosity, and independence, to being active or engaged in something. All this helps us feel that, when we have work, we also have personal value and a place or role. We can even define ourselves by the work we do.

So what happens when the objective you worked so long and hard for is suddenly behind you? All those links disappear. We can't define ourselves the way we did before. We suddenly have time we don't know how to fill. We can't even periodically look in the mirror and pat ourselves on the back anymore. We question ourselves in a million ways.

And if that all seems too simple, you have neuroscience kicking you in the face while you're down. The brain releases dopamine, a hormone associated with both motivation and happiness, in anticipation of reward. So when you plan and know you're going to work for something, you're in biological position to feel good. Each milestone gives you another dopamine hit, which makes you want to keep going with the job. But when you reach your goal, that release of dopamine drops. It's harder for you biochemically to have joy.

Grasping that anticipation of reaching your goal can release soothing dopamine, sometimes people also experience what's known as the arrival fallacy. If you are ridiculously sure you're going to reach the goal, you essentially can trick your brain into behaving like you've already reached the end. The work already seems done or like a mere formality, so dopamine starts to drop off before it otherwise would. Then, when you get to the finish line, it doesn't feel as satisfying. In the worst case scenario, this can lead to you desperately hopping from goal to goal hoping something, anything, will make you happy.

That right there is an order of bleak with sides of apathy, disappointment, and emptiness.

There's a lot of content and advice about how to achieve your goals. What steps you should take and how to never give up in the process of completing the things you want to accomplish. But what I haven't seen much of is advice on what to do once you've reached a goal. Sure, you can always be setting new goals and reaching higher to achieve new things, but what if you're not sure what to do next, but don't want to be complacent with where you are. In other words, how do you continue to grow and set yourself up for success, when you're not sure where you want to go next.

As I mentioned in chapter 8, at the start of the year my goals were; get a mortgage, get a partner, promotion at work and achieve at least 1 World record. Like all good things it took a while and I'm still working on some of these, but I'm happy to say that I have achieved some of these goals. My goals which seemed at the time to be nothing more than a wishes and pipe dreams but now has become a reality. And although I'm so happy with my decisions and achievements, it boasts the question of "now what?"I'm thrilled with my life as it is, but I don't want to get complacent. I've been thinking a lot about how to avoid complacency and continuing to grow, while still recognising that I've made tremendous strides from where I used to be. It hasn't been easy to balance those two thoughts. A lot of times, when I'm feeling frustrated and even stagnant, I have to remind myself to stop and look around me. It's an instant reality check. The only time you should look back is to see just how far you have come on your journey.

It also got me thinking a lot about how I've become very hard to please. I'm always asking what's next and always looking for "more." Is it possible to get to a point where you feel right about where you are and don't want to move any further? I think I'd love to get to that place, but does that place equal complacency? I haven't found the answer yet. Of course, there's always room for growth, but how long are we allowed to bask in the glory of our achievements before setting the next milestone?

Here are a few things I do when I achieve something I've been working hard towards, were I don't want to set another goal immediately.

Celebrate

Take a break and say "I did it!" Even if that just means going out to a nice dinner or putting my phone away or even purchasing something nice that I've wanted. It is important to take time to reflect on the accomplishment.

Set a timeline

If you want to take some time to bask in your current achievement, that's great. To avoid complacency, I set a timetable for how long I want to soak up my current situation before looking ahead. Maybe that means that your next goal is to maintain your current lifestyle for another year and then reassess. You can also use the achievement to fuel your next set of goals, perhaps even set a bigger goal?

Create a maintenance plan

My last big goal required me buying a house. But of course, it'll take more than that to maintain my new lifestyle. So even if I don't have another big goal in mind, my goal now is to figure out how to manage this current lifestyle long term. This is where when you set new targets and ambitions ensure that they are linked to others so that by working towards one you will indirectly make the other ones more achievable.

Try new things

If you feel stuck now that you've achieved your goal, it might be a perfect time to try some new things, and gain new experiences so that you have new things to work towards. There are always new things to be learned and new skills to be had, and all it takes is going out there and doing them. For example, I was a discus thrower for 17years and had competed at 3 Olympic trials and multiple international competitions. The new thing for me was bobsleigh, of which I went on to represent Team GB. After this, I struggled but have my profession which allowed me to live a more fulfilled life through helping others and concurrently helping myself. I have competed in my first strongman competition and went on to win it! So I will now be making best use of my assets and looking to compete in strongman competitions.

Regardless of what your goals are and how long it takes you to achieve them, there's always going to be a time where you're wondering what to do next. For me, as long as I stay grounded and intentional in the goals I set and the actions I take towards them. I've found new ways to stimulate growth and aim even higher. I might not always know what those things are, but I'm still seeking them out and looking for new ways to feel good about the things I achieve.

Depression

There have been some significant events in my life that have made the various sporting accomplishments of more significant to me.

Upon returning from a usual Sunday walk with my mother and sister who had been walking the dog while I was on my mountain bike. Cycling through puddles and attempting to perform some jumps, I was 8 ½ years of age, so they weren't too impressive. Covered in mud and returning home ahead of my mother and sister I turned into the driveway at home, which as I found out had lots of loose gravel on. The front wheel of my bike slid out from underneath me and I subsequently put my hands out to break my fall. However as the force was so great I managed to break my arm.

Initially I was unaware of what I had done, just felt like my arm hurt. At close and delicate inspection I noticed white bits sticking out of my arm. The bones had snapped in my arm and pushed through the skin at which point my hand and wrist was a 90 degrees to my arm. When mum and family returned we called and ambulance and headed over to the hospital where surgery was performed to straighten my arm. The bones were fixed together with 2 metal plates and 9 screws and then the skin sewn back together with 52 stitches. They kept me in a range of different casts for 6 months before releasing my arm and removing all foreign objects from the bone and skin.

One day at school, 9 years of age, I managed to climb up the playground fence and then hang on a basketball hoop. My friend then threw me the ball and I managed to do a dunk. Much to my friends amazement and with do adult supervision I bowed to peer pressure and performed it again but this time with a small crowd. Once I let go of the hoop to drop down to the ground I lost my footling on landing and put my hand down to save myself. At which point the force was so great I managed to break two bones in my arm, which was initially treated with a bag of frozen peas! No surprises I had broken my arm again, which followed another 6 months in casts to put the bones back together.

Having substandard bones in my arm and combined with Ulcerative colitis diagnosis in September of 2013, 6 months before the Olympic games. The Olympic selection process was fierce as one would expect and certainly not one is conducive to symptoms of colitis. However with the opportunity to represent Team GB at the highest level an athlete can achieve in their sport made me determined to fight through it.

Returning from the Olympic games is one of the most surreal experiences of my life. Everyone has the image of athletes being role models and highly focused individuals, you wouldn't be wrong in the assumption. However when the lifestyle, routines and team mates are removed as quickly as collecting your bags from the belt in the airport. It can be a very difficult situation to acknowledge and appreciate. It was at this point that I made a decision to continue with bobsleigh and seek private funding for the upcoming season.

However as a large number of athletes and funding were lost from the sport it became near impossible to proceed. I relocated home and looked for employment while also still trying to keep the Olympic dream alive. It took me from 2014 until now to realise the symptoms of depression and even come to terms with it. This books is a coping mechanism for me while also, I hope, support for others to reset, reach for their goals regardless of the current situation.

Through my time with British Bobsleigh I have made some lifelong friends and one of which reached out to me and asked if I would be interested in being part of a 12 person team to set a 24 hour most weight deadlift by a team world record.

Working as part of a team to help raise awareness about mental health conditions in service men and women who put their lives on the line, daily, to protect our country. In doing so breaking and setting two world records while also raising money for charity and supporting others who are suffering with mental health conditions, myself included. Currently I am still waiting for the certificate to come through from Guinness.

I am now a position to directly impact young people's lives on a daily basis by improving their life chances through academia and choices through education and life lessons. This for me is one of the unique perks of my profession and I still speak with students know who I have and am are helping. Through helping others I can come to terms with my situation and let my light shine. So hopefully helping you to feel confident to do the same.

Dealing with a hidden and unspoken medical condition that is highly embarrassing and debilitating, on a daily basis, that has a huge impact on my; daily life, professional, career, sporting and physical wellbeing.

All of these are key points in my life give and have allowed me to experience a whole range of emotions. I believe that I have worked hard to be in a position to have achieved these and for some of them I am still achieving or working towards these goals. Would you class the above being successful? How would you feel if you had completed all of them? Would you want more? Could you sit back and live to work?

There are a few people who I speak to that would say that the above achievements would command a successful individual. I am just getting started, this is confidence not arrogance, as I believe in myself and my abilities.

If you have given a lot to you and your life and goals then keep giving, don't be afraid. What if you were to die, how would you want people to remember you?

Developing the resilience along with the ability to reflect deeply and appreciate the learning that you have been through on the journey to the goal is, I believe, essential. This chapter will explain how to avoid falling into the gap that lies after completion of goals and dreams.

I have created a personal affirmation that I say to myself when I need to hear it:

"I didn't come this far to only come this far. I always hear people saying things like "when I make it" when I get to the top. Okay working hard until I get to the top.. Until I reach my goal, let me tell you something there is no end winners never stop if you reach your goal server big ago if you get to the top of the mountain to find a bigger mountain it's the journey the continued pursuit of growth constant can of proven improvement the challenge that's what makes life great that's what makes a fulfilled life

I didn't come as far is only come this far when I reach this goal. I will seek more, not more things, more growth. Constantly pushing myself to be better. I didn't come this far to only come this far. I came this far so I could be strong enough to go further. So I would be good enough to push myself harder. I'm only getting started. This is just the beginning.

I'm proud of my achievements but that doesn't mean I'll settle for them. I am proud but never satisfied, proud but forever hungry, proud and always ready, proud but pushing - pushing for more, pushing for greatness. A true winner doesn't seek only the title. A true winner seeks growth, the true winner seeks greatness. It's journey is the challenge don't tell me it's over I'm just getting warmed up if the journey wasn't challenging the destination wouldn't be rewarding. It's the challenge that makes the greatness. You can't have a champion athlete without great competitors pushing them all the way. You can't have the greatest of all time without champions pushing them all the way. Is the journey. The process that makes the greatness if you reach your goal set a bigger goal"

This affirmation is the culmination of hard work and self-worth along with an established growth mindset that has taken me over half a decade to develop and also apply to my everyday life. As I mentioned my journey to representing Team GB at the Sochi 2014 Winter Olympics was not the smoothest. It left a very large void/gap in my life and something that I struggle to deal with every day. I do appreciate that this may be a first world problem but as individuals we may have unfinished business with particular goals or dreams that we came so close to achieving.

Most days I am left feeling that a failure and that I need to prove to myself that I have some value to society and myself. This is my why. A very sore an open wound that never quite seems to heal. The sort that you cant put a plaster on and everyone will notice it. Some will stare and gawp, others will ask and some just don't care and go about their business. It is a challenge to accept these views due to how modern society functions and the impact of social media. Where people can hide behind a phone and appear happy and content but the harsh reality is that we are struggling to cope with our wounds.

Solutions

Create a self-affirmation using the eight steps for creating a highly effective statements. I advise you write these down and leave it by your bed, read it every morning or evening.

1. Start with the words *"I am."* These are the two most powerful words in the English language.

2. Use the present tense.

3. State it in the positive. Affirm what you want, not what you don't want.

4. Keep it brief.

5. Make it specific.

6. Include an action word ending with –ing.

7. Include at least one dynamic emotion or feeling word.

8. Make affirmations for yourself, not others.

If you are unsure of how to start please re-read mine above. Personally a big thing I felt was imperative to include was what I was going to do, set a bigger goal. Now as ludicrous as this may sound, it is something that I thrive on and gives me permission to continue to grow and develop. To find out what my limitations and abilities are. Once I have found them I then set about improving them. For me this is mainly in the form of physiological development in the gym but can this may be different for you as it may be in the form of academically, emotional intelligence, financial development and even professional.

Key learning points.

- Only ever make a decision never a sacrifice
- If opportunities don't exist, make them
- Change try to will and hold yourself accountable
- Create a self-affirmation to read every morning and start your day strong

Tough times never last.
Tough people do.

Final Thoughts

I hope you have enjoyed reading my content and that you to have every opportunity to live your dreams and live to inspire others around you. Our lives are just beginning and at no point is it ever to late to start your journey.

I will leave you with some ideas that may help you to make decisions and hopefully start some thought processes for you to take action.

- What are you most afraid of? Your light or your darkness?
- Would you rather live your dreams or your nightmares?
- You have one life or we only die once and live every day.
- When we are born we are not given a use by date on our life, make the most of every day, every opportunity and everyone around you.
- Get shit done
- IF you feel like you are being shit, stop and start being awesome again. Simply put, change your mindset from fixed to growth.
- If you have a dream, go and get it. Protect it. Don't ever let anyone tell you that you cant do something. Simply because they are too afraid to do it themselves.
- FAIL stands for First Attempt In Life
- Learn from decisions, mistakes or failures. Avoid sacrifices.
- We all have areas for development, there are no such things are weaknesses. Some skills we have are better and more developed than others.
- What is it that you value most? If you can figure this out then apply what you do in everyday life to adding value.
- Time is valued less than Money and Health.
- What is your why?
- If you know this and you can combine it with the process that you value then you are on a winning path. The challenge for most can be to find your why?

This life is not to be forced or resisted.

It is to be fully embraced and accepted.

To be the very best that you can be and to live the life that you dare.

48140526R00074

Printed in Poland
by Amazon Fulfillment
Poland Sp. z o.o., Wrocław

ISBN 978-1-330-95085-2
PIBN 10125423

This book is a reproduction of an important historical work. Forgotten Books uses
state-of-the-art technology to digitally reconstruct the work, preserving the original format
whilst repairing imperfections present in the aged copy. In rare cases, an imperfection in
the original, such as a blemish or missing page, may be replicated in our edition. We do,
however, repair the vast majority of imperfections successfully; any imperfections that
remain are intentionally left to preserve the state of such historical works.

1 MONTH OF
FREE
READING

at
www.ForgottenBooks.com

By purchasing this book you are eligible for one month membership to ForgottenBooks.com, giving you unlimited access to our entire collection of over 700,000 titles via our web site and mobile apps.

To claim your free month visit:
www.forgottenbooks.com/free125423

English
Français
Deutsche
Italiano
Español
Português

www.forgottenbooks.com

Mythology Photography **Fiction**
Fishing Christianity **Art** Cooking
Essays Buddhism Freemasonry
Medicine **Biology** Music **Ancient
Egypt** Evolution Carpentry Physics
Dance Geology **Mathematics** Fitness
Shakespeare **Folklore** Yoga Marketing
Confidence Immortality Biographies
Poetry **Psychology** Witchcraft
Electronics Chemistry History **Law**
Accounting **Philosophy** Anthropology
Alchemy Drama Quantum Mechanics
Atheism Sexual Health **Ancient History**
Entrepreneurship Languages Sport
Paleontology Needlework Islam
Metaphysics Investment Archaeology
Parenting Statistics Criminology
Motivational

THE
PLACE OF WOMEN IN
THE CHURCH

BY

H. L. GOUDGE
DARWELL STONE
W. J. SPARROW SIMPSON
LADY HENRY SOMERSET
GERALDINE E. HODGSON
MARY SCHARLIEB
MRS. ROMANES
MISS E. K. SANDERS

LONDON: ROBERT SCOTT
ROXBURGHE HOUSE
PATERNOSTER ROW, E.C.

UNITED STATES OF AMERICA:
THE YOUNG CHURCHMAN CO.,
MILWAUKEE, WIS.

MCMXVII

CONTENTS

CONTENTS

INTRODUCTION

THE place of Women in the Church is no subject of mere academical interest. It has become increasingly prominent of recent years. To go no further back than 1908, much was said about it in the Papers of the Pan-Anglican Congress. It was maintained by one writer that it was difficult to find any decided rule by which the question what should be considered women's work can be determined " unless we are prepared to admit that a woman should be free to do any work for which she can show herself capable." No reference being made to the principles or traditions of the Church.

Similar uncertainties existed on the status of a Deaconess in the Church. One writer maintained that the order :

" is a Holy Order, a part of the ministry of the Church ; those therefore who are admitted to it cannot be dispensed from it as from a vow, but they receive character which is lifelong. . . . A Deaconess having thus secured her ministry feels that a special grace having been thereby bestowed upon her for her work, she is asked to offer to God her full life. It would outrage her conscience if she married or was otherwise untrue to the requirements of her office."

The Bishops were accordingly called upon by the

writer, herself a Deaconess, to remember " the in-delible character " of the Ordination conferred.

On the other hand the Canons of the General Con-vention of New York rule that " such appointment shall be vacated by marriage." Upon this regulation an American Deaconess observes, in the same series of Papers

" There are those who hold that the Deaconess is, by the laying on of hands, introduced into the lowest order of the Threefold Ministry. The difficulties which confront those who hold this theory are twofold. First, the Deaconess is not commissioned to exercise the full work of the Deacon as defined in the Ordinal ; secondly, the Deaconess forfeits her office if she marries, while to the Deacon marriage makes no difference.

" The more generally accepted theory regarding the authority conferred is that the Deaconess is introduced by the laying on of hands into an Order of the Church which was created in the primitive age for women, which Order, although it gives her a place among the ministers of the Church, is not to be confounded with the Threefold Ministry."

These are illustrations of the diversity of opinion on the Ministry of Women. They imply diverse principles of a far-reaching kind on the nature of ordina-tion and the intention of the Church.

The place of women in the Church came into discus-sion at the meeting of the Representative Church Council in July, 1914.

On the morning of July 10, the Bishop of South-well moved Clause b as follows :

" (b) That if a Diocesan Conference so decides, women may sit as lay representatives on the Ruridecanal Conferences and on the Diocesan Conference of the diocese."

The matter was debated at some length. Opinions

8

INTRODUCTION

were divided and amendments suggested. The last speaker in the debate was Mr. H. W. Hill. The report of his speech which follows is taken from the official *Report of Proceedings* :

"Mr. H. W. Hill said that there was a strong feeling outside that the question had been rather unnaturally forced upon the Council, and that it was one that called for much more deliberation than it had received. Something had been said about the logic which might govern such matters as the present subject, and it was in reference to that particular point that he wanted to say a few words. He wondered whether the Council were aware that steps were really being taken to bring about a conference to discuss the question of the ordination of women to the priesthood.

"A large number of preliminary inquiries had been sent round to women who were supposed to be in favour of such a step. Replies of a favourable character had been received from a great number. He had seen many of those replies. They were very illuminating. The general position was thus expressed : 'Our feeling is that the priesthood is a human office, not at all a sexual one, and since women are human beings it is unreasonable to refuse them an opportunity of holding it, merely because they are women.' Another person let the cat out of the bag. She said: 'The proposal is calculated to alienate many who are now favourable to the suffrage movement.' Another said : 'The time is not ripe. We had better concentrate our energies upon Church Councils.' Another said : 'The time is not ripe. It would hinder suffragism. Work is needed in regard to Church Councils.'

"He was told that amongst women of a certain sort this matter was being very hotly discussed, and that their methods would do no discredit to the most venturesome of higher critics. The Bishop of London rather poured scorn yesterday upon that feeling which regarded the dangers of the thin end of the wedge. The thin end of the wedge was already inserted. It was in no narrow spirit that he ventured to offer information upon the particular development to which he had referred. The Bishop of Southwell, in his speech on the previous day, had said that the time had come for giving to women the power of ministering. Mr. Hill asked the Bishop whether the use of such language was not calculated to

9

create some false hopes among such people as those whose opinions he had quoted. He was in favour of using the good offices of women in all sorts of ways, both in the Church and in the State ; but with regard to Church matters, as the Council had been reminded by Mr. Howard, there was such a] thing as catholic order. If the Council disregarded that fact it would go some way towards making itself the laughing-stock of the rest of Christendom."

There can be no question that Mr. Hill's speech was one of warning. Immediately he resumed his seat, the Archbishop of Canterbury stated that he would put the motion as a whole as it stood. In reply to questions from the Bishop of Winchester and Lord Parmoor His Grace said they could not follow House of Commons rules, adding, " I think that I will put this as a Resolution which is capable of amendment. If it is completely rejected, *cadit quæstio*, if it is not then it becomes the substantive Resolution which can be amended in any detail."

On the demand of the Bishop of St. Albans the Council voted by Houses. The motion was lost, the voting being as follows :

	For	Against
Bishops . .	13	8
Clergy . . .	36	39
Laity . .	27	94
	76	141

It will be seen that the motion was carried by the Bishops, but rejected by the clergy and laymen.

The place of women in the Church has been forced into prominence in connexion with the National Mission. The subject was introduced by the Central Committee of the National Mission.

By that Committee the principle was laid down

of the equality of men and women in the sight of God, and went on to explain the meaning to be, " equality in privilege, equality in calling, equality in opportunity of service."

Following upon this declaration of principle by the Central Committee, there came the definite action of some individual Bishops for their own dioceses. Women were under certain clearly defined conditions allowed to preach.

The conditions laid down by the Bishop of London for Women preachers were as follows : -

" (1) They must only speak to women and girls.

" (2) They must in all cases have the permission of the Bishop.

" (3) They must have the full consent of the incumbent.

" (4) They must not speak from the pulpit, lectern, or chancel steps.

" This permission only holds good up to the end of the period of the National Mission."

The approval given by certain Bishops to the introduction of women preachers as part of the agencies in the National Mission met with very considerable opposition both from Evangelicals and High Churchmen. The former did not see their way to reconcile it with the teaching of St. Paul. The latter were unable to reconcile it either with St. Paul or with the tradition of the Church.

Opposition on the High Church side was led by Mr. Athelstan Riley, whose correspondence with the Archbishop of Canterbury upon the subject, when published in the newspapers, awakened considerable attention within the Church and beyond it.

The correspondence did not reach any harmonious conclusion. His Grace complained of the tone of Mr. Athelstan Riley's letters. And Mr. Athelstan Riley considered the Archbishop's replies evasive and unsatisfactory.

Mr. Athelstan Riley contended that the notion,

"That women should speak in the churches is in direct conflict with Holy Scripture, with the express injunctions of St. Paul in the First Epistle to the Corinthians and with the common order of the Catholic Church. If this innovation is to be imported into the methods of the National Mission disaster must inevitably follow."

He also claimed that :

"this resolution to allow women to speak in our churches, carried in an unguarded moment by the Council [of the National Mission], is the first recognized step in an organized movement to claim the priesthood for women." [1]

Mr. Riley reminded the Archbishop that the Representative Church Council, at its session in July, 1914, was warned of this movement.

"I now turn to a graver matter which has no connexion with the National Mission except to show the need for caution in dealing with the Women's Movement and some of the ladies connected with it. For this resolution to allow women to speak in our churches, carried in an unguarded moment by the Council, is the first recognized step in an organized movement to claim the priesthood for women. It is not generally known that just before the great war, when the Suffragettes were being guilty of all kinds of offences against law and order, even to the extent of burning churches, a section of them were secretly preparing for an attack upon the ministry of the Church. The Representative Church Council at its session in July, 1914, was warned of this conspiracy. But it looks as if the warning had been unheeded by the rulers of the Church. .   I need not say more about this as all the documents connected with the case, documents indicating the methodical way in which the priesthood is to be won by women step by step, have been placed in your Grace's hands."

The Archbishop in his reply extenuated the move-

[1] *Church Times,* July 28, 1916, p. 80.

ment. He said he had observed with much appreciation what is being done both in England and in France by " women who have quietly gathered a few girls and children in church, and helped to guide their prayers."

Much controversy ensued. Attention was called again to the fact that the question of women preachers, and also women priests, had already been the subject of correspondence in a section of women interested in the women's movement. We have already seen that public reference had been made to this correspondence by Mr. H. W. Hill at the meeting of the Representative Church Council in 1914. But his emphatic warning seems somehow to have escaped the attention of his clerical and lay hearers.

A few months before the beginning of the War an effort was made to organize a conference to discuss the question of the Ordination of women to the priesthood. A circular letter was sent to about a hundred and fifty women, in which the authoress said ·

" Our feeling is that priesthood is a human office, not at all a sexual one, and that since women are human beings it is unreasonable to refuse them an opportunity of holding it merely because they are women. I know at least one woman who feels that she has the vocation ; and this woman would have made, so far as one can see, an almost ideal priest. The weight of custom seems to us to be quenching the Spirit of God. The loss to the Church appears to us lamentable."

A summary of about ninety answers received was drawn up at considerable length.

Some were unfavourable. One thought the proposal premature, and calculated to alienate many who are now sympathetic towards the Suffrage movement. Another thought the limitation of the priesthood to men not an accidental, but an essential part of the Catholic Faith. Another held that ordained or official priests must be men, because they must be ready to celebrate Holy Communion at any moment. Women cannot, because of their potential motherhood. Another urged that there was no woman among the Apostles. Another, that our Lord never contemplated it; it would do much harm to the Church.

Some were interested, but not convinced. One felt that the proposal to admit women to the priesthood was enormously revolutionary, yet a logical outcome of the Women's Movement. Another saw grave practical objections to a mixed priesthood of men and women. Another thought that as motherhood is the supreme vocation of women, possibly the priesthood is the supreme vocation of men. Another held that such a movement could only be justified if it came in response to a felt need. That need was not felt at present. It must be felt by the Church at large, and not only by the women who may desire the privilege. It would be an obstacle in the way of reunion with the Eastern Church. It would hinder the progress of the deaconess movement if it was thought that the diaconate of women was to be a stepping-stone to the priesthood.

Some were favourable. One held that women should be qualified to hold services and to preach, but because it is necessary that the Church hold fast to the doctrine of the Apostolic Succession passing through a male priesthood, it is not fitting that deaconesses should administer any of the sacraments. Another was only doubtful whether the present hour is the tactful moment to begin to agitate. Better get the vote for women first. At present we should shock many earnest-minded women, more than we should win over. Indeed, until the Catholic Church is once more united, and we can have our restored Council of the whole of undivided Christendom, she did not see where valid orders could be obtained. We Anglicans are a branch of the Catholic Church, and not a sect to do what pleases ourselves apart from the whole undivided Church. Another was sure that the time was not ripe for making any kind of claim. Another would like to see priestesses and women Bishops in due course, but thought there were other things to make sure of first. Another complained that the Church had no room for educated women. Another agreed with the idea, but felt that all the energies of women should be first given to winning the vote. The struggle for entrance into the priesthood will be hard and prolonged. Another did not think that the time will be ripe for this momentous change until two generations after the vote has been won, and after the Church has been disestablished.

The existence of this Conference among women had been known for at least a year to many persons. As we have said public attention had been called to it in the Representative Church Council of July, 1914. Several remarkable extracts from the correspondence, showing the nature of its tendencies and principles, had been repeated in the presence of the Bishops, priests and laymen of that Council. But hitherto the correspondence had not been in public circulation. Those who knew of its existence considered that the warning given in the Representative Church Council

should be sufficient, and had no desire to give unnecessary publicity to a movement which they deplored.

However now, after the failure of his correspondence
with the Archbishop to reach any reassuring result, Mr.
Athelstan Riley thought it well to enable Churchmen
to realize the nature of the movements which had been
hitherto confined to unpublished documents. The
publication of the women's circular letter and the
answers sent in response to it evoked much surprise.
It appeared that some in high positions, and some
sympathizers of the Women's Movement, were not
aware that in discussion among women their claims
to be preachers and priests were being freely and
frankly advanced.

Subsequent events have shown that this Conference
of Women by no means stands alone. Their claims,
at any rate to the office of preacher, have been
advocated in many directions since.

The immediate effect of the publication of the
report of the Women's Conference was unquestionably
to strengthen the opposition to women preachers.

In the London Diocese a memorial appeared, signed
by many leading clergy, complaining that the sanction of women preachers would compel them to
withdraw from all co-operation with the National
Mission.

" We, the undersigned priests of the diocese of London,
under a grave sense of responsibility, feel it our duty to
declare that we cannot continue our preparations for the
National Mission in union with the Central Council, neither
can we accept a ' messenger ' to be sent to our parishes as
part of the scheme formulated by the Central Council. We
are driven to this conclusion because of the resolution of the
Council urging upon the Bishops ' the importance of giving
definite directions as to the best ways of using the services

and receiving the message of women speakers whether in church or elsewhere.' We believe that to grant permission to women to preach in our churches is contrary to the teaching of Holy Scripture and to the mind and general practice of the whole Catholic Church. Still more, we believe that such permission will be an encouragement to those women who publicly claim their right to be appointed to the priesthood and Episcopate of the Church, which claim is heretical."

It was highly probable that a similar memorial might appear in other dioceses also.

Here then was a critical time. It looked as if the forces of the English Church would be divided just at the very moment when the National Mission required fullest harmonious co-operation ; and divided by the sanction given to the preaching of women.

An article by Dr. Percy Dearmer in the *Guardian* supported the preaching of women on the ground that St. Paul by his injunction that women should keep silence in the churches was only forbidding them to chatter while men were speaking, and further that St. Paul permitted women to prophesy in church. He held that the prejudice against women taking services was an Anglican peculiarity.

To these assertions the Principal of the Pusey House replied complaining that Dr. Dearmer's inter-pretation of St. Paul was " as perverse as his article was clever "; that it " ran counter to the general mind of the Church, as well as to the teaching of St. Paul." He concluded with an appeal against the introduction of such a subject at a moment when unity was essential.[1]

" I write as one who has much sympathy with many fea-tures in what is known as the ' Women's Movement.' For years I have done what I could in what seemed rightly my

---

[1] P. 387.

sphere to promote the increase of women's influence in political affairs and in many Church matters. But the claims suggested by Dr. Dearmer's article run counter to the general mind of the Church as well as to the teaching of St. Paul. And what a tragedy it is that, when we should all be united for the work of the National Mission, there is a project for promoting such ministrations of women as would make it necessary for those women and men who pay regard to Holy Scripture and the traditions of the Church to stay away from and discountenance the services in which these take place ! "

Meanwhile the movement within the English Church upon the subject was being watched, with curious and critical eyes, in the Roman Press.

The *Tablet* remarked that :

" The wonderful movement within the Anglican Church in favour of allowing women to deliver what are called ' messages ' in church continues to excite a wide attention, and also considerable opposition. It seems not unlikely, indeed, that the movement may even spoil the success of the proposed National Mission. In the diocese of London the clergy are being invited to sign a protest. . . . It is considered probable that the clergy of the diocese of Chelmsford will take similar action. The London News Agency has been informed by Mr. H. W. Hill, secretary to the English Church Union, that such action is certain to be taken in every diocese where Bishops allow what is described as this ' grave departure from Catholic order.' So far only two Bishops appear to have announced their intention of allowing women to talk in church : the Bishops of London and Chelmsford. . . . Happily there is always the well-known ' comprehensiveness ' of the Church of England to encourage us to hope that within the wide borders of the Establishment room may be found for all : and that those who accept the teaching of St. Paul, and those who reject it, may continue to find themselves equally at home there."

The Bishops who had sanctioned the innovation appeared to agree with the Principal of Pusey House to this extent : that a subject which created disunion in the National Mission was clearly inexpedient. Accordingly their sanction was withdrawn from women preachers : so far as addresses in consecrated buildings were concerned.

The agitation on the subject of women preachers in church produced the following letter from the Bishop of London · [1]

" SIR,—

" I find that during my absence from London on a visit to the Grand Fleet, during which I had no time to read either the London daily papers or the Church papers, a considerable controversy has arisen with regard to women having classes for women and girls during the mission in church, and the matter has apparently been mixed up with the question of a woman priesthood.

" I had never even heard of the movement for a woman priesthood until I read the correspondence unearthed by Mr. Riley, and should most strongly oppose it as both undesirable and uncatholic. But I confess I thought that, with hundreds of women taking classes for girls and children, and even boys, in churches now every Sunday, it was not a great concession to allow them during the few weeks of the mission (which in London does not begin till November) to enlarge their classes for women and girls.

" The absolute barring of official places, such as pulpit and lectern, and also of the chancel steps (when it was pointed out to me that this, too, had grown to be an official place), was meant to emphasize the strictly limited concession made. To talk of women being ' allowed to preach in church ' is an unconscious or deliberate perversion of the facts. But, quite as clearly, this limited concession has been widely misunderstood, and must be reconsidered. Nothing must be allowed to harm the mission ; the devil is, no doubt, working for some way of doing it, and he must not be allowed to succeed. I take the whole blame of any harm which has been done, and only ask for a truce to all protests and counter-protests.

" No women messengers have received any licence yet in London to give their message either in or outside a church, and I am certain that the high-minded women who will be entrusted with the responsibility will only wish to act as is thought best for the Church and nation at large. After visiting twenty-five dioceses to start the mission, and giving

[1] *Daily Telegraph*, August 17, 1916.

eight or ten addresses every day during my visit to the Fleet, I am not ashamed to say that I am having a few weeks' rest ; but I return to London on September 4, and I ask the London clergy at any rate to await my return and come and confer with me after my return on the whole subject.

" Yours faithfully,

" *August* 15. " A. F. LONDON.

" P.S.—I have reason to believe that the Bishop of Chelmsford will follow the same line which we take in his old diocese of London."

The Bishop of London further issued the following announcement :

" Pending a decision by the united Episcopate as to the Church's use of the ministry of the laity, both men and women, the Bishop of London has decided that those of his messengers who are women will deliver their message during the Mission in parish halls or schoolrooms. The Bishop desires above everything else that on the eve of this momentous enterprise, which must claim the united strength of the whole diocese, the work should be in no way weakened by controversy on any matter."

The Bishop of Oxford, on the other hand, in his Diocesan Magazine entered a strong protest against endeavours to innovate by individualistic enterprise and without corporate action.

" Once more, I am asked to sanction women giving addresses in church. That again is a matter so plainly contrary to the tradition of the Church that I think it will be disastrous to leave it to this Bishop to allow or that Bishop to prohibit. There must, first of all, be some corporate action of the Church. What we are being encouraged to scrap, it seems to me, is something much more important than the Act of Uniformity, or a particular tradition which may be mistaken. It is the principle of the corporate action of the Church and of corporate loyalty. Laity, clergy, and Bishops, we all alike need to realize that the only way of salvation for the Church of England is the way of corporate government. Bishop Ellicott used to say that however much the Bishops confer, after all they remain ' toparchs,' local rulers, each ruling according to his own judgment. He might have said the same thing sub-

INTRODUCTION

stantially of incumbents in their parishes. This 'toparchy'
or individualism has gone much too far. I do pray that this
National Mission, while it emphasizes and deepens our sense of
needful change, will deepen even more our sense of the need
of the great change, the restoration to the Church of the
power which it ought never to have parted with, the power to
bind and loose, the only power which can lift us out of the
peril alike of Erastianism and of Protestant particularism :
the only power which can restore the sense of corporate
loyalty, which is the essence of Catholic order."

Much correspondence ensued in the journals devoted
to religious interests. It was pointed out that the
distinction between women preaching in church (meaning thereby consecrated buildings) and women preaching in unconsecrated places, was superficial, and was
not contemplated by St. Paul (as there were no consecrated buildings in his day). The real question
being the official position of women in the Church,
meaning thereby the Divinely founded Society, or
Corporate Institution ; or, to put it in other words,
in the public services of the mixed congregation of
men and women.

The discussion on women preachers and priestesses
entered widely into the pages of the general press.
Among the arguments propounded by women were
the following :

A lady of social distinction was quoted in the press
as having defended the cause of women preachers in
the following way :

"The question, Should women preach ? could never have
arisen but for certain very doubtful and uninspired writings
in the New Testament, which are diametrically opposed to
Christianity : if by Christianity is meant the teachings of
Jesus Christ."

Another said :

" There is one question I should like to put to the Bishop of

21

London. When he consented to allow women to preach in church, but only to women and children, is that because he thinks women and children of so little value that it really does not matter whether they are left to unordained preachers or not ? or does he consider them so good that they do not need an ordained priest to guide them ? "

Another was a great deal more emphatic :

" If women by reason of their sex are forbidden access to the sacred precincts of the church, it may safely be predicted that in a few years' time no self-respecting woman will be seen entering the door of any church that offers this supreme insult to her sex and to her personality."

Both the *Nineteenth Century* and the *Contemporary Review* inserted articles on the Ministry of Women. In the *Nineteenth Century* for September, 1916, Miss Picton-Turbervill complained in a somewhat impassioned article, that artificial restrictions and paralyzing customs had excluded women from that exposition of religion before the world which is her rightful prerogative :

" for throughout the ages one half of humanity alone has been called to guide in thought the Church of Christ. At once we recognize the exceptions, Catherine . of Sienna, Santa Theresa, and others ; but in the main man has reserved to himself the power to express fully to the world his conception of the mind of God, and in the aggregate woman has been told that to the world at large she can have no such message to give."

Mr. Athelstan Riley replied in *The Nineteenth Century* to Miss Picton-Turbervill's article on the place of women in the coming order in the Church of Christ. The reply is entitled " Male and Female created He them," and the main purpose is to insist that diversity of constitution implies diversity of function.

" As between the sexes I say boldly there is inequality in privilege, inequality in calling, inequality in opportunity of service. There is one set of physical functions peculiar to the man, and there is another set peculiar to the woman, and no 'movement' will ever succeed in making them interchangeable. So there are certain moral qualities conspicuous in the man and other moral qualities in the woman. Even in their sins they differ : temptation to sexual immorality is far weaker in the woman than in the man, while the consequences of the sin to the character are more serious in the woman, and the injury done to the family by the mother more profound. No Acts of Parliament can alter these fundamental facts. Who does not know that man energizes more by reason and woman more by instinct ; that deliberation is the safety of the one, quickness of apprehension of the other ? . . .

" Now, if all this be true in the natural sphere, is it unreasonable that it should be true in the supernatural sphere, and that here too there should be inequalities and differences in callings and functions ? " [1]

The *Contemporary Review* for October, 1916, inserted an article entitled " Should Women Speak in Church ? " The writer maintained that 1 Corinthians xiv. 34

" would in itself be final but for two considerations : (1) St. Paul himself states a higher principle superseding this rule ; (2) woman's status to-day and our whole social environment are totally different from St. Paul's day."

The higher principle is :

" there is neither Jew nor Greek, neither bond nor free, there is neither male nor female ; for ye are all one in Christ Jesus." [2]
" These principles," the writer urges, " implicit in Christianity from the first, spell death to Jewish exclusiveness, slavery, sex-inferiority, as Paul foresaw. The retention of any one of these barriers maims Christianity and convicts it of failure."

The author accused Catholics with still clinging to the letter of an isolated precept of Paul " voiced to meet a local and temporary case at Corinth, and ignoring the whole spirit of Paul and his Master Christ " They are " making a fetish of Paul's theology, exactly as the Jews did of the Mosaic Law."

[1] *Nineteenth Century* October 1916, p. 838.
[2] Gal. iii. 28.

23

But presently it was admitted that Catholics share this narrowness with St. Paul.

" St. Paul's whole teaching of women and ascetic views on marriage are surprisingly narrow for a liberal Paul, survivals of his Rabbinic teaching, an old garment showing around the rest of his new cloth."

The author did not attempt to define how far this equality of function is to extend ; and whether the priesthood and the Episcopate are also on Christian principles assignable to women. This would appear to be logically involved in his proposition.

Miss Picton-Turbervill wrote in the *Nineteenth Century* for November, 1916, a further statement of her opinions on the Ministry of Women. She reasserted that

" in the teaching of Christ, not only is there nothing contrary to the inclusion of women in the ministry of the Church, but by His attitude to women and by His teaching it is clear that they, equally with men, are His channels."

This proposition was apparently meant to affirm the vocation of women to the priesthood and Episcopate equally with men. The writer said that a clergyman, on reading her previous article, wrote to say that it was a revelation to him, and that he considered it unanswerable. The writer, however, did not herself endorse this view. For she says :

" Answerable, however, it admittedly is, if argument be built upon Church tradition and ecclesiastical history, but unanswerable, we believe, if the answer be sought for in the teaching of Christ.

" The teaching and tradition of the Church is contrary to the full inclusion of women within its ministry ; it has yet to be shown that it is contrary to the teaching of the Church's Founder. Church tradition is, we are well aware, no mere report, and has its weight which must not be ignored, yet it cannot be considered final unless it can stand that test."

INTRODUCTION

The discussion is also being further extended in pamphlets.

A pamphlet by Miss Maude Royden on *Women and the Church of England* expressly demands discussion on the subject of the priesthood, and presumably also the Episcopate for women. The author challenges Churchpeople to give reasons why women should not be ordained.

" The mere question, ' Why should not women be admitted to holy orders ? ' causes some Churchmen to cry out and cut themselves with knives, while others, more reasonable, answer us that there are indeed reasons, but of a character so fundamental as to prohibit their being put into words. With this it is expected that women, women of the twentieth century, will be content ! But, alas ! *somehow this comment does not now satisfy.* We desire reasons, and it seems to us nothing but a comedy to suggest that this desire is monstrous, and that no such question should be so much as discussed by the people whom it most intimately concerns. Where, then, have these gentlemen who deny us lived ? In what little island of thought have they been segregated from the contagion and movements of modern life, that they honestly believe they can by loud shouting and abusive language silence the demand for reasons when any great monopoly is on its defence ? It is possible that women have not the vocation for the priesthood ; but it is not possible to persuade them that they commit a crime when they raise the question and ask for an answer. Nor will they consider their doing so as a conspiracy."

Another pamphlet by Mr. John Lee, entitled *The Church and Women*, is important because it is an address delivered in the Church of St. Martin-in-the-Fields. The author recognized that " there was some justice in the contention which was made editorially by a Church paper that the Church of England did not possess sufficient power of discipline to enable her to keep within proper bounds a concession or a development which, in itself, was quite legitimate."

But he held that " though that contention was just, it is infinitely pathetic." But he took comfort in the reflection that " If the Church of England cannot control a development of women's work she is equally incompetent to choose her hymns." [1]

The author pleaded for " a just attitude to the relationship between man and woman." He contended that

" It is not a question of women for the priesthood : that question cannot be reached until the Church has her discipline, until she has authorized more hymns than one, and at long length succeeded in electing her own Bishops. It is a question of attitude to women."

But no attempt was made to go down to principles whether of human nature or of the Catholic Church. He omitted to say what the basis was on which a just attitude was to be determined.

The subject is still being eagerly debated. A tract *Concerning Churchwomen*, or " a plea for admission to the Councils of the Church," by Miss Gertrude Bayley, second edition, revised, holds that the teaching of St. Paul is by no means decisive for Christian women whatever it may be for Christian men.

" One prominent Churchman has said that 'St. Paul's statement that women were not to speak in the Church is absolutely decisive for Christian men.' But even if St. Paul's words really had that meaning (which is more than doubtful), they would be by no means decisive for Christian women, who hold fast by the teaching of the Lord Jesus Christ, Whose they are and Whom they serve, and to Whom alone they owe implicit obedience. Surely it is against all reason and common sense, and contrary to that law of progress which works in the world, that the regulations which St. Paul may have thought fit to make for his Corinthian convert

---

[1] P. 6.

should be for ever observed by the women of all nations. The Holy Apostle St. Paul was subject to human limitations. He not only admits the fact, but passionately asserts it. He was not God Incarnate, and to treat his words as equal to those of the Lord Himself is idolatry." [1]

Then again a public meeting in London was reported in *The Times* for January 8, 1917, in which it was declared that St. Paul was not a guide in social and political matters.

" Lady Selborne, speaking yesterday at a meeting at St. George's Vestry Hall, Bloomsbury, on the subject of women in the Church, said she represented the moderate party and Miss Picton-Turbervill the forward movement.

" The Church was, she said, obviously not getting the best it could out of women, but the form of their ministry should be a question for the Church to settle. Even taking the traditions of the Church, there had been prophetesses from the time of Deborah, who delivered the message of God to the people, and this method of delivering a message might be restored. Such women as Josephine Butler and Octavia Hill delivered their message, but not with the authority of the Church or in the Church. Such women as these should have been enlisted in the service of the Church. There were many devout women with the gift of speech who would be efficient evangelists, and it was regrettable that the Church was driven to use inferior men when they had good women at their disposal.

" Miss Picton-Turbervill said in an invitation recently issued on a Church anniversary it was announced that the Vicar would speak on the history of the Church, the Curate on women's work for the Church, and the churchwardens on their office, and in small print it was announced that the ladies would give the tea and coffee. Before a congress of Churchwomen some time ago she approached a Vicar for the use of the chapel-at-ease for a meeting of prayer and intercession for women. He agreed until he heard that a woman was to lead in the intercession. ' You can't do this,' he said. ' The place is consecrated.' The idea seemed to be that the fullness of the grace of God flowed only through men. This attitude was entirely opposed to that of the Founder of the

---

[1] P. 3.

Christian Faith.   There was no trace of sex or class distinction in His teaching, and the first Easter message of life and power was given to women.   In the Early Church women had a far larger share in the ministry than they had to-day ; then for a time there was a return to the Eastern idea of women.   In the Middle Ages women were again heard in the Church. There was, for instance, Hilda of Whitby.   Then by degrees they received a crushing ecclesiastical set-back.   A Bishop had given as the reason that women were over-sexualized. In the Church, year in and year out, nonsense was being preached, and women had to listen Sunday after Sunday to young callow parsons telling them of their conception of the mind of God.   Through ages man had reserved to himself the power to explain the mind of God.   The Church would have more influence to-day if the attitude of Christ towards women had been more closely followed.

" In a discussion, the question of St. Paul's teaching that women should be silent in the Church was raised.   Lady Selborne answered that St. Paul was not a guide in social and political matters, that he had defended slavery, and that his views were urged by the opponents of the emancipation of slaves.   It was suggested by Miss Picton-Turbervill that women might be given licences to preach in a Church in the same way as a layman."

This summary of recent discussion on the place of women in the Church shows plainly enough that the subject has taken hold upon the modern mind.   It has become a matter of serious attention among thoughtful men and women.   This interest was not created by the National Mission.   It was a natural result of the Women's Movement.   Discussion on the place of women in the political order inevitably led to discussion on their place in the Church.

Many persons no doubt have carefully followed the course of this debate.   Some would call it desultory and superficial.   It has been characteristically English.   It has concerned itself far more with expediency than with principles.   It has shown no little confusion of thought. There has been an element of wildness and rhetoric not conducive to a reasoned conclusion. Far more has been written in attack of the Church's tradition than in support of it. And the attack has been conducted from many conflicting points of view, with assumptions as to the value of Apostolic teaching, or of the Church's practice, which naturally lead to results which a Catholic is unable to accept.

It further appears that sanction was withdrawn from women preachers during the National Mission on the motive of expediency : in order that no controversy, and no division among Churchmen should be permitted to thwart their harmonious co-operation. But this only postponed the subject and with an evident intention to resume it at a later date.

The Bishop of Oxford had said that to sanction women giving addresses in church was so plainly contrary to the tradition of the Church that it would be disastrous to leave it to individual Bishops to allow or prohibit. " There must first of all be some corporate action of the Church " In the Upper House of the Canterbury Convocation, February 8, 1917, the status of women in the work of the Church was mentioned, and the Archbishop, before proceeding to the order of business, announced that the Archbishops had appointed a Committee of Bishops and scholars to consider and report to the Archbishops upon (a) " The sanctions and restrictions which govern the ministrations of women in the life of the Church," and (b) " The status and work of deaconesses." Its Chairman would be Bishop Ryle, and its members would include the Bishops of Winchester and Southwark, the Dean of Wells, Dr. Frere, Dr. Headlam, Dr. Weitbrecht, and Miss Alice Gardner.

Meanwhile it is but natural and right that those who adhere to the principles of the Catholic tradition should bear witness at a time when, as it seems to them, there is a curious undervaluation of apostolic precedent even in quarters where they had every right to look for stronger things.

The Teaching of St. Paul as to the Position of Women

By THE REV. CANON GOUDGE,
Principal of Ely Theological College

IT is, as all Christians will agree, a matter of great importance which is the subject of this paper. The mind of the Church as to the position of women has been formed by the teaching of St. Paul more than by the teaching of any other writer of Holy Scripture. Indeed, it would scarcely be too much to say that Holy Scripture contains no teaching on this subject, which St. Paul does not recognize. He reasserts all the highest teaching of the Old Testament; he follows closely the example and teaching of the Lord; and when other writers of the New Testament deal with the subject, they deal with it exactly on the lines which St. Paul has already laid down. Moreover, to all this the controversy, which has arisen in our own day, gives the clearest confirmation. The teaching of St. Paul lies at the root, both of that wide emancipation of women, with which the Church has so deep a sympathy, and of that caution, by which in the Church's wisest teachers that sympathy is always accompanied. Where, on the other hand, the Church's caution is disliked or repudiated, the teaching of St. Paul is disliked and repudiated also. Frequently he is charged with being inconsistent with himself. On the one hand, it is said, he lays down a grand principle, entirely inconsistent with any restrictions upon a woman's freedom, and, on the other hand, in his detailed instruction, lamentably fails to be faithful to it. He is still a slave to Oriental prejudice and encumbered by the small-clothes of Judaism. He bases his case for the continued subjection of women not only upon the assumption that the primitive folklore of Genesis is literal history, but upon a forced and unnatural interpretation of the language of that folk-lore itself. What is permanently valuable in St. Paul is the grand principle which he lays down, that in Christ " there can be no male and female " [1]; and our right course to-day is to hold fast his principle, while we ignore the timid and inconsistent limitations which he unhappily attaches to it. Now it is the justice of this attitude towards St. Paul's teaching which we must examine, and we can only do so by careful consideration of the teaching itself. St. Paul is not a very lucid writer, but he is an extremely deep and acute thinker ; though he is frequently " rude in speech," he is never rude " in knowledge." [2] He combines quite marvellously the wide grasp of the Christian theologian with the practical common sense of the Christian ruler and guide of souls. Thus it is very foolish to charge him with inconsistency, before we have carefully examined all that

[1] I Gal. iii. 28.   [2] 2 Cor. xi. 6.

he says, and considered the circumstances under which he says it. We do not at all wish to brush aside all criticism of St. Paul as necessarily irreverent and presumptuous. He himself appeals to our reason and conscience, and speaks at times as one who has " no commandment of the Lord." [1] His education was a Jewish education, and he was undoubtedly ignorant of much that we now know as to the character of the Old Testament literature. But he certainly regards his teaching as to the true position of women as having a far higher authority than his own individual judgment, and it will be time enough to set it aside, when we have learned, like Queen Esther with Mordecai's lamentation, [2] both what it is and why it is.

Now, before addressing ourselves to St. Paul's actual teaching, it may be well briefly to consider the supposed Orientalism of his outlook. It is one thing, when we have convinced ourselves that St. Paul's teaching is unworthy of him, to make the charitable suggestion that his Oriental training is the explanation of the fact: it is quite another to approach his teaching with the assumption that he thought of women like a potentate of the Arabian Nights. St. Paul was not a Turk, but a Hebrew of the Hebrews, and, if we suppose that the Hebrews of St. Paul's day held degraded views of women, we suppose what is not the fact. Both the teaching and the language of the Old Testament with regard to women no doubt at times leave much to be desired, but our Lord has taught us how to regard them. He contrasts the Old Testament at its highest with the lower standard

[1] 1 Cor. vii. 25.   [2] Esther iv. 5.

33

permitted because of men's " hardness of heart." [1]
His own reference is to the permission of divorce,
but His words have a wider application. The grand
ideal of marriage, to which He refers us, is as much
the condemnation of polygamy as it is of divorce.
Now polygamy and divorce, however necessary for
men's hardness of heart before the " grace and truth " [2]
of our Lord have come to them, are institutions cruelly
unjust to women. Not only do they involve a different standard of purity for men and for women,
and ruin the home ; they degrade women both directly
and indirectly. A further injustice follows. Such
a writer as Ecclesiastes not only regards women from
the standpoint of the Oriental harem ; he proceeds
to abuse them for being what the harem makes them.
But then, as we have now come to understand, the Old
Testament must be judged rather by its general tendency than by the standards accepted at a particular
moment. The Divine Teacher takes us as we are, that
He may gradually train us to be what at present we
are not, and the general tendency of the Old Testament, in regard to the position of women, is in the
right direction. Even in the law itself, we find a
tenderness for the slave-woman, for which it would
probably be impossible to find a parallel in the legislation of other ancient peoples. [3] Though polygamy
is permitted, it is not in the least encouraged ; [4]
indeed, throughout the narratives of the Old Testament, it hardly ever appears without bringing disaster in its train. What sort of encouragement to
polygamy would Israel have found in such family

[1] Mk. x. 5.　　[2] John i. 17.　　[3] Exod. xxi. 7-11.
[4] Deut. xvii. 17—probably a reference to Solomon.

34

histories as that of David, or of Solomon, or even of Abraham himself? So it is with divorce. It is permitted, but that is all; and the Old Testament ends with a denunciation of the practice as full of tenderness for women as it is of understanding of the purpose of the family. "Ye cover with tears the altars of Jehovah, with weeping and with groaning, because respect is no longer had to the offering and acceptable gifts are not taken from your hand. And ye say, Why? Because Jehovah has been witness between thee and the wife of thy youth, with whom thou hast broken faith, though she is thy mate and thy wife by covenant. . . . Take heed, then, to your spirit, and be not unfaithful to the wife of thy youth. For I hate divorce, saith Jehovah, God of Israel."[1] Nor is this all. We shall not understand the estimate of women, which the Old Testament tended to create, without paying attention both to the honour accorded to the mother, and to the place of women in Hebrew story. In the home the Hebrew woman is not a slave, but a ruler, sharing the authority of her husband over their children. The books of Proverbs and Ecclesiasticus make this entirely clear. "My son, hear the instruction of thy father, and forsake not the law of thy mother."[2] "The Lord hath given the father glory as touching the children, and hath confirmed the judgment of the mother as touching the sons. He that honoureth his father shall make atonement for sins: and he that giveth glory to his mother is as one that layeth up treasure."[3] With such conceptions as these the "Oriental" view

---

[1] Mal. ii. 13–16 (G. A. Smith's trans.).
[2] Prov. i. 8   [3] Eccles. iii. 2–4.

of women cannot coexist. Just as little can it coexist with the Hebrew understanding of their place in the Divine purpose, both in the past and in the future, with the stories of Deborah and Esther and Judith, and with the anticipation of the outpouring of God's Spirit upon them. " It shall come to pass afterward, that I will pour out My Spirit upon all flesh ; and your sons and your daughters shall prophesy, your old men shall dream dreams, your young men shall see visions : and also upon the servants and upon the handmaids in those days will I pour out My Spirit." [1]

Thus the belief, so often entertained, that St. Paul as a Jew must have held " Oriental " views of women, rests upon a misunderstanding. Need we add that he was a follower of our Lord, fully acquainted with his Master's teaching by precept and example, and with the place which women had occupied in His life and ministry ? His own practice exactly resembled his Master's. He did not call women to positions of authority in the Church any more than the Lord had called them. But his own relations with women were close and affectionate, and he valued most highly their co-operation in his work. To his mind the Church was one great family, in which all the elder women were to be treated " as mothers "—we have seen what this would mean to a Jew—and the younger " as sisters, in all purity." [2] The mother of Rufus, probably the widow of Simon of Cyrene, is not the mother of Rufus only ; she is to St. Paul his own mother also.[3] The long series of salutations in the Epistle to the Romans is throughout most illuminating. Phœbe, the deaconess, is apparently sent upon

[1] Joel ii. 28, 29.   [2] Tim. v. 2.   [3] Rom. xvi. 13.

a mission to Rome; Mary has "bestowed much labour" upon the Church there. It is the same with Tryphaena and Tryphosa, and with "Persis the beloved." Still more remarkable is the position of Prisca or Priscilla, St. Paul's "fellow-worker in Christ Jesus," to whom all the "churches of the Gentiles" are in debt. Almost always, when she is mentioned with her husband Aquila, her name stands before his as the more important of the two, and we find her with her husband the means of the instruction of Apollos in the Christian faith.[1] All this we shall have to remember presently, when we come to consider St. Paul's supposed refusal to allow women to teach. Other instances of St. Paul's regard for women crowd upon us in other Epistles. At Philippi the position of Lydia [2] did not stand alone; Euodia and Syntyche were evidently very prominent also.[3] At Colossae Apphia is the recipient of St. Paul's letter with Philemon and Archippus; at Lystra Lois and Eunice are St. Timothy's examples in faith,[4] and evidently his instructresses in early years in the Scriptures of the Old Testament.[5] Now it is just these incidental references to women, which are the best revelation of St. Paul's mind. As we shall presently see, the few passages in his writings which give a different impression are all written when he has to deal with particular dangers, arising out of the noble position which belongs to women in the Church. We shall deal with their teaching in due course quite frankly, but we must explain St. Paul's incidental

[1] Rom. xvi. 1, 2, 6, 12, 3, 4; Acts xviii. 26.
[2] Acts xvi. 15.   [3] Phil. iv. 2, 3.   [4] 2 Tim. i. 5.
[5] 2 Tim. iii. 14, 15.

and occasional teaching in accordance with his general mind and practice, and not his general mind and practice in accordance with his incidental and occasional teaching. The fact is that St. Paul is particularly favourable to women, and that no other writer in the New Testament, except his friend St. Luke, approaches him in the position which he gives to them.

It is now time to turn to St. Paul's positive teaching. It has two aspects. On the one hand, he is the preacher of an universal gospel, the Apostle of an universal Saviour and an universal Church. So far there can be no difference between the position of men and the position of women : " the same Lord is Lord of all, and is rich unto all that call upon Him." [1] On the other hand, he teaches that there exists within the family by God's appointment a real subordination of the woman to the man, and that the discipline of the Church must recognize the fact. How far this subordination should go is a question which needs careful thought, and St. Paul's words may not answer all the questions we should like to ask. But that the subordination exists, and should be recognized, he is entirely clear, and those who would deny it are right in their recognition that they have St. Paul against them.

Let us begin with his grand assertion of the universality of the Gospel. " There can be neither Jew nor Greek, there can be neither bond nor free, there can be no male and female : for ye are all one man in Christ Jesus." [2] To this great principle St. Paul gives glowing expression several times in his writings. We find it not only in the Epistle to the Galatians,

---

[1] Rom. x. 12.   [2] Gal. iii. 28.

but in the Epistles to the Romans and to the Colossians, and in the First Epistle to the Corinthians.[1] But it is only in the Epistle to the Galatians that we find it applied to the relations of men and women. This, however, does not mean that St. Paul is less sure of its applicability here than in the other cases ; it is rather that its applicability here is so obvious, that there is generally no need to insist upon it. It may be, though we do not know this, that the churches of Galatia needed a clear assertion of the rights of women, while other churches did not. But does this assertion of the universality of the Gospel involve a denial of the subordination of women ? Certainly not. The context makes St. Paul's meaning entirely clear. All, he has just said, who have been " baptized into Christ " have " put on Christ " ; all are alike children of God, " through faith in Christ Jesus "[2] In Him the old differences of race and sex and status have lost their power to sever us ; we are all one in the one body of the Risen and Ascended Lord. But this unity in no case involves a bare and barren uniformity of position, by which all previous differences pass away. The examples which St. Paul takes are very different one from another. One, the difference of sex, is a difference which must ever remain while man is man ; another, the difference of race, goes very deep, so deep that the common relation to the Lord has thus far but little affected it ; while the third, the difference of status between bond and free, is but artificial, as we actually find it in human life. If, as Aristotle thought, there are those who are by nature bondsmen, they

---

[1] Cf. Rom. x. 12 ; Col. iii. 11 ; 1 Cor. xii. 13.   [2] Gal. iii. 26, 27.

were to be found in St. Paul's day, it must be feared, quite as often among the free provincials of the Roman Empire as among the slaves. But in no case did St. Paul teach that within the Church the difference must pass away. He had no objection to a Jew practising circumcision, and observing the customs of his forefathers ; indeed he himself " to the Jews became as a Jew " that " he might gain Jews," [1] and on one occasion actually took part in the sacrificial worship of the Temple.[2] Nor, again, did he teach that within the Church there could be neither slave-owners nor slaves. His sympathy with the slave is plain in the Epistle to Philemon ; doubtless he would have wished that all slaves might become free. But he never for a moment suggests that such a change is either possible or desirable under the existing circumstances of his day, and he regards it as of great importance that slaves should not bring discredit upon the Church by lack of respect and obedience to their masters.[3] Rather he says beautifully that Christian slaves are the Lord's freedmen, and that Christian freemen are the slaves of Christ ; though the old relation stands, the common relation to the Lord sweetens and transforms it.[4] Now just as little is it possible to maintain that St. Paul's assertion of the universality of the Gospel destroys the differences between men and women, or their practical consequences. How far these differences, as we know them to-day, are innate and unavoidable, and how far they are artificial, is a question of great complexity ; it

---

[1] I Cor. ix. 20.   [2] Acts xxi. 26.
[3] Cf. Eph. vi. 5–8 ; Col. iii. 22–25 ; I Tim. vi. 1, 2 ; Tit. ii. 9, 10.
[4] I Cor. vii. 21, 22.

is quite possible that we regard many differences as innate which are really the consequence of differences of education. But the physical difference goes very deep—Christianity in no way affects it—and we do not know how far the mental and spiritual differences depend upon the physical. We are not asserting at this point that these differences, whatever they may be, carry with them the subordination of women to men ; we are but pointing out that, if they do, and so far as they do, the universality of the Christian gospel can have no power to override them, and that to quote St. Paul's words as meaning that no subordination of women to men can exist is altogether to misunderstand their meaning.

But there is more to say than this. Nothing is surely more foreign to St. Paul's mind than the idea that the common relation to the Lord, and to the Father through Him, is that of a number of individual men and women, with none but self-chosen relations one with another. He regards the Church as an organized body, in which the place and office of each member has been settled by the gifts which God has been pleased to bestow. " Now ye," he says, " are the body of Christ, and severally members thereof. And God hath set some in the Church, first apostles, secondly prophets, thirdly teachers, then miracles, then gifts of healings, helps, governments, divers kinds of tongues. Are all apostles ? Are all prophets ? Are all teachers ? Are all workers of miracles ? Have all gifts of healings ? Do all speak with tongues ? Do all interpret ? " [1] Obviously, if the universal character of the Gospel makes impossible the subordin-

[1] I Cor. xii. 27–30.

ation of women to men, it must also make impossible
the subordination of men one to another. What,
then, becomes of " governments " of every kind,
not to say of that Apostolic office upon which St. Paul
so strongly insists ? But nothing is further than all
this from St. Paul's mind. On the contrary, the body
is built up in love " according to the working in due
measure of each several part." [1] Will it be answered
that all this has to do with the differences constituted
by the gifts of the Spirit, and has nothing to do with
the natural differences between men and women ?
No hard and fast line separates natural from spiritual
gifts. The spiritual gifts, which the Lord left behind
Him when He went into " another country," are
distributed to each of His servants " according to
his several ability " [2]; the natural gifts determine
the form which the spiritual gifts will take. So it
is in the case of men and women. The highest (or
almost the highest) spiritual gifts are open to all ;
if there are no women-apostles, there are women-
prophets. [3] But even these gifts are bestowed upon
man and woman according to the several ability of
each ; they do not make the man less a man, or the
woman less a woman. " God is not a God of confusion, but of peace " [4]; and the natural differences
which His creating Hand has constituted are not
destroyed by the gifts of His Spirit, but consecrated
to their highest ends. It is on the same principle
that St. Paul teaches that existing differences of race
and status, as we have already seen, continue to hold
within the Church, and that " each man, wherein he

[1] Eph. iv. 16.   [2] Matt. xxv. 14, 15.
Cf. Acts xxi. 9 ; 1 Cor. xi. 5.   [4] 1 Cor. xiv. 33.

was called," should "therein abide with God."[1]
The great consolation for those who seem the less gifted
or the less advantageously placed, is that they, as
well as those they may be tempted to envy, are necessary to the welfare of the whole body, necessary, not
in spite of their differences, but because of their differences.[2] So is it with man and woman, "Neither is
the woman without the man, nor the man without the
woman in the Lord."[3] If they are necessary one to
the other, mutually helpful one to the other, outside
the limits of the Church, much more must they be
so within the life of that body, to which the Spirit of
God imparts so careful and complete an organization.
But the man must remain the man, and the woman the
woman.

> For woman is not undevelopt man,
> But diverse ; could we make her as the man,
> Sweet Love were slain ; his dearest bond is this,
> Not like to like, but like in difference.

Yes : and not only that " sweet love," which is the
basis of the family, but that wider, that supernatural
love, which is the bond of unity in the Church. It
rests not on the abolition of differences, but upon the
reverent recognition of them, and upon the mutual
service which that recognition brings. Not husbands
and wives only, but all the members of the Church
must

> walk this world
> Yoked in all exercise of noble end.
> Each fulfils
> Defect in each, and always thought in thought,
> Purpose in purpose, will in will, they grow.

---

[1] I Cor. vii. 17-24.   [2] I Cor. xiv. 14-25.   [3] I Cor. xi. 11.

So St. Paul teaches. The differences within the Church are all " unto the building up of the body of Christ : till we all attain unto the unity of the faith, and of the knowledge of the Son of God, unto a full-grown man, unto the measure of the stature of the fullness of Christ." [1]

It may be hoped that it is now clear that, when St. Paul says that in Christ " there can be no male and female," he says nothing inconsistent with a difference of position and function, which the Church is bound to recognize. But it will be urged with truth that thus far nothing has been said positively to justify the subordination of women to men. On the contrary, " gifts must prove their use," and St. Paul's view, that the organization of the Church depends upon God's free bestowal of the gifts of the Spirit, must carry with it the consequence that women must be just as unfettered in the use of their gifts as men themselves. Now this contention, unlike the contention which has been just dismissed, is one worthy of the highest respect ; it is indeed the great argument which St. Paul's teaching has to meet. It is by no means obvious that a woman with gifts of leadership should be subordinate to a man who has none, Queen Margaret, e.g. to King Henry VI ; or that a woman endowed with great gifts of teaching should be refused permission to exercise them. Do we propose to condemn Deborah, or St. Catherine of Sienna, or Elizabeth Fry ? St. Paul, as his teaching is generally understood, appears to condemn them all. It is not a question, be it observed, of the rights of women ; it is the far more important question of their duties. To subject the competent

[1] Eph. iv. 12, 13.

44

to the incompetent, or to "quench the spirit," [1] involves most serious injury to the Church itself. Is it conceivable that St. Paul, of all people, desired to do either ? Plainly, before we admit this, we must submit his teaching to the most careful examination, and consider the exact circumstances which led him to give it. We shall find that this teaching has been misunderstood in a very serious way.

But, before addressing ourselves to his actual teaching, it is necessary to explain a very important distinction. Subordination is entirely different from subjection or inferiority. St. Paul's doctrine as to the position of women is a doctrine of their subordination within the family, and not of their inferiority, or of their subjection. The words "subject" and "subjection" are indeed unhappily employed of the position of women both in our Authorized and Revised Versions of the New Testament. But these words, with the colour which they bear to-day, give a wrong impression of St. Paul's meaning. Especially is this true of the latter word.[2] There is something slavish about its

---

[1] 1 Thess. v. 20.

[2] The use of such words needs the utmost caution, if a wrong impression is not to be given. We have e.g. no objection to saying that we are British subjects, but we should strenuously deny that we are living in subjection. The former statement simply conveys the idea of loyalty to a not unwelcome rule ; the latter bears an entirely different colour. Thus the language of the English versions in 1 Tim. ii. 11 ; 1 Pet. iii. 1, 5 ; Eph. v. 22 (R.V.) is seriously misleading. In the last passage, the R.V. substitutes the words "be in subjection," for the A.V. "submit yourselves," without any justification whatsoever in the Greek. Bengel well points out that children and slaves are commanded to "obey," but that this word is not used by St. Paul of the duty of women. See his note on Eph. v. 22. "De liberis et servis dicitur, obedite. Conjugum, major paritas."

45

associations, something which seems to speak of an inferior race held down by a stronger. But St. Paul's view of women is not this. He does not hold that women as a class are to be subject to men as a class, or that each individual woman is to be subordinate to each individual man with whom she comes into contact ; what he holds is that each woman should be subordinate to her own husband or to the head of her family. Now subordination is one thing, and inferiority is altogether another. If we think otherwise, the confusion is probably due to our own pride. Too often we like to dominate others, and make the supposed blessing which we thus confer our justification for doing so. As our Lord caustically said, " The kings of the Gentiles have lordship over them ; and they that have authority over them are called benefactors." [1] Too often, again, we dislike to be subordinate, and justify our insubordination on the ground that we know quite as well what to do as those who claim to direct our action. For both reasons we come to confuse subordination with inferiority. Now no doubt, *ceteris paribus*, it is desirable that the wisest and best should rule. But it cannot always be so. The necessity of subordination does not depend upon the fact that some are wiser and better than others, but upon the necessity of mutual co-operation in human society. Rule there must be, and if we wait for it until we are agreed as to who are the wisest and the best, society will have dissolved before we have reached a conclusion. Thus it is that everywhere we find human rule resting in fact upon a different principle. A ruler is accepted because he is regarded as

[1] Luke xxii. 25.

appointed to rule; " the powers that be are ordained
of God " ; and we willingly subordinate ourselves to
them, " not only because of the wrath, but also for
conscience sake." [1] But in doing so, we make no admission of inferiority ; either the question does not arise,
or, if it occurs to our minds, we dismiss it as irrelevant.
And if this be so even in the life of the world, how
much more is it so in the life of the Church ! " He
that is the greater among you, let him become as the
younger ; and he that is chief, as he that doth serve." [2]
How can a Christian ever be guilty of confusing subordination with inferiority ? What did his Lord and
Master but take " the form of a servant, being made
in the likeness of men," and become " obedient even
unto death " [3] not only to His Father in heaven, but
to Joseph and Mary in their place, and even to those
" meaner miserable," the rulers of His day ? Did He
regard Himself as inferior because He was subordinate ?
Very far from that. One day He would reign, and
realize that true aristocracy, that rule of the wisest
and the best, which we all desire. But the time for
that is not yet. Meanwhile " as He is, even so are we
in this world," [4] and with us too willing subordination
is no confession of inferiority whatsoever.

What then exactly is St. Paul's fundamental teaching on the question before us ? He holds that within
the Church, as well as without it, woman is meant to
render obedience to her husband. She is to render
it, not because she is his inferior, but because he is
under the Lord her appointed head. " I would have
you know, that the head of every man is Christ ; and

---

[1] Rom. xiii. 1, 5.   [2] Luke xxii. 26.
[3] Phil. ii. 7, 8.   [4] 1 John iv. 17.

47

the head of the woman is the man ; and the head of
Christ is God." [1] The Apostle's point is that the
principle of subordination prevails everywhere, and
runs up into the life of heaven itself. Are we inclined
to. exclaim against a difference of position so slight as
that of man and woman being compared with a difference so vast as that of man and the Lord ? If so, we
have only to consider the third and loftiest example
of subordination which St. Paul gives to see that no
depreciation of woman's position is involved. There
can be no higher example of glad subordination than
that of the Ascended Lord to the Father. That perfect submission to Another's will, which we see throughout the Lord's earthly life, has not passed away ; still
in His new sphere of heavenly glory, " the life that He
liveth, He liveth unto God." [2] But this willing subordination, complete as it is, implies no inferiority of
nature ; in the Blessed Trinity there is no greater or
less, but the whole Three Persons are coeternal together, and coequal. But St. Paul has probably more
in mind than this, as he shows us in the Epistle to the
Ephesians. " The husband is the head of the wife,
as Christ also is the head of the Church, being Himself
the Saviour of the body." [3] That is the principle of
all true subordination, as contrasted with slavery or
subjection. The higher has a duty to the lower (if
higher and lower be the right terms to use) as well as
the lower to the higher. " As the living Father sent
Me," says our Lord, " and I live because of the Father ;
so he that eateth Me, he also shall live because of
Me." [4] The Son's obedience and dependence is

[1] i Cor. xi. 3.   [2] Rom. vi. 10.
[3] Eph. v. 23.   [4] John vi. 57.

48

answered by the Father's unfailing support; the obedience and dependence of the member of Christ is answered by the Lord's unfailing supply of spiritual life. So says St. Paul also. The Lord is not only " the Head of the Church "; He is also " the Saviour of the body." He " loved the Church, and gave Himself up for it; that He might sanctify it, having cleansed it by the washing of water with the word, that He might present the Church to Himself a glorious Church "; daily, moment by moment, He " nourisheth and cherisheth it." [1] So it is, St. Paul teaches, with the Christian husband and wife. It is not a relation of slavery, but a relation of corporate unity. The duty of subordination on the one side is in no way more imperative than the duty of love and sacrifice and cherishing on the other. The wife " sets herself " to her husband, not as a slave to her master, but

Like perfect music unto noble words,

that the two may be together what each alone could not be. Her loving subordination has no other aim, and the husband, as the stronger, gives to the wife, not the proud condescension of conscious superiority, but honour " as unto the weaker vessel, as being also joint-heirs of the grace of life." [2] Were it otherwise, their " prayers " would be " hindered," for they would be violating that law of their common being, which they draw from the relation of Christ to His Church. Will it be urged that in the First Epistle to the Corinthiaus and in the First Epistle to Timothy St. Paul dwells more upon the duty of the wife to the husband than upon the duty of the husband to the wife? If it be so, that is only because of the immediate purpose

[1] Eph. v. 25–27, 29.   [2] 1 Pet. iii. 7.

which he has in view. At Corinth and Ephesus it was the women who were setting the true relation aside, and St. Paul's own insistence upon liberty may have been the occasion of their doing so. His teaching is not usually one-sided. As a rule, he deals with all human relations in a thoroughly impartial way. It may be the relations of husbands and wives, or of parents and children, or of masters and slaves, or of the scrupulous and the free, or of the highly gifted and those with lesser gifts; always, having dealt with the one side of the relation, he turns immediately to the other. The Church too often has insisted on authority in a one-sided way which has lent itself to tyranny, but St. Paul does not. His teaching is just as clear and emphatic as to the duty of the stronger to the weaker, as it is as to the duty of the weaker to the stronger. And this brings us to another point of the utmost importance for the understanding of his teaching. Just as he teaches that even the poor slave is the Lord's freedman, and the master the Lord's slave,[1] so much more does he teach that the Christian wife, like all Christians, shares in the " freedom," with which " Christ set us free," [2] and that the Christian husband, as the slave of the Lord, may ask of her nothing but what the law of Christ allows him to ask. The common subjection to the law of Christ rules every relationship in the Christian family, " for the same Lord is Lord of all." [3] That is why Christians must marry " only in the Lord." [4] Why was it, do we suppose, that when one party to a heathen marriage became a Christian, and the other did not, the

---

[1] I Cor. vii. 22.   [2] Gal. v. I.
[3] Rom. x. 12.   [4] I Cor. vii. 39.

heathen partner was not always willing to continue the relationship? Simply because the Christian re-fused to act as he or she had done before. In the religious chaos of the Roman Empire there was the widest choice of worships; there was nothing unusual in husband and wife worshipping different gods. But the heathen cults made no difference to conduct, while Christianity did. If the husband asked what was unlawful, the Christian wife refused, and was " not put in fear by any terror," [1] and so the heathen hus-band refused to live with her, and dissolved the mar-riage.[2] Now all this is of the utmost importance. The promise of obedience, which the Christian woman makes to her husband on her wedding day, is a promise which is made in a Christian church and a Christian atmosphere; every prayer that is there offered " through Jesus Christ our Lord " is an assertion that in all that is said and done the Lordship of Jesus Christ is presupposed. If the wife may not thereafter repu-diate her promise of obedience, neither may the hus-band repudiate the conditions under which that promise has been given. Does any one suppose that the duty of a soldier to obey the officer set over him involves the duty to obey him, if he commands his company to desert to the enemy? That would indeed be for the sake of obedience to forget the purpose of obedience. So it is in Christian marriage. The wife's promise of obedience is given after the purposes of Christian marriage have been clearly explained, and no obedience can be lawful which sets them aside. When St. Paul says that " the head of every man is Christ, and the head of the woman is the man," [3] the

[1] I Pet. iii. 6. [2] Cf. i Cor. vii. 12–15. [3] i Cor. xi. 3.

former truth limits and explains the latter. So far from denying the immediate responsibility of the woman to Him Who is the head of the whole body of the Church, it asserts it. The whole teaching of the Apostle throughout his Epistles is addressed to the whole Church, and not merely to the men, who form but a part of it; and the woman, who like the man, must one day be " made manifest before the judgment-seat of Christ," must attend to it, and obey it, as fully as the man himself. And so the Church, in her representation of Christ, has ever taught. Ever the Church has claimed to deal directly with women as responsible beings, and not merely through their husbands, and to bring under her discipline the relation of husband and wife, as every other relation. Though she respects and upholds the husband's authority, she knows that all authority, unchecked by higher authority, tends to become tyranny, none more so than the authority of men over women. It is precisely because in our own day the Church fails so greatly in this part of her duty, that there is so widely a demand for complete emancipation. The authority of the husband, which St. Paul so plainly recognizes, is one thing, when kept under control by the effective teaching and discipline of the Church; it is quite another when the husband in the exercise of his authority becomes altogether untrammelled, and recognizes no authority but his own sweet will. In the one case, we have but a beautiful subordination, which makes for good in every way; in the other we may have a subjection so detestable as to explain, if not altogether to justify, every rebellion against it.

We see then what St. Paul's fundamental teaching

is, and how carefully it is guarded. Why then does it often cause so much annoyance to those who have the highest ideals of married life, and are in no wise unwilling to be to their husbands all that St. Paul would have them be ? We have touched upon this point before. St. Paul does not confine himself to explaining and guarding the true ideal of the relation of man to woman. He gives reasons for his teaching which occasion real difficulty, and makes applications of it which do not immediately commend themselves to the minds of our own day. By so doing, he to many people discredits his teaching as a whole, and affords an excuse for setting it aside.

To these difficulties therefore we now turn. But before doing so, there are a few preliminary remarks which it may be well to make.

In the first place, the truth of St. Paul's, as of any other teaching, depends upon all the reasons which can be given for it, and not upon the reasons which under particular circumstances he actually gives. The most profound reasons for our beliefs are frequently obscure even to ourselves ; and, even when they are clear to us, we do not as practical teachers always place them in the foreground. On the contrary, we speak or write with the needs of particular people in view, and we employ the arguments most likely to convince them. Now St. Paul was a Jew, trained in the school of Gamaliel, and his converts, even in the Greek cities, were for the most part either Jews, or Gentiles who had long been subject to Jewish influences, and instructed in the Old Testament Scriptures. His view of these Scriptures, whether right or wrong, was the view current in his day. As far as we can judge from his language, he regarded the stories of the Old Testament as historically true, and the language employed as full of Divine meaning, and of instruction for ourselves. Now, assuming all this, no one, who really understands his words, is likely to deny that he interprets the language of the Old Testament in a most penetrating way. Nor will it be denied that, given hearers who interpret the Old Testament as St. Paul does, his arguments are practically effective. The difficulty is that the great majority of educated people to-day find themselves, rightly or wrongly, unable to accept St. Paul's standpoint. They regard, e.g., the early chapters of Genesis merely as interesting examples of primitive science and folklore. Thus, when St. Paul argues as he does from these early narratives, his words are not only meaningless to them, but even a hindrance to the acceptance of his teaching. It is at this point that we would ask for attention to two considerations. Regard these stories as we may, they are in fact instinct with most valuable religious teaching. If they were originally but popular science and folklore, they have been transfigured by contact with the illuminated mind of the people of God; and the religious ideas that are found in them must have a basis, independent of the primitive stories, into which they have been introduced. Moreover, as we shall shortly see, it is the mind which possesses independently the religious ideas which discovers them in these primitive narratives. Thus, in the question before us, the arguments which St. Paul adduces for his conclusions as to the right relations of men and women, strange as they are to our modern minds, are not a proof that he possesses no deeper reasons, but a proof that he does possess them, and that the Hebrews of far-off days possessed them also.

In the second place we must be careful to distinguish applications which are of permanent value from applications which, though true and valuable in St. Paul's day, no longer follow from his principles under the different circumstances and sentiments of our own. We may not all apply this distinction in the same way, but we should all recognize its importance. St. Paul himself here helps us greatly, since, in the applications which he makes, he does not simply rely upon his personal authority, but argues at length for the directions which he gives. In considering his arguments, and deciding for ourselves whether they hold under our own circumstances, we are only doing what he would wish us to do. The Church herself has not permanently upheld all St. Paul's rulings in the questions before us.

We turn then to these minor difficulties, with full willingness frankly to face them, but in no way disposed to set aside the broad principles of the Apostolic teaching, if he fails to satisfy on these minor points. The first with which we shall deal is his teaching in the First Epistle to the Corinthians as to the veiling of women in the public assemblies of the Church. Full understanding of St. Paul's mind is here impossible for two reasons. In the first place, the passage in question contains a sentence, to the meaning of which we have lost the key.[1] The Authorized Version renders it word by word correctly enough, except that " authority " should be substituted for " power."

[1] I Cor. xi. 10.

" For this cause ought the woman to have power on her head because of the angels." This unhappy sentence has probably never conveyed a meaning to a human intelligence. The Revised Version succeeds in conveying a meaning, but only by introducing words that have no place in the original text. " For this cause ought the woman to have a sign of authority on her head because of the angels." It is possible that this speculative addition may give St. Paul's meaning correctly, but to what angels he refers, and what they have to do with the matter, no one has ever satisfactorily explained.[1] In the second place, St. Paul's instructions rest upon current ideas of etiquette and good manners. Such ideas vary continually. The young University man who goes to work among people in England of a different class from his own, if he would avoid giving offence, has laboriously to learn a new social code ; he finds to his surprise that his free and easy ways, though they may be acceptable in the lowest ranks of the population, are regarded as improper by the better-class artisans. Missionaries in such countries as China and Japan are at first still more at sea. And, when we come to deal with a passage of St. Paul's writings like the one before us, we must recognize that a full understanding of it is beyond our attainment. What St. Paul teaches

[1] The best explanation is perhaps Tertullian's, that Paul has in mind Genesis vi. 1-4. This strange story took a strong hold of the mind of the Jews, and received great development in that Book of Enoch, to which they and the Apostolic Church attached such great importance. St. Jude apparently regards the Book as authentic prophecy (Jude 14), and we find references to this fall of the angels in Jude 6 and 2 Pet. ii. 14. Jewish belief is well illustrated by the part played in the Book of Tobit by the evil spirit Asmodaeus.

is substantially this. When women attend and take part in the assemblies of the Church, above all when they take part in, or perhaps even lead, the Church's prayers, they must be becomingly attired, and they must respect the general sense of the Church as to what becoming attire is. When St. Paul says, " Doth not even nature itself teach you ? "[1] he means by " nature " the general sense of mankind, and the general sense of which we must take account, is the general sense of those with whom we have to do. " Whatsoever things are honourable, whatsoever things are pure, whatsoever things are lovely, whatsoever things are of good report, take account of these things."[2] The rules of etiquette are occasionally tiresome, but they generally rest upon practical experience of what is best, and this is especially the case in the relations of men with women. To an argumentative disregard of the *convenances*, we do not reply by argument ; we reply, " My good sir, it isn't done." So, though with reference to a common sense more inspired than that of the world, does St. Paul also. " If any man seemeth to be contentious, we have no such custom, neither the churches of God."[3] Now all this suggests no difficulty, when we understand St. Paul's meaning. Nor does it create any difficulty when St. Paul says that misbehaviour on the part of a woman " dishonoureth " that husband who is " her head." When a man outrages the *convenances*, his doing so causes great pain to his wife. But when a woman does so, especially when she does so in a way which is understood to be a repudiation of her husband's authority, she causes to him far greater pain.

[1] I Cor. xi. 14.   [2] Phil. iv. 8.   [3] I Cor xi. 16.

He knows that everybody is saying that he ought to put a stop to it, and despising him for his apparent inability to do so. The woman is not held responsible for the misbehaviour of her husband, while the man is held responsible for the misbehaviour of his wife, and is injured in his honour as a man, when she does misbehave. Where St. Paul's language gives offence is that he seems at first sight to put the woman in a position of insupportable inferiority by the language which he employs. The man is " the image and glory of God : but the woman is the glory of the man. For the man is not of the woman ; but the woman of the man : for neither was the man created for the woman ; but the woman for the man." [1] It is here that what has already been urged as to St. Paul's use of Holy Scripture comes to our assistance. St. Paul's reference is to the second chapter of the Book of Genesis. The Book of Genesis begins with two stories of the Creation, which are placed side by side. In the former, woman equally with man is said to have been created in the image of God " God created man in His own image, in the image of God created He him ; male and female created He them." [2] The word " man " is here generic ; it is not man as contrasted with woman, but the human race as contrasted with the rest of the creation. But in the second and more primitive story, nothing is said about the image of God. Man is created first, and woman afterwards to be " an help meet for him." [3] " The Lord God caused a deep sleep to fall upon the man ; and he slept ; and He took one of his ribs, and closed up the flesh instead thereof : and the rib which the Lord

[1] Verses 7–9.   [2] Gen. i. 27.   [3] Gen. ii. 18.

God had taken from the man, made He a woman, and brought her unto the man."[1] St. Paul, in the offending passage of his Epistle, follows the second story, and it is this which occasions the difficulty. He does not deny that the woman is made in the image of God; probably he thought that she was so indirectly, since she was to be a " help answering to "[2] the man already made in His image. But the Apostle keeps to his text. He says that the woman was derived from the man, because the text says so; he says that the woman was created for the man, because the text says so. But he also says that " the woman is the glory of the man."[3] To be the glory of the man is far indeed from being his plaything or his slave; playthings and slaves are no glory to anybody. The woman glorifies her husband, as he, and indeed she also, glorify God, by the free use of her splendid powers in glad co-operation with him. She stands to him, like the will to the understanding in South's splendid simile, " not as a servant to a master, but as a queen to her king, who both acknowledges a subjection, and yet retains a majesty." Is St. Paul one-sided, in that he does not add that there is a true sense in which the man was created for the woman? He is necessarily one-sided, because he is dealing with a practical situation, in which it was women who were at fault. But he feels the one-sidedness, as we feel it, and at once corrects it: let us quote his words once more. " Howbeit neither is the woman without the man, nor the man without the woman, in the Lord. For as the woman is of the man, so is the man also by the

---

[1] Verses 21, 22.   [2] Gen. ii. 18, margin of R.V.
[3] 1 Cor. xi. 7.

woman ; but all things are of God." [1] What could he more say ? Every man has a mother ; without her he would not be here at all. Moreover, in that immeasurable dependence which belongs to us all alike, how little meaning there is after all in our talk of the higher and the lower, the greater and the less ! " All things are of God." Dependent upon God as we are for all that we are and for all the conditions of our life, what does it matter whether the dependence be more or less direct ? St. Paul asserts the subordination of women to men in this passage, as he always does, but he asserts it in the kindliest and gentlest way that is consistent with the maintenance of his position. As we have previously seen, we shall be much lacking in intelligence if we repudiate his teaching for no better reason than that he bases it upon the primitive story in Genesis. For on what does the story rest ? Simply on the observed facts of human life. Those facts are not true because they are found in the Book of Genesis : they are found in the Book of Genesis because they are true. Suppose that in some story, which the Church maintained to be inspired, the opposite position had been adopted. Suppose that the Book of Genesis related that woman was first created, then the animals, and then man ; and that, it not being good that the woman should be alone, man was taken out of woman's side to be a help meet for her. The subordination of man to woman would then be as clear in the narrative as the subordination of woman to man is now. The faithful in this case would be hard put to it. The uncultivated unbeliever in Hyde Park would caustically observe

[1] Verses 11, 12.

that, if that were the Creator's purpose, His arrangements appeared to be singularly ill-adapted to its
realization. He made man far the stronger physically, and never in his capacity of a father laid aside,
as woman is in her capacity as a mother. He gave
to him, not necessarily higher and better mental and
emotional gifts, but certainly far more of those which
lead to command. Everywhere in the world man is
dominant as a matter of course. How absurd, then,
the unbeliever would urge, is the Bible narrative,
which asserts the contrary ! Now does not everybody
see that St. Paul's position rests ultimately upon
facts, and upon nothing else ? In the Women's
Movement to-day there is much that is noble, and
much that is true. But when its apostles repudiate
the subordination of women in any and every sense,
they have not merely St. Paul against them, but the
ordinances of the Creator Himself ; and the under-
current of bitterness which is sometimes to be traced
in their words is really a recognition of the fact. May
we, with respect, utter a word of remonstrance ?
Woman has her own peculiar burdens, but man also
has his, and which are the heavier it is idle to specu-
late, since there is no one who can have both lots and
so compare them. Women to-day are often eloquent
in their own cause, but men have a case too, though
they are generally silent about it. Greater freedom,
greater responsibility, do not necessarily bring greater
happiness.

> Why doth the crown lie thus upon his pillow,
> Being so troublesome a bedfellow ?
> O polish'd perturbation ! golden care !
> That keep'st the ports of slumber open wide
> To many a watchful night.—Sleep with it now !

But not so sound, and half so deeply sweet
As he whose brow with homely biggin bound,
Snores out the watch of night. O majesty!
When thou dost pinch thy bearer, thou dost sit
Like a rich armour worn in heat of day,
That scalds with safety.

The Book of Genesis, with profound insight, speaks of the differing burdens of women and of men.[1] Each may resent, and seek to escape, the lot ordained, but only in the long run to the grievous hurt of each. Better far to recognize that in some mysterious way the sorrow of the world is bound up with the sin of the world, as the Book of Genesis says that it is, and that it is by men and women bearing patiently, each the burden ordained for them, that they will ultimately be delivered. Every man worthy of the name is overworked, but it is by " bearing about in the body the dying of Jesus " that " the life also of Jesus " will one day " be manifested in " his body.[2] So says St. Paul. And of woman he says, " She shall be saved through the child-bearing ".(it is that of which the third chapter of the Book of Genesis speaks) " if they continue in faith and love and sanctification with sobriety." [3]

The second difficulty which we have to meet is St. Paul's apparent refusal to allow women to teach, or even to speak in the public assemblies of the Church. His " rudeness of speech " and want of lucidity are here almost at their worst, and it is most difficult to make sure of his exact meaning. In the passage which we have just considered, St. Paul says, " Every woman praying or prophesying with her head unveiled dis-

[1] Gen. iii. 16–19. [2] 2 Cor. iv. 10. [3] 1 Tim. ii. 15.

honoureth her head." [1] To all appearance he is speaking of the public assemblies of the Church, and we should never suppose from the language which he here employs, that he objected to women praying aloud or prophesying there, if only they were suitably attired. And yet three chapters later we read : " Let the women keep silence in the churches : for it is not permitted unto them to speak ; but let them be in subjection, as also saith the law. And if they would learn anything, let them ask their own husbands at home : for it is shameful for a woman to speak in the church." [2] So also in the First Epistle to Timothy St. Paul says, " Let a woman learn in quietness with all subjection. But I permit not a woman to teach, nor to have dominion over a man, but to be in quietness. For Adam was first formed, then Eve ; and Adam was not beguiled, but the woman being beguiled hath fallen into transgression." [3] Two solutions appear to be possible. The first is that St. Paul forbids women to join in the public discussions, which took place in the Christian assemblies, and to engage in the work of public teaching ; but that, regarding praying and prophesying in the Spirit as Divine manifestations, in which the human agents are no more than passive instruments, he does not venture to suppress them even in women. The second is that, though St. Paul recognizes the existence of prophetic and teaching gifts in women, he would forbid their public exercise, and

[1] I Cor. xi. 5.   [2] Chap. xiv. 34, 35.
[3] I Tim. ii. 11–14. The words translated "dominion over a man" may perhaps better be translated "dominion over her husband," as the reference to Adam and Eve would suggest.

insist in all cases on the silence of women in the assemblies. The second view is the more probable, and will be here adopted. The first presupposes a conception of prophecy which seems to be inconsistent with St. Paul's mind, since he regards the power of the teacher as well as the power of the prophet as bestowed by the Spirit of God, and insists that even prophecy should be regulated, so as to respect the due order of the Church.[1] But then, if we adopt the second view of his meaning, we do undoubtedly find a limitation placed upon the activity of women in the Church, which we should hardly have expected, in view of their undoubted mental and spiritual gifts, and two questions arise. In the first place, was St. Paul right ? And, in the second place, if he was right under the circumstances of his own day, are the restrictions which he lays down necessarily permanent ? Christianity, in the course of the centuries, has greatly raised the position of women ; and in our own day, their education has been immensely improved. They are in fact intellectually, to say the least, far more the equals of men than they were in the time of St. Paul. Now the Apostle, as was previously pointed out, does not merely give his decision ; he also gives his reasons for it. Our duty then is to consider his reasons, and ask ourselves whether they hold now, as they held at the time when he gave them.

St. Paul's first reason is this. The spectacle of a woman publicly teaching her appointed head is not seemly. St. Paul has no objection to a woman being a teacher. Those labours for the benefit of the Church, which he so highly praises in the Epistle to the Romans,

---

[1] Cf. 1 Cor. xii. 28 ; xiv. 26, 33.

almost certainly included teaching, _and he himself most wisely says that it is for the elder women to teach the younger their duties.[1] Nor has his prohibition, as the English reader of his words might at first think, anything to do with any supposed impropriety in their speaking in consecrated buildings. The Church of St. Paul's day, as far as we know, possessed no such buildings; "the churches," in which women are to "be silent," are not buildings at all (this use of the word does not belong to the Apostolic age) but the public assemblies of Christians. St. Paul's prohibition rests upon his old point, that women are by the Divine ordinance subordinate to their husbands or the heads of their families, and within definite limits under their authority. Now the public teaching of the Church is, or ought to be, always an exercise of authority. "If any man speaketh," he should speak "as it were oracles of God."[2] The Christian teacher, as St. Paul thinks of him, is exercising a gift bestowed upon him by the Holy Spirit. Those who listen should indeed "discriminate"[3]; they should employ their own God-given spiritual insight, in deciding whether what is said to them really comes from God or not. But if it does, it is not something to be taken or left according to the will of the hearer; he must receive "the word of the message, even the word of God . . . not as the word of men, but, as it is in truth, the word of God, which also worketh in" those "that believe."[4] Moreover, this word of God (especially if it comes in that awe-inspiring form which St. Paul calls "prophecy," welling up from the depths of subconscious

---

[1] Titus ii. 3-5.
[2] I Pet. iv. 16.
[3] I Cor. xiv. 27.
[4] I Thess. ii. 13.

E

life) appeals to something far wider than the intellect. It is " living, and active, and sharper than any two-edged sword and piercing even to the dividing of soul and spirit, of both joints and marrow, and quick to discern the thoughts and intents of the heart."[1]   The hearer, as St. Paul says, is " reproved " and " judged " ; " the secrets of his heart are made manifest."   He is awed, overwhelmed ; he falls " down on his face " in worship, recognizing the Divine presence which will alone account for his experience.[2]   We see then what St. Paul means when he permits " not a woman to teach, nor to have dominion over her husband, but to be in quietness." [3]   Inspired Christian teaching involves authority, and thus, when it is given publicly by a woman to her husband, it oversets the true relation between them.   Every sensible man, who has a wife worthy of him, knows that very often she knows better than he does, and finds the greatest advantage in listening to her advice.   To receive correction in private is no injury to the dignity o' his manhood, nor, unless he is eaten up with pride, does he suppose that it is.   But it is essential to the utility of his wife's action that it should take place in private.   For a man to be publicly corrected by his wife not only mortifies his pride (that might be very good for him) it injures him in his honour and proper self-respect ; no good ever comes of it.   And if this be so, even with the most ordinary correction in the affairs of the world, much more is it so in the things of the Spirit.   St. Paul would not " quench the Spirit,"[4] but he regulates

---

[1] Heb. iv. 12. [2] I Cor. xiv. 24, 25.
[3] I Tim. ii. 12. [4] I Thess. v. 20

its manifestation in women, as he also does in men,[1] in the interest of due order in the Church. That great saying of his, " That is not first which is spiritual, but that which is natural," [2] has this application among others, that the natural order is not overridden by subsequent spiritual endowment. The true relation of man and woman is a part of the natural order, and the gifts of the Spirit are not intended to override it.

Secondly, St. Paul says that women should be "in quietness." Their whole nature demands it, and it is almost always injurious to them physically, mentally, and morally, to set this claim of their nature aside. They have their own burden, which men cannot share with them ; it is wrong in principle that they should have man's burden too. Public speaking and teaching is exhausting work for body, mind, and spirit ; it involves a great strain upon the nervous system. The ground of man's heart, like that tilled by the husbandman, brings forth to the cultivator, as St. Paul knew well, thorns and thistles [3] ; and it is for man rather than for woman to endure the toil of dealing with it. So it is also with public debate, such as that which took place in the Jewish synagogues, and in the Christian assemblies at Corinth. It is exhausting ; it may easily be demoralizing ; it is better for women, with their strong emotions, to stand aside, and " be in quietness." It is not that women are bad speakers ; that they certainly are not ; indeed, unless they speak better than the average man, they do not as a rule attempt to speak at all. It is that their success is purchased at too great a cost in nervous energy. The

[1] Cf. 1 Cor. xiv. 26–33.   [2] 1 Cor. xv. 46.   [3] Gen. iii. 18.

dreadful violence and fanaticism, exhibited in the years before the war by so many of the advocates of women's suffrage, did not at all prove that their cause was a bad one; what it proved was the exceeding danger of political agitation to the mental and moral nature of women. The reason why men do not behave in a similar way is not that they are better or wiser than women, but that their nature is made for conflict, while that of women is not. Thus St. Paul's prohibitions, rightly understood, are as kindly as they are wise. We must not, of course, forget the truth contained in the proverb " Necessity knows no law." Many of the noblest women, who take part in public agitation, take part in it with the clearest consciousness of its injurious character, but they think that duty demands the sacrifice. Like Deborah of old, they take a prominent part because men will not act unless women do.[1] Such women deserve nothing but honour. But St. Paul's principle is entirely sound, and it is for men to see that they do not discredit it by their own neglect of their duty to women. For the deplorable disturbances, which have disgraced the women's movement, men have certainly their own responsibility.

Of St. Paul's third reason it is less easy to speak. But we are dealing with a subject of great importance, and it is necessary in the interests of truth to present an " unexpurgated case." He holds that the special gifts of women are not such as to make them good guides to religious truth. Here as before, we shall be very foolish, if we set aside what he says because of the apparent foolishness and ungenerosity of the

---

[1] Judges iv. 6-10.

argument which he adduces. " Adam was not beguiled, but the woman being beguiled hath fallen into transgression." Let us observe, firstly, that St. Paul's interpretation of the narrative is entirely correct. In the story of the Fall, Eve is deceived by the serpent, and pleads the fact in extenuation of her fault [1]; Adam is not deceived, but yields to his wife's solicitation.[2] But, we say, even if we accept the narrative as historical, how foolish to base an universal law upon a particular instance ! Very foolish, doubtless, if St. Paul does so. But let us look a little deeper. Two questions immediately arise. Firstly, what makes the narrative what it is? Secondly, what is it that quickens St. Paul's insight into its meaning ? The answer in both cases surely is that it is practical experience. Women, as a rule, are more timid than men ; they have more of the fear of God. Thus, when they sin, they are usually in greater or less degree deceived first, or they deceive themselves, while men sin with a high hand. Moreover, the cause of this is not merely timidity. In women, as a rule, emotion is stronger than in men, and reason weaker. They are more apt than men to think that what they want to do is right, and that what they want to believe is true. As a rule, they are less disposed to look at truth in an objective way, and to follow truth for truth's sake. It is quite possible that a different education to some extent accounts for this, but facts are eloquent even in our own day. Women think about the problems of life and religion, and read poetry, far more than men do. But their contributions to philosophy and theology, and even to poetry, are

[1] Gen. iii. 13.   [2] Gen. iii. 12.

comparatively almost negligible. Their peculiar powers of sympathy and patience make them admirable instructors of the young, but, in times of religious and intellectual change like the age of St. Paul and our own age, they easily lose their way. They are creative in their capacity as mothers ; they are not as a rule intellectually creative, nor have they that power of taking a wide view, and balancing one consideration against another, which the teacher requires. Men will often see the truth, and maintain it, even while in their wilful disobedience they have no intention of acting upon it. With women it is generally otherwise.

The last consideration which St. Paul brings forward is one that it is not easy to estimate, for reasons which we have considered already. " It is shameful for a woman to speak in the church." St. Paul had evidently no doubt that the general sense of Christians would endorse his verdict, but it is not easy to say how far the feeling which he expresses rests upon permanent grounds, and how far upon grounds which may no longer hold. There is indeed not much here to add to what has been said already in speaking of the veil. But it seems to belong to the innate modesty, or " shamefastness," [1] of the best and purest women to shrink from anything which unnecessarily calls attention to themselves, especially in public assemblies where men are present. Just as they feel that the extravagant adornment of their persons has about it something of immodesty, so they feel that public speaking has it also. They would rather that their teaching, like their adornment, should be " through good works." [1] We ourselves in England

[1] 1 Tim. ii. 9

70

probably feel this less strongly than other peoples ; we should probably say that, though there may be something in this, there may be higher considerations to set it aside. But we must remember the point for whatever it may be worth, and remember also, as St. Paul ever remembers, how important it is to the Church's good name that public sentiment should not be outraged by the action of her members.[1] That sentiment is of course always more or less fluid and uncertain, but what St. Paul feels is felt by the best English people of all classes more than is sometimes recognized. The time may come when it will be otherwise, but we cannot foretell the future, and it is better in such things to lag behind public opinion than to advance in front of it.

We see then St. Paul's mind as to the position of women, in so far as his words reveal it to us. It is a mind absolutely consistent with itself, with the highest teaching of the Old Testament, and with the Lord's own teaching and example. The main principles which he lays down are as true to-day as they were when he first expressed them, and it is for the Church not to be ashamed of them, but to see that her members understand and act upon them. If they are set aside to-day, and that with disastrous consequences, it is men at least as much as women who are to blame. It is because men so widely neglect their duties that women so widely desire to be free of their subordina tion. Let us, in conclusion, make this last point as clear as we can.

Firstly, then, the subordination of women to men presupposes that it is the duty of men, at whatever

---

[1] Cf. Titus ii. 5. .

cost to themselves, to provide for the bodily needs of the women who are subordinate to them. St. Paul's teaching on this point is as clear as the day. It is not merely that the husband must provide for his wife, and the father for his daughters; elder women may claim support from their children and grandchildren. "If any widow hath children or grandchildren, let them learn first to show piety towards their own family, and to requite their parents: for this is acceptable in the sight of God.   But if any provideth not for his own, and specially his own household, he hath denied the faith, and is worse than an unbeliever." [1] St. Paul would have been the last to wish women to lead useless lives. Not only would he have them "workers at home," [2] but he would have them employed beyond their homes in works of piety and charity. Consider what the past life of a woman must have been for her to be fit for enrolment among the "widows" of the Church. "Well reputed of for good works; if she hath brought up children, if she hath used hospitality to strangers, if she hath washed the saints' feet, if she hath relieved the afflicted, if she hath diligently followed every good work." [3] The vicious idleness of the Oriental harem, the aimless existence so long forced upon English womanhood, are entirely alien from St. Paul's mind. What is intolerable is not that women should work, but that they should have to work for their living. What would St. Paul have thought of the working classes of our great towns, where even the married women, neglectful of their homes and their children, toil in the factories, thereby too often throwing the

[1] I Tim. v. 4, 8.   [2] Titus ii. 5.   [3] I Tim. v. 10.

men out of work, and depressing the standard of wages ? What would he have thought of the girls of the middle classes, damaging their physical and intellectual health, and endangering their capacity for motherhood, by spending their girlish years in preparing, with a girl's terrible conscientiousness,_for a series of exhausting examinations, and then going out to sink or swim in the whirlpool of modern life ? The woman has her own characteristic burden, that man cannot share with her ; the very facts of her life render it necessary that her work should be a work that can be laid aside at such times as she is not fit to perform it. It is infamous that she should shoulder man's characteristic burden in addition to her own, and in the sweat of her face eat bread, till she return to the ground. The will of God, that women should be subordinate to men, is not written upon the facts of nature one whit more plainly than His will that they should be free from such labour as this. And if it be said that these things are unavoidable, we ask, What makes them unavoidable ? The laziness of men, the love of luxury among both men and women. Men must work harder, and spend far less upon themselves ; men and women alike must lower their standards of living. War conditions may make the toil of women inevitable, but the conditions of peace do not. It is for the Church to set her face against it ; she has no right to maintain the subordination of women to men, without maintaining the corresponding truth of the duty of men to provide for women. *No-blesse oblige*, and all true Christian authority, as St. Paul says, is for " building up," and not for " casting down." [1]

---

[1] 2 Cor. x. 8.

Secondly, if, as men are so fond of saying, " the sphere of women is the home," it is the business of men to see that this sphere is provided for them   " I desire, therefore," says St. Paul, " that the younger widows marry, bear children, rule the household, give none occasion to the adversary for reviling · for already some are turned aside after Satan." [1] St. Paul, needless to say, sets the highest value upon the celibate life, not as a purer life than that of marriage, but as one which offers greater facilities for the service of God. [2] But the celibate life, to be lived worthily, requires a special gift [3] ; the majority of women desire to be wives and mothers ; and, if they are baulked of their natural desire by the evil conditions of modern life, they are restless and unhappy, and tempted to " turn aside after Satan " in a variety of ways. Now the Frenchman knows this, and acts upon it.   If his daughter is without any special religious vocation, he regards it as his duty to deny himself in order to provide her with a dowry suitable to her position, and actively to interest himself in her marriage.   No doubt the marriage customs of the French have their own danger, but they are far nearer to the mind of St. Paul than our own.   The danger of tyranny inherent in the French method is no more than a danger ; there is no necessity that Frenchmen should be overcome by it, or behave themselves " unseemly toward their virgin daughters " [4] in any way. The English method is wrong fundamentally. Its necessary consequence is that a multitude of women, who

---

[1] 1 Tim. v. 14.   R.V. margin has " younger women."
[2] 1 Cor. vii. 32–35.   [3] 1 Cor. vii. 7   [4] 1 Cor. vii. 36.

74

are without any special religious vocation, " pass the flower of their age " without any reasonable chance of becoming happy wives and mothers. What wonder that there forms upon them

> the crust of iron moods
> That mask them from men's reverence,

and that they exhibit a violence and discontent with their lot which French women do not ?

Thirdly, the duty of men to provide for women applies not only to their physical and emotional needs, but to their mental and spiritual needs also. When we read St. Paul's words, " If they would learn anything, let them ask their own husbands at home," [1] do we always consider what is presupposed ? Plainly such a direction is meaningless, unless their husbands are ready and competent to provide the knowledge which they desire. If women are priest-ridden, their husbands have generally only themselves to blame. If they are competent to help their wives and daughters in spiritual things, they will have no trouble. But all this has a wider application. Women can attain no adequate mental and spiritual culture without study and experience and free discussion of both ; and, if St. Paul's teaching sets a limit to their activities, it as clearly demands that men should be prepared to give them access in other ways to all the knowledge which they require. If they do not, they themselves suffer, and not women only.

> If she be small, slight-natured, miserable,
> How shall men grow ?
>   As far as in us lies
> We too will serve them both in aiding her—

---

[1] I Cor. xiv. 35.

Will clear away the parasitic forms
That seem to keep her up, but drag her down—
Will leave her space to burgeon out of all
Within her.

Exactly so. Once more, *Noblesse oblige.* If men
are to rule, they must not only be intellectually fit
to rule, as too often they are not; they must be ready
to make their rule tolerable by making it intelligible.

Lastly, what of those who have no men at once
bound to protect them from the world, and able to
do so? What of widows who are " widows indeed,"[1]
and of unmarried women in no better case. St. Paul's
answer is clear. They are the charge of the Church.
" Honour widows that are widows indeed." [2] The
word " honour " here, as in the fifth commandment,
means " support." She that is desolate must " set
her hope on God," and God by His Church will take
the father's place, while the desolate, who receives
the Church's " honour," must requite the Church by
her labour and her prayers.[3] The Early Church perfectly understood this duty; she did not insist upon
the subordination without accepting its necessary
outcome. She had her bands of consecrated widows,[4]
and soon her bands of consecrated virgins also. We
must revive her practice. Such institutions as the
Béguinages of Belgium are grievously needed in
England to-day.

[1] Tim. v. 16.   [2] 1 Tim. v. 3.
[3] 1 Tim. v. 5.   [4] 1 Tim. v. 9.

Ministrations of Women in Church

By Dr. Darwell Stone

D R. DEARMER discusses three passages in the Epistles of St. Paul : "Let the women keep silence in the churches, for it is not permitted unto them to speak ; but let them be in subjection, as also saith the law. And, if they would learn anything, let them ask their own husbands at home, for it is shameful for a woman to speak in the church" [1] ; "Every woman praying or prophesying with her head unveiled dishonoureth her head" [2] ; "Let a woman learn in quietness with all subjection ; but I permit not a woman to teach, nor to have dominion over a man, but to be in quietness." [3] He explains the first as simply a prohibition of women chattering with one another while men are speaking with tongues, and the second as allowing women publicly to pray and preach in

[1] I Cor. xiv. 34, 35.
[2] I Cor. xi. 5.
[3] I Tim. ii. 11, 12.

church. On the third, after saying that he himself thinks it " superstitious to let our services be governed by St. Paul's advice to his converts," he bases a *reductio ad absurdum* addressed to those who appeal to the authority of St. Paul in such matters : namely, that, if they cite St. Paul against the public preaching of women, they must sweep away all our girls' schools and denounce the memory of such teachers as St. Hilda and St. Teresa.

Dr. Dearmer's interpretation of St. Paul is as perverse as his article is clever. As to 1 Corinthians xiv. 34, 35, the frequent use of "speak" throughout the chapter to denote public utterance, the relation of the particular verses to the general context, which is concerned with public utterance, the addition in verse 35 of the further point implying that women are not even to ask a question publicly at the time in church, combine to show that the words in verse 34, " it is not permitted unto them to speak," prohibit women from teaching or preaching to the congregation in church. In 1 Corinthians xi. 5 St. Paul may allude to a practice of women " prophesying " in church at Corinth, and for the moment condemn only the abuse which concerns his present argument in such " prophesying" being by one " unveiled," but, if so, that he does not deal with two points at once does not show that he approved of that on which he does not comment, and he is already moving towards the general prohibition of women speaking in church in the light of which the earlier passage must be read. And in 1 Timothy ii. 12 the natural meaning suggested both by the context, which has to do chiefly with public worship, and by use of the word " teach " in the two other places in the Epistle in which it is used,[1] is that what it forbids to women is public teaching in church. St. Paul is consistent throughout. He prohibits the public ministrations of women in church. He none the less refers to and approves of many kinds of private teaching by them. He is entirely consistent when in I Timothy ii. 12 he forbids women publicly to teach in church, and in Titus ii. 3–5 declares that aged women are to be " teachers oft hat which is good," to "train the young women" in the duties of their station. And this consistent attitude was based on principles of permanent value, whatever might be required in some particular detail affected by considerations of time and place. As thus based on permanent principles, St. Paul's teaching became a foundation for the general method of the Church. When the Gallican Canons, which are known by the name of the " Fourth Council of Carthage," decreed that a woman was not to teach in the general congregation, however learned and pious she might be, and also that the widows and consecrated virgins were to teach ignorant women catechumens the Baptismal Responses, and how to live after Baptism (12,99), and when in a very different locality the "Apostolic Constitutions," while allowing some ministrations of women, forbade them to teach in public worship (iii. 6), such instances are alike significant of the mind of the Church and an echo of the teaching of St. Paul.

Dr. Dearmer's perversity in interpretation affects his whole article. In attempting to discredit " the prejudice against women taking services" by describing it as " an Anglican peculiarity," he refers to the saying

[1] I Tim. iv. 11 ; vi. 2.

of Litanies or the Rosary by women abroad. It is well known that when this is done the woman acts as a member of the congregation and not as a minister. One who joined (to mention two instances frequent abroad) in prayer begun by a little girl in a multitude of school children or a hymn started by a woman might well go out of church at once if a woman stood up to preach in the pulpit or on the sanctuary step or in some other ministerial way. Dr. Dearmer refers also to a private chapel "where the lady of the house regularly serves at Mass," and to religious Houses where "nuns officiate at the Altar as deaconesses." He must know that any priest celebrating under such conditions is liable to severe censure. In the Church of Rome, if there cannot be a male server, a woman is allowed to "make the responses" on behalf of the congregation. But in accordance with the Canon Law she is forbidden to be near the Altar for this purpose or to assist the priest by handing the Elements to him (*Decret.*, I. xxiii. 25 ; *Decretal. Greg.*, III. ii. 1 ; *cf.* e.g. Lehmkuhl, *Theol. Mor.*, ii. 244).

I write as one who has much sympathy with many features in what is known as the "Women's Movement." For years I have done what I could in what seemed rightly my sphere to promote the increase of women's influence in political affairs and in many Church matters. But the claims suggested by Dr. Dearmer's article run counter to the general mind of the Church as well as to the teaching of St. Paul. And what a tragedy it is that, when we should all be united for the work of the National Mission, there is a project for promoting such ministrations of women as would make it necessary for those women and men who pay regard to Holy Scripture and the traditions of the Church to stay away from and discountenance the services in which these take place!

III

The Ministry of Women and the Tradition of the Church

By W. J. Sparrow Simpson

THE recent discussion on the claims of women to official ministry in the Church, whether as preachers or as priests, shows very plainly indeed how necessary it is not only for principles to be considered in the light of modern needs, but also modern needs in the light of principles.

The claim of women to exercise the official ministry of the Church must be considered·from the standpoint of the Church itself, and in the light of its principles and practices. Neither the office of a preacher nor that of a priest can be self-imposed. No man and no woman can take this honour to themselves. They cannot rightly preach the Church's doctrine except they be sent, nor consecrate the Church's Sacraments except they are authorized and commissioned by the Church to which those Sacraments are divinely entrusted. It is, therefore, the Church which must decide, and not the persons by whom the office is desired.

The evidence of Scripture to the place of women in the Church has been considered in a previous essay. Our attention is to be fixed on the Church's practice.

WOMEN AND THE CHURCH'S TRADITION

I

The history of the early Church shows that :

1. There were *prophetesses* in the second Christian century as well as prophets. " At Hierapolis in Phrygia the prophetic daughters of Philip enjoyed great esteem ; Papias, amongst others, listened to their words." [1] But the prophetess was a gifted individual, the possessor of personal endowments of a religious kind. She was not a member of an official order, formally instituted and recognized by the Church as such. Her gifts were clearly personal and not transmitted. The prophetess as such had no successor.

Prophetesses seem to have been more conspicuous in religious movements outside the Church than within it. There were the well known prophetesses Maximilla and Priscilla in the Phrygian Montanist movement. But an essential feature of that movement was that it expressed individual religion as opposed to corporate. Harnack says that " Among the Gnostics especially women played a great rôle, for the Gnostic looked not to sex but to the spirit." [2]

Harnack recognizes the difference in ministerial function between women in the Church and women in other forms of religion. He attempts to account for the difference as caused by reaction of the Church from other religions.

" It was by its very opposition offered to Gnosticism and Montanism that the Church was led to interdict women from any activity within the Church ; apart, of course, from such services as they rendered to those of their own sex." [3]

---

[1] Harnack, *Expansion*, ii. 228.
[2] *Expansion*, ii. 229. [3] *Expansion*, ii. 230.

THE PLACE OF WOMEN IN THE CHURCH

The place of women in the Church was discussed by ecclesiastical writers as early as 200. Tertullian, in the Catholic period of his life, held that women had no authority to teach doctrine.[1] Baptism could be administered by laymen in cases of necessity. But that a woman should baptize he regarded as an extravagance of which no example had arisen. The story which ascribed to Thecla a liberty to teach and baptize was a fiction of a certain presbyter who for writing it was deposed from his office, as doing discredit to St. Paul. For seeing St. Paul held that women should be silent and consult their own husbands at home, it was unthinkable that he had given them the power to teach and baptize.[2]

Tertullian taught again categorically that

" it is not permitted to a woman to speak in the church ; but neither is it permitted her to teach, nor to baptize, nor to offer, nor to claim to herself a lot in any manly position, not to say in any sacerdotal office." [3]

Bishop Firmilian, contemporary of St. Cyprian, cites a case of a woman who ventured not only to baptize but to celebrate the Eucharist, and who in so doing kept close to the usual ecclesiastical language. The act in his opinion was utterly null and void.[4]

Ambrosiaster regards the ordination of Deaconesses as an innovation of the Montanists, an act for which there was no apostolic precedent—an act which was due to entire misunderstanding of St. Paul.[5]

The ministry of women in the Church was regulated by various Canons, dating from about A.D. 380. Thus

[1] *De Baptismo*, ch. i.   [2] Ch. xvii.
[3] *On the Veiling of Virgins*, ch. ix.
[4] *Ep.* 75 St. Cyprian Hartel, ii. 819.
[5] P. 470.

84

it was ruled that women must not draw near to the altar, that is in any ministerial capacity.[1] That they should undertake any quasi-levitical ministrations was considered in 394 as an unheard of innovation and expressly prohibited.[2] As late as the time of Charlemagne a reforming Synod of Paris complains of instances in certain provinces of women serving at the altar, and assisting in distributing to the faithful the Lord's Body and Blood. This the Council regards as an intolerable abuse and in contradiction to the ancient rules of the Church.[3]

These facts suggest a very necessary caution. A careful distinction must be drawn between the fact of an occurrence and the legitimacy of an occurrence. It is one thing to collect a number of incidents from history. It is another thing to assign them their proper valuation. There are facts which are the logical result of a Society's principles, and there are facts which are in contradiction with its principles. It is not enough to say that a thing has been done. The question is, whether that thing is, or is not, irregular. Hence the ecclesiastical maxim : It has been done : let those who did it be responsible. It is clearly possible to collect a number of examples to show that women here and there have served at the altar, or helped in the administration, perhaps by taking the reserved Sacrament to the sick. But those examples must be balanced by the fact of the Church's regulations about them. Viewed in this connection they are seen to be abnormal, irregular. They are not the product of the

---

[1] Synod of Laodicea. Hefele, ii. 159
[2] Synod of Nîmes, 394. Hefele, ii. 248.
[3] Synod of Paris §29. Hefele, v. 261.

Institution collectively. They do not express its mind or its tradition. They were done in contradiction to its intentions.

The ministry of women is also seen in the office of the Deaconess.

The Syriac Document (*Didascalia*) which professes to contain instructions delivered by the apostles, but which is in reality a series of ecclesiastical regulations compiled in the third century, probably by a Bishop for the guidance of the Syrian Church, gives the earliest directions on the subject of Deaconesses. It is very probable that this compilation includes material of a yet earlier date.

The Didascalia directs the Bishop to appoint Deacons " and a woman for the service of women." For there are houses to which you cannot send a Deacon to minister to women, because of the pagans. There are also many other matters in which the employment of a Deaconess is necessary. They are to attend upon the women at baptism.[1] The Deaconess is to receive the women after they have been baptized and to instruct them, apparently in practical duties.

For this ministry of the Deaconess appeal is made to the ministry of women to our Lord. It is also added that since many believing women were inmates of pagan households, the Deaconess was required to visit them in illness and to provide for their needs.[2]

The Syriac Didascalia of the third century is largely incorporated in the curious fiction called the Apostolic Constitutions. This highly imaginative work includes much of the devotional and practical life of

[1] *Nau,* p. 134.   [2] P. 135.

the early centuries. It probably belongs to the fourth century and represents the Church of Antioch.

There we find that the Deaconess was a recognized institution. She was intended for ministrations among women. She was to visit the sick, to act as doorkeeper at the women's entrance into the church, to enforce discipline on the women in church during the time of service. She was to attend upon the women who came to be baptized.

Deaconesses were not allowed to teach in the church, still less to act as priests.

" If in the foregoing constitutions we have not permitted them to teach, how will any one allow them, contrary to nature, to perform the office of a priest ? For this is one of the ignorant practices of the Gentile atheism, to ordain women priests to the female deities, not one of the constitutions of Christ." [1]

It is pointed out that our Lord sent men but no women to baptize. It is urged that if this office had been designed for women, our Lord would have been baptized by His mother and not by St. John.

But it must be observed that if in these Apostolic Constitutions Deaconesses are forbidden to baptize, so also are the Deacons. [2]

" A deacon does not bless, does not give the blessing, but receives it from the bishop and presbyter : he does not baptize, he does not offer." [3]

His functions are compared with those of a Deaconess, of whom it is said

" A deaconess does not bless, nor perform anything belonging to the office of presbyters or deacons, but only is to keep the doors, and to minister to the presbyters in the baptizing of women." [4]

---

[1] *Apost. C.*, iii. 9.   [2] iii. 11.   [3] viii. 28.   [4] Ib.

The important question arises here : What was meant by the " ordination " of a Deaconess ?

The Apostolic Constitutions seem to apply the title " ordination " to the appointment of a Deaconess as well as of a Deacon. And the form of their appointment is somewhat similar. Both Deacon and Deaconess are appointed by the laying on of the Bishop's hands in the presence of the presbytery.

The central portion of the office " concerning the ordination of a Deacon " is as follows :

" O God Almighty, . . . cause the light of Thy countenance to shine upon this Thy servant who is to be ordained for Thee to the office of a deacon ; and replenish him with Thy Holy Spirit and with power, as Thou didst replenish Stephen, who was Thy martyr, and follower of the sufferings of Thy Christ. Do Thou render him worthy to discharge acceptably the ministration of a deacon, steadily, unblameably, and without reproof, that thereby he may attain a higher decree, through the mediation of Thy only begotten Son," etc.

The prayer " Concerning a Deaconess " is ·

" O Eternal God, the Father of our Lord Jesus Christ, the Creator of man and of woman, Who didst replenish with the Spirit Miriam, and Deborah, and Anna, and Huldah ; who didst not disdain that Thy only begotten Son should be born of a woman ; who also in the tabernacle of the testimony, and in the Temple, didst ordain women to be keepers of Thy holy gates : do Thou now also look down upon this Thy servant, who is to be ordained to the office of a deaconess, and grant her Thy Holy Spirit . . . that she may worthily discharge the work which is committed to her to Thy glory, and the grace of Thy Christ," etc.[1]

Here then in the dedication of a Deaconess reference was made to the Prophetesses of the older dispensations, to the selection of the Blessed Virgin, and to the appointment of women to the office of doorkeepers of the Jewish Sanctuary.

[1] Trans. in *Ante-Nicene Library*, p. 239.

Both these forms of ordination are framed in such general terms that it is impossible to gather from them precisely what the functions of either office were understood to be, or what precisely was the nature of the ordination conveyed. The one is appointed to " discharge the ministration of a deacon," the other to " discharge the work which is committed to her." Both expressions are quite indefinite. One distinction between the two forms is clear enough. The ordination of a Deacon is regarded as a stage of transition to a higher degree of ministry. There is nothing corresponding to this in the case of the Deaconess. The Apostolic Constitutions give a form for the ordination of a priest but not of a priestess : of a Bishop but not of a Bishopess. And of course the whole principles of instruction which the work contains exclude the possibility of any such thing.

These references throw much light on the Church's intention in appointing the Deaconess. And when it is remembered that the *Apostolic Constitutions* expressly refuse to permit women to teach in the church, and appeal to the fact that our Lord " nowhere sent out women to preach, although He was not wanting in such," it becomes quite clear what the office was to which a Deaconess was " ordained." [1] As Dean Howson said when writing on this subject :

" We must not allow ourselves to be misled by the meaning of the word ' ordination ', as we now employ it. The imposition of hands had a wider range in the Early Church than it has with us ; and distinctions must be drawn with regard to the import of the ceremony on different occasions. In the case of the Bishop and Presbyter, it is a solemn consecration. In the case of the Deaconess it is only an official blessing." [2]

---

[1] *Apost. C.*, iii. 6.   [2] Howson, *Deaconesses*, p. 243.

The only question is what that laying on of hands denoted. That depends on the intention of the Church. We must clearly distinguish between the act and the intention, because the act of laying on of hands may represent many things; and did represent various things in the primitive Church. A sign which denoted Confirmation and Absolution, as well as Ordination, must be carefully distinguished according to the intention with which it was employed. It may denote the conferring of a blessing, or it may denote the transmission of apostolic ministerial power.

A Syrian form of appointing a Deaconess expressly directs that " the Bishop places his hand upon her head, not in the manner of ordination but blessing her." [1]

This subject of the appointment of Deaconesses came into discussion as early as the Council of Nicea.[2] The language of its ruling is obscure and has been the subject of much debate among the learned. On the whole the line adopted by the Council appears to be that if the laying on of hands was understood in the sense of a blessing, then it was true that the deaconess had been ordained ; but if it was understood in the sense of Holy Orders, or the Apostolic ministry, then it was true that the deaconess had not been ordained. This interpretation was given by the historian Baronius, and is accepted by the greatest modern student of the Councils, Hefele.[3]

It seems clear that the office of Deaconess not only

[1] Robinson, *Ministry of Deaconesses*, p. 224.
[2] Canon xix.
[3] Baronius, *Annals*, An. 34, 283. See also Goschler's translation of Hefele, i. 420.

originated in the East, but was only congenial to the East. It never took any real hold upon the Church of the West. It is probable that the reason for this was the different status of women in the two spheres of the Church's operation, women in the East being more secluded than those in the West.

Bishop John Wordsworth, of Salisbury, held that the practical development of the Deaconess movement was " confined to the East, and more particularly to such centres as Antioch and Constantinople, though it appears elsewhere. There is scarcely any mention of the office in the West.in the first four centuries, and when it is afterwards noticed, it is usually with disfavour." He held that various Western benedictions of Deaconesses which have been collected were blessings of Deacons' wives.[1]

The real meaning of this appointment of women in the Church becomes plainer still when we contrast the language directed to be used in the same *Apostolical Constitutions* at the appointment of a Bishop.[2]

" Thou Who didst appoint the ruler of the Church through the word of Thy grace ; . . . grant that this Thy servant whom Thou hast chosen to the holy office of Thy bishop, may discharge the duty of a high priest to Thee   that he may present to Thee the gifts of Thy Holy Church, and in the spirit of the high priesthood have power to remit sins according to Thy commandment, to loosen every bond according to the power which Thou hast given to the Apostles."

This makes the intention and the spirit of the Church quite unmistakably clear. Certain subordinate func tions, invaluable indeed, and such as none can do but

[1] *Ministry of Grace*, 1901, pp. 276, 277.
[2] *Apost. C.* viii. 5, p. 214.

they, are herein entrusted to women; but the whole apostolic ministry, prophetic and priestly, is entrusted to men. That is obviously what is implied in these forms of ordination. It is not conceivable that the Church would use the latter form in the appointment of a woman.

2. It has indeed been argued that the priestly work of offering the Eucharist was in the primitive period confined exclusively to the Bishop; consequently that the priests only offered in precisely the same manner as the women in the congregation.

This seems to miss the point.

For the priest, although not actually exercising his ministry was nevertheless a potential offerer in the sense in which the Bishop was, and the congregation was not. Moreover it is incorrect to say that the actual offering was confined to the Bishop. St. Ignatius clearly contemplates the priesthood celebrating the Eucharist in place of the Bishop.

And further, the recipient of the apostolic commission was invariably a man. There is not a solitary instance in primitive Church history of the Episcopate being conferred upon a woman. Therefore, while no doubt it is true that priests who were not celebrating, but were present simply as members of the Church, offered the Eucharist precisely in the same manner as the women in the congregation, the conspicuous distinction is that the celebrant, or official offerer, was invariably man.

3. The doctrine of the Western Church in the Middle Ages may be ascertained from the greatest of the Latin theologians. St. Thomas maintained that to confine Ordination to men belongs to the essential nature of that

Sacrament; and that if all the forms and signs of Ordination were bestowed upon a woman she would receive nothing more than an outward form destitute of reality. In other words, he taught that Ordination cannot be conferred upon a woman.[1]

This is still the teaching of the Roman theologians. Lehmkuhl declares that it is certain that women are by the Divine Law excluded from ecclesiastical office. A woman is incapable of being a subject for Ordination.[2]

It would not be difficult to add other examples. Gasparri argues that the Ordination of a woman cannot even be called irregular, for only those are capable of irregular Ordination who are capable of being ordained, which a woman is not.[3] Ordination of a woman would be in the same category as the Ordination of the unbaptized. It would be null and void.

Pesch declares that the perpetual doctrine and practice of the Church is that women are never permitted to become priests. Men alone are subjects capable of being ordained.[4]

Suarez goes further still, and affirms that no woman may serve a priest at the altar in the celebration of the Mass.[5] In saying this, Suarez only repeats the principles of the Canon Law.

No doubt the question whether women can be preachers of the Church is separable from the question whether they can be priests. As to the latter, it is

---

[1] St. Thomas, *Summa*, Suppl. Q. xxxix., A. 1 : *Works*, tom. iv. 506.

[2] Lehmkuhl, *Theologia Moralis*, ii. 420 (1896).

[3] Gasparri, *De Ordinat.*, i. 121, 122.

[4] Pesch, Prælect. Dogm., vii. 319.

[5] Suarez, *Works*, xxi. 922.

certain that no orthodox Bishop in all Christendom would venture to go through the ceremony of ordaining a woman. If such an action were performed, it is certain that its agent would be repudiated alike in the East and in the West, and the action itself pronounced to be utterly null and void.

The question whether women can be preachers of the Church is obviously on a different level. For it is a recognized thing that laymen, when authorized by their Bishop, may preach. But here too the tradition of the Church is unmistakable. The practical interpretation which the world-wide Church, East and West, has put upon the matter is unquestionable. It has entrusted the official ministry of the Church, whether prophetic or priestly, exclusively to men. There have been preaching orders of men but none of women. Women have never been authorized by the Church as preachers to the general congregation. They have taught children. They have instructed women. They have advised and guided in private. They have instructed all alike by their writings. Their sphere of religious influence has been immense, both in depth and in extent. But they have not been placed hitherto in the official ministry as instructors of the mixed assembly in public worship.

Nearly two thousand years, the whole of its duration hitherto, the Church has had one rule. It has confined official ministry to men. The work of a deaconess is no real contradiction. The legend of a woman Pope, which no one credits, only throws this fact into stronger light. It may have been a satire to represent the power behind the throne, the days when a Pope had sold himself into the hands of a woman. But no woman as yet has ever ministered at the altars of Christendom. No woman as yet has been authorized as preacher in the Church's official ministry. This is the Catholic custom, universal in East and West.

No doubt the case has been otherwise in certain Protestant denominations in America. Nor is this a matter for surprise. A land with no ancient buildings, and no traditions, dominated by a sturdy individualism and independence of the past, is the natural sphere for the production of eccentricities and novelties in religion, as well as in all other things. This only makes the Catholic tradition stand out in stronger relief.

II

But it would be a most inadequate account of the place of women in the Church if little more were observed than their exclusion from the official duties of the preacher and the priest.

Nothing could be more mistaken than the notion that in consequence of the official ministry being restricted to men, women in the early Church could neither express their faith nor make their influence adequately felt. It is difficult in a limited space to give any idea of the immense influence exerted by women in the Church during the age of the Fathers.

St. Gregory of Nyssa reports in a lengthy treatise the instructions given by St. Macrina,[1] sister of St. Basil, on the Soul and the Resurrection of the Dead. Gregory calls Macrina "the Teacher," and circulates her teaching for the benefit of the Church. Gregory writes

[1] ? A.D. 380.

as one profoundly indebted to the religious medita-
tions of Macrina.[1]

St. Gregory Nazianzen in his funeral oration on his
sister Gorgonia draws a picture of remarkable religious
influence exerted by a woman over the circle of her home
and of her city. There was no sense of limitation
because she was neither a public preacher nor a priest.

Gregory could ask :

" What could be keener than her intellect ? She was
recognized as a common adviser, not only by those of her
family, those of the same people, and of the one fold, but even
by all men round about, who treated her counsels and advice
as a law not to be broken. What more sagacious than her
words ? What more prudent than her silence ? "[2]

Or again let any one read the story of the religious
women in Rome in the time of St. Jerome ; the lives
of St. Melania, St. Paula, and her daughters. It is
difficult not to be astonished by the Biblical studies
of these women, and their knowledge of the Hebrew
language, their community life, and their powerful influence. Cardinal Rampolla's *Life of St. Melania*, 1908 ; or
the *Histoire de Sainte Paule*, by Mgr. Lagrange, former
Bishop of Chartres, 1901, seventh edition, have placed
these lines within easy reach of the general reader ; and
they certainly might contribute to remove misconc-
ceptions.[3]

These allusions are wholly insufficient to represent
the immense influence in religion exerted in the past
by women over men. It may be perfectly true that
the woman's influence has not been as public or con-

[1] See Gregory of Nyssa, *Life of S. Macrina*. Transl. by the
Rev. W. K. Lowther Clarke, in Early Church Classics.

[2] § 11, translation, p. 241.

[3] For Melania see also Duchesne, *Histoire ancienne de
l'Eglise*, iii. 189.

spicuous as that of the preacher or the priest. But it is not always the most conspicuous influences which are the deepest. Woman has fully expressed to the world her conception of the mind of God, not in the pulpit, indeed, but assuredly in the home. To ignore that quiet, persistent, constraining influence is to misrepresent the facts of religious history to a most serious degree. Think of the influence of St. Monica on Augustine, of Anthusa on St. John Chrysostom, of Nonna upon Gregory Nazianzen.

The fact is that behind each of these great preachers was the spiritual influence of the mother. It was the woman's religious ascendancy which guided these great men to the service of the Church.

" Gregory," says his biographer, " had the inestimable advantage of being reared at the knee of a mother of conspicuous holiness." [1] He acknowledged in the In Memoriam Poems that he owed her everything. Nonna controlled his destiny. She gave him to the priesthood.

Of the mother of St. John Chrysostom it has been said :

" All her love, all her care, all her means and energies were concentrated on the boy destined to become so great a man, and exhibiting even in childhood no common ability and aptitude for learning. But her chief anxiety was to train him in pious habits, and to preserve him uncontaminated from the pollutions of the vicious city in which they resided. She was to him what Monica was to Augustine and Nonna to Gregory Nazianzen." [2]

" Anthusa did not marry again ; very possibly she was deterred from contracting a second marriage by religious scruples which Chrysostom himself would certainly have

---

[1] *Mien Lib.*, p. 187.
[2] Stephens, *Life of St. John Chrysostom*, p. 10.

approved. The Pagans themselves admired those women who dedicated themselves to a single life, or abstained from marrying again. Chrysostom himself informs us that when he began to attend the lectures of Libanius, his master inquired who and what his parents were; and on being told that he was the son of a widow who at the age of forty had lost her husband twenty years, he exclaimed in a tone of mingled jealousy and admiration: ' Heavens ! What women these Christians have.' " [1]

Judging the value of a life by its effect, whether on the Christian or on the Pagan mind, it seems quite clear that Anthusa's devotion was the best adapted to her age. It is not at all clear that she would have served her generation better, nay, as well, if she had occupied the pulpit instead of training her son.

It is a mere acknowledgment of a simple fact that multitudes of the Church's noblest priests are accounted for by their mothers' religion. The religious communities of women are an enormous strength in the education of every country where they are admitted. The Western Church has known how to direct and utilize the gifts of women, whether spiritual, intellectual, or practical, in a very wonderful way. The Church which excluded them from the priesthood is the Church which has consecrated their labours and canonized their saintliest. The place held by them in Christendom during their lifetime, and still more since their death, by such women as St. Catherine of Siena, and St. Theresa, only illustrates a woman's spiritual powers and the immensity of her religious influence.

Catherine of Siena, a middle-class tradesman's daughter, " full of practical wisdom no less than of the highest spiritual insight," " entered into correspondence with the princes and republics of Italy ; and

[1] Stephens, *ibid*. p. 12.

was consulted by papal legates about the affairs of the Church."

We are told that a Carthusian Prior led all his monks to the house where she was staying and begged her to address them, which she did. She began to speak of Temptation and of Victory, so that all her audience were filled with amazement. The Prior remarked that if Catherine had heard the confessions of all the brethren she could not have said anything more to the point.

" She neglected nothing they needed, and did not utter a useless word. It is evident that she possesses the gift of prophecy, and that the Holy Ghost speaks through her mouth."[1]

How Catherine counselled and directed Pope Gregory XI is simply wonderful. She made so profound an impression upon his mind that in spite of the opposition of the French King, and almost the whole of the College of Cardinals, he left Avignon and returned to Rome. Her letters are described as " a wonderful mingling of the humility of a pleading child and the stern voice of a prophet of old."[2] Few things are more singular in Papal history than the picture of the Pope, who fearing to compromise the Papal dignity if he appeared publicly among the crowd of visitors at Catherine's house, visiting the saint in disguise, to strengthen his weak and vacillating disposition by the aid of her guidance and advice.

" The Pope had turned from his Cardinals to seek the advice of the dyer's daughter : the one being in the world in whom he trusted perfectly, and who, he knew, would not fail him. And Catherine of *Siena* did not fail him. Her hand it was that steered the barque of Peter back to Rome " (A.D. 1376).[3]

---

[1] Antony's *Life of St. Catherine of Siena*, p. 104.
[2] P. 119.   [3] P. 136.

Afterwards when Gregory was dead and Urban VI was deserted by his cardinals, and the great schism was created by their election of another Pope, Catherine assumed the rôle of Urban's chief defender.

Her canonization by a grateful Church was the thankful acknowledgment of her sanctity and her ascendancy. Any one who has read her *Dialogues* knows the force and severity with which she rebuked the defects and failings of the clergy of her time. Her denunciation of evil and unworthy priests is scathing, her moral anger tremendous. If the Church honoured her goodness it was not because it put restraints upon her freedom. She was a reverer of sacred office, but she was no respecter of persons.

St. Theresa is another conspicuous example of a woman's ascendancy in the work of the Church. She was an inspiration to priests and Bishops. That she was entrusted by her Bishop with the delicate task of determining which of the Biblical expositions of four priests was most in accordance with Catholic truth shows the deference paid to her spiritual insight and her critical abilities.[1] The inimitable character of her criticisms shows how thoroughly she deserved the trust. Gregory XV did not hesitate to say that her writings on mystical theology were among the treasures of the Church.[2] She fulfilled a most noble mission in religious literature.

" From the beginning of English Christianity," says Archdeacon Hutton, " the Church joyously availed itself of the national respect for women. Women were among the earliest agents of the conversion, or at least of the establishment of religion in settled resting-places."

---

[1] Bouix, *Lettres de Sainte Thérèse*, ii. 253, L. cxlvii.
[2] *Ibid.*, iii. 603.

The writer mentions several who " all helped to spread the faith, to build churches, or to encourage the religious life." [1] " Among the earliest English missionaries," he adds, " to the Germans were many women ; and they, too, after the manner of St. Hilda, were missionaries of culture as well as of Christianity. . . . Thus from the first days of mission work Englishwomen have understood how great a part they might play in the turning of the nations to Christ." [2]

The correspondence of St. Boniface, the English Apostle of the German people, is a remarkable testimony to the influence of women in the missions of the Church. We read how Boniface entrusted to the Abbess of Thanet the work of producing a copy of the Epistles of Saint Peter [3] to be written in letters of gold " that the Holy Scriptures may be honoured and reverenced when the preacher holds them before the eyes of the heathen." [4] Boniface called women to aid in the work of his missions. Among them Lioba, who is said to have been learned in the Holy Scriptures and the Canons.[5] She presided over a convent at Bischopheim, and with other women " carried the spirit of Christian piety and virtue among German women and into German homes." They educated girls, taught handicrafts and fine art, embroidered vestments and altar hangings, and in the dignity of their spiritual office as abbesses ruled the daughters of Christ.[6] Missioners addressed them as their spiritual mothers, asked their prayers, and sought their counsel.[7] These women were notably identified with the service of the Church and the conversion of the people. They

---

[1] Hutton, *The English Saints*, pp. 305, 306.   [2] P. 310.
[3] *The English Correspondence of S. Boniface*, 1911, in The King's Classics, Letter xiv.   [4] P. 90.   [5] P. 13.   [6] P. 98.
[7] P. 101.

sustained and cheered the Apostolic labours of such men as Boniface and Luk, who constantly asked to be consoled and rescued by their prayers.[1]

Nor can we as English people forget St. Hilda of Whitby, " a woman of wise rede and mighty influence," " the mother whose advice was sought by princes, and who held out to many at a distance an example of the works of light." [2] " A noble woman, we may well say, strong and wise, true-hearted and firm of purpose, with warm affections and clear discernment, using her great capacities for rule and guidance in the true spirit of a mother in Israel "[3]; " making her monks, as Bede says, give so much time to the study of Scripture, and so much heed to the practice of good works, that Bishops came to think of her house as the best place for supplying competent ordinands, and five of the brethren, whom Bede enumerates, ' all of them persons of signal worth and holiness ' attained the Episcopal dignity." [4]

In the Anglo-Saxon converts of the seventh century the authority of the Abbess was most remarkable. She was at the head of both Communities : that for men as well as that for women. St. Hilda ruled in this capacity for thirty years. Bishop Aidan and many other religious went to converse with her on the love of God. Kings and princes consulted her. She was a mother to the countryside. The Venerable Bede becomes eloquent in her praises. She encouraged the study of the Scripture in the Community of men with such effect that this monastery ruled by a woman

[1] *Ibid.*, p. 147.
[2] Bright, *Early English Church History*, p. 273.
[3] P. 274.   [4] P. 275.

became a seminary of missionaries and of bishops.[1]
John of Beverley, for instance, owed his training to
Hilda's influence.

This ascendancy of women continued to the thirteenth century. It was authorized by Papal regulations. Monks were bidden to see in the presiding
Abbess an application of the text, "Son, behold Thy
mother."

Neither can we omit one who has come into much
favour of late years among English people : Juliana
of Norwich, whose writings have been called "the
most perfect fruit of later mediaeval mysticism in
England."

Broadly speaking the action of the Church with
regard to women's work has been governed by the
principle that women should teach in their private
capacity, but that the authorized official exponents of
the corporate belief should be exclusively men. Thus
women have been recognized as teachers, as writers,
as professors of theology ; none of these being officers
of the Church, but individual cases of learning or
literary ability. But women have never been called
by the Church to become authorized mouthpieces of
the Church's Faith.

III

The mind of the Church of England on the subject
of women's ministrations as it has existed hitherto is
well represented in the words of Bishop Jeremy Taylor.
He is discussing the commission to preach the Gospel
as being entrusted by our Lord to the Apostles. He

[1] Montalembert, *Les Moines d'Occident*, iv. 65–67.

then goes on to consider the plea that the descent of the Holy Ghost was upon women as well as men, and that sons and daughters also did prophesy. Consequently that the case was now altered ; that whereas Christ gave the commission exclusively to men, it was now shared alike by men and women. " Priscilla sat in the chair with her husband Aquila, and Apostles sat at their feet." " And therefore although the commission went out first to the Apostles, yet when by miracle God dispensed great gifts to the laity, and to women, He gave probation that He intended that all should prophesy and preach, lest those gifts should be to no purpose." Such was the argument against the Catholic tradition.

Bishop Jeremy Taylor replies, " This must be considered." Accordingly he proceeds to consider it. He holds that such gifts were exceptional and extraordinary and that

" These extraordinary gifts were no authority to those who had them, and no commission, to speak in public. And therefore St. Paul forbids the women to speak in the Church, and yet it was not denied that some of them might have the spirit of prophecy. Speaking in the Church was part of an ordinary power, to which not only ability but authority also and commission are required. That was clearly one separation ; women were not capable of a clerical employment, no, not so much as of this ministry of preaching."

He then refers to the ministry of the Deaconess and maintains that :

" Whatsoever these deaconesses could be, they could not speak in public, unless they did prevaricate the Apostolical rule given to the Corinthian and Ephesian Churches. And therefore though Olympias was an excellent person, yet she was no preacher ; she was a philosopher, not in her discourse, but in her manner of living and believing : and that could not be by preaching : but these deaconesses after the Apostolical age, were the same with the good women that did domestic offices and minister to the temporal necessity of the Churches in the days of the Apostles ; such a one was Phoebe of Cenchrea : but they were not admitted to any holy or spiritual office : so we have certain testimony from antiquity, whence the objection comes."

Bishop Jeremy Taylor then appeals to the Council of Nicæa, which he considers to teach that " deaconesses are to be reckoned in the laity, because they have no imposition of hands, i.e. for any spiritual office ; for they had imposition of hands in some places to temporal administrations about the Church, and a solemn benediction, but nothing of the priestly power." He illustrates the case of other women, not deaconesses, who " were solemnly ordained and set over the women in such offices, yet pretended to nothing of the clerical power, or the right of speaking in public." [1]

Bingham reports as the result of his studies in history that deaconesses were ordained and that they were consecrated to a certain office in the Church. Her ordination consisted in the laying on of hands joined with a prayer of benediction for grace to discharge that office aright. But he adds she was not consecrated to any office of the priesthood.

" Yet we are not to imagine that this consecration gave them any power to execute any part of the sacerdotal office, or do the duties of the sacred function. Women were always forbidden to perform any such offices as those. Therefore the author of the Constitutions calls it a heathenish practice to ordain women-priests ; for the Christian law allowed no such custom. Some hereties, indeed, as Tertullian observes, allowed women to teach and exorcise, and minister baptism ; but all this, he says, was against the rule of the Apostle." [2]

---

[1] Bp. J. Taylor, *Works* i. 18.
[2] Bingham, i. 330, 331.

The same learned writer Bingham sums up the duties of the Deaconess as being :

1. To assist at the baptism of women.

2. To be a sort of private catechist to the women candidates for Holy Baptism. Though they were not allowed to teach publicly in the church, yet they might privately instruct and teach the women. This was called the private ministry of the Word. For this purpose a deaconess was required to be a well instructed woman.

3. To visit and attend women in sickness or distress.

4. To minister to those in prison.

5. To attend the women's gate in the church.

6. To preside over the women, assigning them their places and regulating their behaviour in church.[1]

The learned Anglican Hammond says of the deaconesses that " their ordination was performed by imposition of hands ; but it was not such an ordination as conferred authority to discharge any priestly office." [2]

IV

Such, then, is the tradition of the Church. Now, we know that such a tradition will make a very different impression on different minds. One type of mind regards it with impatience, another with deference. To one it is a burden to be escaped ; to another a guide to be followed. A leading lady advocate of priesthood for women says that in her opinion " the weight of custom seems to be quenching the Spirit of God." And certain supporters of women-preachers declare

[1] Pp. 332–336.   [2] Hammond, *Definitions of Faith*, 1843, p. 35.

reproachfully that the Church is bound by a cast-iron tradition. Others, on the contrary, apply the Apostle's language, " We have no such custom, neither the Churches of God." These are the two estimates of tradition. What is their value ? How are we to decide between them ?

In the first place, we are bound to utter the warning : Take care how you disparage tradition. Why ? Simply because tradition is essential to the Christian religion. Many things you cannot afford to lose depend upon tradition. We are sometimes told that certain practices must not be introduced into the English Church. The reason given is that the custom of the Church of England since the Reformation is against them. But if the traditional custom of three hundred and fifty years is a powerful argument, what will you say to the traditional custom of almost two thousand years ? Can you consistently claim credit for a custom of a local Church if you refuse to credit the custom of the world-wide Church ? Then, again, upon what authority do you receive the Scriptures ? How do you know that the New Testament contains precisely the documents which ideally it should contain ? You can only know this by the authority of tradition. Would not, then, to undermine this tradition be a very dangerous thing ? Or, again, upon what authority do you accept the Episcopate ? Upon what else than the authority of tradition ? What is a Bishop but the very embodiment of tradition ? For him of all men to disparage tradition would be suicidal ; for it would be to cut away the very foundation upon which his own authority reposes. If a tradition continuing from the beginning uninterrupted by adverse facts, coextensive with the world-wide Church, is undermined, then many other elements of Christian development are liable to be overthrown.

But, secondly, there is more than this. Different estimates of the value of a universal tradition are in reality caused by different beliefs concerning the Church's nature. If there is no such thing on earth as a Divinely created Institution, if the Church is nothing more than an aggregate of man-made independent assemblies, then its traditions and its customs have no more than a human authority, and may conveniently be set aside. But if, on the contrary, there is on earth a Church which Christ created and His Spirit has guided, if the visible Church is indeed a Divine Institution, then its universal traditions possess a Divine authority. Certainly in this case there can be no stranger proceeding than to pray to the Holy Spirit to guide us, while we ignore the guidance which He has given persistently and invariably in the age-long experience and practice of the Christian Church.

It may, however, be suggested that such a tradition of exclusive official ministry for men may have been advisable and even necessary, considering the status of woman in the past, but that this exclusiveness is no longer necessary or advisable under the totally changed conditions of womanhood in the modern world. It may be asked whether, if Christendom should last for tens of thousands of years, it is of necessity bound in perpetuity to the customs of that small fragment of its duration and development realized hitherto. This is undoubtedly a plea which sounds effective to many minds.

Whatever answer may be rightly given, one thing

at least is clear. The question is, Who has the authority to change the customs of the Universal Church? The answer ought to be beyond dispute.

The authority to change a world-wide tradition cannot be found in any diocese taken by itself. No Bishop has authority to alter the Church's traditions. He is of all men entrusted with the duty of their preservation. A diocese is but a fragment of the Church. It is bound by the customs of the world-wide Church.

Neither does authority to change the world-wide customs exist in the local or national portion of the Church. For the part is subjected to the whole. The local cannot lawfully override and contradict the universal, of which it is but the partial expression.

Least of all can the Church of England afford to act independently of the traditions of Christendom. Our confusions, our contradictions, our unhappy divisions, ought to make us more careful than any other Church in Christendom not to complicate our relationship to the rest of the Catholic Church by raising suspicions of our indifference to its continuous traditions. We do well to lay to heart the criticisms, the sarcasms to which we have been recently subjected, on this very subject of women preachers, from other portions of the ancient Church. We need to remind ourselves very definitely and resolutely that, whether such traditions are within the Church's power to change or not, it is absolutely certain that no change whatever can be made by any authority less than that of the Catholic Church in its entirety. No desire to conciliate, no prospect of capturing a movement, no local advantage or apparent expediency can justify us in a violation of this essential principle. For upon this principle our very status as a Church is based.

IV

The Claim of the Priesthood for Women

By Lady Henry Somerset

THOSE who have worked for and advocated the claims of women's political and industrial freedom, have seen with real rejoicing the gates of opportunity flung open to her one by one: and have watched women go out gladly to take up their new tasks and new toil.

At such a time it seems doubly regrettable that a discussion should arise and an agitation be set on foot which can be interpreted to mean that women are claiming now, or intending to claim at some future time, equality with men in the Priesthood of the Church. And I can only believe that those who take such a position have failed to realize what is implied by their claim.

The leaders of the agitation state quite frankly their demands "that women shall be admitted to the Priesthood," and as frankly state their reason for the demand because women "have gifts for that work and would supplement and inspire the work of men."

Presuming that this demand is made by women

who hold and love the Catholic Faith, I would venture to point out to them that these claims are made under a misapprehension of what the Catholic Faith teaches about the office of the Priesthood, and its place in the Church.

The arguments I use may not appeal to any one outside the Catholic Church, but I trust that even those who differ from me will realize that, granting our belief in the Church, our position is at least logical.

We believe that in the Catholic Church, we have a

" God-given order, something which is necessarily and unalterably right, something which we own to be, in just this shape, indispensable. We could not ask that it should be accepted for any other reason or in any other way." [1]

For in God's Church we see the Divine ideal of human society, and this Divine Ideal has been given to us, we believe, by the guidance of the Holy Spirit working in and through His Church.

Far from this being an arrogant claim, it is founded in man's deep sense of his own limitations. Our Faith is not in what man can do or what man is, but in what God is, and what God has done.

This great principle lies at the root of Church order and Church Sacraments. " Revelation turns our thoughts away from all merely self-formed ideas ; it bids us put our trust not in the virtues, righteousness, actions which we possess or perform, but in what Christ has done for us."

Women are asking to be admitted to the Priesthood ; some go so far as to say " The sex bar should be removed," others, that " The struggle for entrance into

[1] *The Church and Religious Unity*, by the Rev. H. Kelly, from whom I have freely quoted.

the Priesthood will be hard and prolonged. It will be well for us to enter into the fight armed with the weapon of the vote."

However sincere and earnest these women are, their point of view is fundamentally inconsistent with Catholic teaching. The firm hold that the Catholic Faith has taken on the hearts and minds of millions of men and women is due to the fact that their Faith offers them an escape from their own utterly unworthy, sin-stained, weak and foolish personality. There is nothing we have found in our own selves to warrant a belief that we have any power to teach or uplift or inspire others. It is not only the fact that we can come to God that comforts us, but the far greater fact that in spite of our faithlessness and unworthiness, God comes to us. He comes by His own appointed means, the Sacraments. The Priest is the channel through which these Sacraments are administered. It is to no personal quality or aptitude of his that we owe the validity of these gifts of God, any more than it is to our own worthiness that we receive them. " The Priest himself has neither skill nor holiness nor privilege in the matter." He is a servant, an official, and all that we ask of him is that he shall do rightly that which he is bidden to do. He is the Steward of the Mysteries of God, and it is of supreme importance that we realize that they are God's Mysteries. The Gift in the Sacrament is God's act. But the appreciation, discernment, appropriation are ours. This is the point of the Catholic expression " To assist at Mass." And a child in the congregation saying his prayers, or the charwoman washing the floor of the church, who pauses for ·a moment to worship the

Presence of Christ, is a factor in that service and contributes to its completeness.

We read passionate complaints that women have been " ousted " from their place in the Church, and that the Church has not assigned to them the position and influence " which Christ gave them." Are they sure of this ? Or is it not that they despise the place which He has given them and have not recognized its dignity ? The necessity of woman's share in the religious life has been recognized all through the progressive revelation of the old dispensation. The importance of the woman's position was equal but not identical. To her the office of priest was never entrusted. She might not stand in the temple and offer sacrifice, but to every woman in Israel was given the hope of all hopes, that she might be the chosen mother of the great coming Deliverer. And this inherent dignity was the birthright of every woman : it was her calling in the sight of God and of man, until the fulfilment came in Mary the Blessed Mother of the Lord. And only because the prejudice of Protestantism has so warped the minds of men have we ceased to see that the greatest human figure in our religion, except that of the Divine Son, is a Woman.

It is undeniable that the Catholic Church in the past recognized the office of woman at the head of the great religious orders in a way wholly different from anything that we see to-day. It would be very desirable that dedicated women should receive more definite official recognition from the Church. But surely it is not position that women are fighting for, but for greater opportunities of service. This desire is seen at the root of so many of the present movements among women, such as the Pilgrimage of Prayer and other legitimate ways of widening their spiritual life.

It may be that a recognized order of women teachers should be admitted to the service of the Church. The dignity of the early Methodist women preachers that George Elliot portrayed in her " Dinah Morris," the power of a Mrs. Booth in our own time, and the persuasive poverty and simplicity of the Salvation Army lassie to-day, should give us food for serious thought on this subject. But this does not imply admittance to the priesthood.

We are face to face with the fact that even were it possible we are at present powerless to make any such change in the Sacrament of Holy Orders. For such a matter can only be dealt with by " The Church," and the Church as at present constituted cannot take action. For the Church of England to admit women to Holy Orders would be an act of suicide, it would dissociate us as a Church from Catholic Christendom throughout the world and throughout history. No National Church has the right to innovate independently upon an immemorial and universal practice of the whole Catholic Church. An Œcumenical Council could alone rightly institute such a change.

If we turn to the basic teaching of the Catholic Church, we get back to the true proportions of the woman question.

The war has done us all great service in bringing us back to the fundamental principles underlying our civilization. A long period of the development of peaceful prosperity had produced many false standards, and, for all except the wisest thinkers, had obliterated the clear lines of the elementary truths of human nature. And just as classes and individuals had lost sight of their necessary functions in the community, so woman had to some extent lost sight of her special inheritance. But the War has brought us face to face again with the fundamental difference of sex. We have returned to the primitive ideal of man as the defender, the protector of the home. It is a man's duty to give his life for the community when the safety and well-being of the community is threatened. No one questions this. It is his vocation. Woman has instinctively taken again the place she occupied in the most primitive society : and, to-day, just as the majority of our men are soldiers or defenders, so the majority of our women are tending the community.

The natural instinct in woman is the instinct of sacrifice. In the animal life this is the instinct of maternity only, but in the developed human life it is the instinct not necessarily of personal motherhood, but of a " motherliness " which cheerfully sacrifices itself for the good of humanity. This argument holds good for all women's work to-day. It is not only in nursing the sick and wounded that she is fulfilling her destiny. Every woman who is driving a motor ambulance to pick up the wounded at the Front, or a lorry to facilitate the distribution of food at home, who is helping on the land, helping in a canteen or preparing the needful requisites for the troops, is working in harmony with her calling. An unerring instinct, which is true as the needle to the pole, has called her at this time to take up the work which is inherently hers.

It is true we heard a whisper of a Woman's Corps to be trained for actual fighting, but this flickered out like a tiny flame before the wind as the great majority of women swept forward to take the places national exigency had assigned to them.

When Ibsen's " Norah " said to her husband " I am a human being with the same rights as yourself," it was at a time when such a statement of truth was as valuable as it was necessary. We have but to read mid-Victorian literature with its belittling of the elderly woman and the unmarried to understand how necessary, and how valuable. But what many people do not understand is that Ibsen's heroine was only insisting on the recognition of a great Catholic truth. It was not the present generation that first made the discovery that women had as good a right as men to political freedom. In the thirteenth century Pope Innocent IV declared that all election rights should belong to all human beings over fourteen years of age, whether they were men or women and whether the women were married, unmarried or widows. No one who has read the history of the Church will be surprised at this, for the Catholic Church has always dignified women. It was left to Lutheran Germany to degrade woman, to regard her as a mere appendage of man. Luther's views of women, instanced by Baron von Hugel in *The German Soul*, page 168, are revoltingly coarse and brutal.

It is easy to trace, side by side with the influence of German Protestantism in England, the mean low view of women held in the Georgian and Victorian age, but happily we have come back to a more Christian estimate of the deep facts of life.

Quite lately I asked one of the clearest thinkers of our day what was, in his opinion, the spiritual difference expressed by sex. I cannot do better than give his answer to my question.

"I would say it is only a difference of emphasis. Spirit expresses itself and is known to itself by its absolute values, and these are, and must be, the same for all spirit. The absolute values of men and women are the same. But each sex has a greater sensitiveness to certain values than the other. For this reason they are so useful to each other in freedom and equality; they enrich each other's values. Only they must always follow their own values, passionately, as they feel them."

And here, it seems to me, we come to the fact that by nature the woman's value will always be that she is destined to be the figure at the world's hearth. And though some women may be found to repudiate or minimize this vocation, it cannot be denied that the natural instinct of the great majority of young women is to regard every occupation as more or less temporary, pending the taking up the responsibility of a home of their own. Every employer of women's labour is aware of this, and it is one of the economic facts that has tended, however unjustly, to keep down women's wages.

I would instance the literature and the public utterances of the extremists in the woman movement, as evidence that seems to point to pitiful discontent with their own achievement, which, taken with their clamour not only to be allowed to rival men but to be men, prove that they are on the wrong lines, though they know it not, and are hungering for a truth they have scornfully set aside.

The God-given instinct of motherliness in no way cramps or dwarfs a woman's life. In what possible way can it belittle any woman to be "as the heart within the breast," the life, the warmth and the consolation of a home ?   Those who are in close touch with the thought and feeling of the young girls of the present day recognize the beauty of this inheritance as the root of so many of the numerous " War-weddings." It is her instinct of motherliness that binds the girl to her bridegroom at the Front : her desire that whether she is nursing in some hospital, or making munitions in some great manufacturing centre away from her home, she may be in herself his home.   She is " the figure at the hearth " to which he looks from the loneliness and desolation and the utter fatigue of the actualities of war.   Far deeper and more fundamental than her love of him as her lover, is her mother-love for him as she realizes his childlike need of her. Esoterically every woman looks on every man as a child.   The women who do not marry but carve out careers for themselves outside the limits of a home, are generally women to whom many look for help, women of many friends, many interests bound up with other people's homes, friendships and interests, which, if we analyze them, bring us back to the essential motherliness of the true type.

The sword which pierced the soul of Mary has to-day pierced the hearts of thousands of women, revealing to them the depth of the great Catholic truth that sets in the centre of humanity the Holy Mother and the Divine Child.

V

The Ordination of Women

By Geraldine E. Hodgson, Litt.D. (Trin. Coll.,
Dublin)

WHEN, in August, 1916, the English Church
Union published some documents, viz. two
letters and replies thereto, revealing the efforts of a
band of women to pave their way to obtain Holy
Orders, there was an outburst of amazed-disgust ;
though unfortunately one or two priests expressed
the opinion (their usual acumen being surely at fault)
that the movement could and should be regarded with
contempt.   Indeed, in the *Church Times* of August 18,
Mr. Lacey went so far as to write ·

" The scheme of the ladies who desire ordination has for
a long time been familiar to me. . . . I have never found
occasion to do anything but laugh at it."

But unlike less well-informed critics he did admit the
fact : while other people were reckless enough to charge
the objectors to this scheme with a desire to wreck the
National Mission, a charge as regrettable as it was
baseless.   Though the letters published by the E. C. U.
were explicit enough, they did not prevent the foolish
statement that " no woman ever thought of asking for

Holy Orders." As a book may have a less precarious life than a pamphlet, the covering letter may well be reproduced here, just to prove, once for all, that some women did cherish these aspirations. It is always sound policy to face facts and not to underrate your opponent.

"C—— Rectory,
"R——.
" (Private.)   "March 26, 1914.
"Dear Madam,

"Your name has been suggested to me as that of a Church-woman who might possibly be sympathetic towards an attempt which I am making to organize an informal Conference to discuss the ordination of women to the priesthood. I have written to about 150 people and have received favourable replies from between thirty and forty. Miss Maude —— Dr. Jane —— and Miss Elizabeth —— have consented among others to read papers. The Conference will probably be held on September 18 in London. It is hoped that in coming together for prayer and discussion we may be shown more clearly what is the will of God in the matter.

"Our feeling is that priesthood is a human office, not at all a sexual one, and that since women are human beings it is unreasonable to refuse them an opportunity of holding it merely because they are women. I know at least one woman who feels she has the vocation; and this woman would have made, so far as one can see, an almost ideal priest. The weight of custom seems to us to be quenching the spirit of God. The loss to the Church appears to us lamentable.

"I enclose a summary of the answers I have received. I shall be very glad to hear from you, if you are interested.
"Yours faithfully,
(Mrs.) —— ——."

Now, at least three considerations should have prevented any Catholic from meeting this document merely with amusement and derision.

(1) The body might be small, but it was, at least, in process of careful organization (private information shows it to be widely spread, and well if cryptically

organized) ; and it had a definite programme. It is a matter of experience (an illustration may be found in the Deceased Wife's Sister Bill) that practically any movement can succeed ultimately in England, if it be skilfully engineered, and persistently pushed over a long period.

(2) Setting aside the strange statement, as it may merely be clumsily expressed, that the priesthood is a " human " office, most of us having supposed it was spiritual, the non-Catholic spirit escapes in a single adjective, *unreasonable* · " it is unreasonable to refuse them an opportunity." Rationalism may be, has been, the basis and *raison d'être* of religious bodies outside the Catholic Church. But the Church repudiates Rationalism as its Charter, relying on the guidance of the Holy Spirit and tradition ; in other words, the doctrine and practice of the Catholic Church rest on the teaching of its Founder, given to the Apostolic College, and, under the direction of the Holy Spirit, transmitted to their successors. People who organize their religious life and base their religious practice on the dictates of reason may be very wise and very successful : but they have no claim to belong to or speak for the Catholic Church. This is not to say that the Church is irrational, but it is to say that she obeys her Lord's teaching, not because it strikes her as reasonable or unreasonable, but because, so far as she knows, it is His.

(3) This claim to the priesthood is based on the " feeling " of a woman or of women about " vocation." No doubt some systems of philosophy have rudely depreciated or even unwisely ruled out feeling. Catholic doctrine and practice neither rule it out nor leave

it triumphant : they regulate, discipline and guide it. But the Church has never accepted a vocation solely on an individual's feeling.

It surely is best and wisest to take this movement on its own showing. By its publications (to wit the aforesaid documents, Miss Picton-Turbervill's article in the September *Nineteenth Century*, sundry letters, speeches and lectures) we are led to suppose that this is a deliberate, thought-out plan of people, whose minds, if not always particularly well informed, are made up. The best way to meet it is by the more deliberate and thought-out, longer-tried order and discipline of the Catholic Church.

The letter already quoted, was sent seemingly to 144 persons (presumably women) in March, 1914. The " summary of the answers " shows that fifty-nine made no reply, seventeen answered so as to be marked " unfavourable," twelve as " interested but not convinced," fifteen as " favourable but will take no action." Besides these, eleven (described as " Agnostics, Quakers, Romans or Nonconformists ") were classed as " favourable but not Churchwomen." It is straining credulity to ask us to believe that " Romans " replied favourably : practising Roman Catholics could not do so.

The class marked " favourable " numbers thirty, but a careful scrutiny shows that of these only fourteen can be considered so without qualification. The rest hesitate : " the time is not ripe," or they are " doubtful whether this is the tactful moment to begin to agitate," or " all our energies should first be given to the winning of the vote." The conclusions justified by a critical perusal of these papers seem to be ·

(1) That it is a *deliberate, definitely organized movement*.

(2) Its methods are *concealed and cryptic*. (Private information shows that as in Pacifist circles, and some of the people concerned belong to both movements, the propaganda is largely carried on in private drawing-room meetings.)

(3) That *fear of wrecking it prematurely* checks or keeps silent some who would, had they a little more confidence, be supporters.

(4) That a *determined bid for power* will be made. One correspondent urges this : " I hope very much that you will *from the first* secure the co-operation not only of Churchwomen, but also of Churchmen, specially of some priests if possible."

If these conclusions be justifiable, and I think any one who reads the documents carefully will admit they are, the gravity of the matter is established.

It is worthy of note that the published " aim " of the Church League for Women's Suffrage, of which the Bishop of Lincoln is president, is " To secure for women the vote in Church and State, as it is or may be granted to men ; to use the power thus obtained to establish equality of rights and opportunities between the sexes ; to promote the moral, social and industrial well-being of the community."

It is difficult to see how any accurate interpretation of this mixed multitude of aspirations could clear their " onlie begetters " from the charge of aiming at the priesthood for women.

About ten years ago, some of us who had for years been and are still " suffragists " with no ulterior motive whatever beyond serving our country and the Church to that limited extent whereby political power ever can serve her, received veiled warnings that sinister intentions lurked behind the movement. No inquiry or urging could disinter these : certainly they were concealed with remarkable skill from those whose unyielding opposition, if this Holy Orders proposition were among them, was a foregone conclusion.

The aim of the movement, like those of some other religious or political activities, has become somewhat obscured in controversy. There are, as some of the controversialists have been careful to state, two questions, and they are distinct, viz. :

(1) Can women be admitted to Holy Orders in the Catholic Church ?

(2) Can they lawfully be allowed to preach or speak in Church ?

No doubt some people will say that even if the second could, in theory, be answered affirmatively, yet in consideration of our antique friend, " the thin end of the wedge," it should in practice be met by a determined negative. No one can have a more lively sense than I of the triumphant value, specially in a country like ours where you can obtain most things by " worrying on " of " the thin end of the wedge." But in the interests of truth, it surely is desirable to meet these demands by an appeal not to expediency, but to principle. First then, comes the question of Holy Orders, which we are told are to be sought through the present deaconesses. Here is the advice of one of the " favourable thirty " ·

" Since we have working in the English Church a large number of episcopally ordained deaconesses, ought not the new movement to originate with them, or, at least, if possible,

125

with their co-operation? . . . I think that our ordained deaconesses should ascertain whether they have been admitted to the diaconate or not. If there is any doubt about this, they should ask to be re-ordained with the Form regularly used for the Ordering of Deacons. In any case, the Form used for men and women should surely be the same in future."

So far as I have observed, the deaconesses of the English Church have not intervened in this controversy. But it surely is a well-known fact that they are not admitted " with the Form regularly used for the Ordering of Deacons "; and it surely is a rather gratuitous assumption that they need to ask any questions about their status. It is difficult to believe that they accepted solemn functions without acquainting themselves with all the pertinent facts.

Though it does not seem in the least to countenance the claim for women's priesthood, Deaconess Cecilia Robinson's *The Ministry of Deaconesses* is one of the books recommended by the Movement's pioneers for study. It is a valuable account of the origin of the diaconate, and in Chapter V a brief but clear summary of the work of deaconesses in the Primitive Church is given. A learned Appendix by the Dean of Wells brings together in convenient compass all relevant references from early documents and from the Fathers. It is worth notice that Miss Robinson's book seems to answer the two questions raised by the present controversy in the negative.

There is not the slightest indication in the book that women could receive Holy Orders, for after a discussion on the XIXth Canon of the Council of Nicæa, the decision appears to be " these women must in all respects be reckoned among the laity " (p. 233).

A remark in an earlier chapter incidentally indicates the Primitive Church's refusal to allow women to *teach* in public. Speaking of the deaconess Syncletica (in the first half of the fifth century) Miss Robinson writes :

"She was a remarkable woman, for the poet Sedulius speaks of her to Macedonius as one to whom any writer might be proud to dedicate his work. He says she was of noble blood, and so learned a theologian as to be capable of teaching, did not her sex forbid."

If we turn to the New Testament, it would appear that deacons " served tables," [1] i.e. attended to the material wants of the Faithful ; and that they *taught*.[2]

St. Irenaeus speaks of " Stephen, who was chosen the first deacon by the Apostles."[3] Though we learn from the Acts of the Apostles that St. Stephen " did great wonders and miracles among the people,"[4] this was surely not through his diaconate, but as the recipient of *charismata* : because the gift which comes by Orders is " grace," " not a charismatic gift but a gift of the Holy Spirit for the rightful discharge of official duties."[5]

The Council of Trent elucidated the point :

"Whereas by the testimony of Scripture, by Apostolic tradition, and by the unanimous consent of the Fathers, it is clear that grace is conferred by sacred ordination, which is performed by words and outward signs, no one ought to doubt that Order is truly and properly one of the Seven Sacraments of Holy Church." (Sess. xxiii. c. iii. can. 3.)

Primitive custom appears to have prohibited deacons from offering the Holy Sacrifice, or even from dis-

---

[1] Acts vi. 1–6.   [2] Acts vii. 2–53, and Acts viii. 5.
[3] Irenaeus, *Against Heresies*, iii. xii. § 10.
[4] Acts vi. 8.
[5] H. Ahaus, *Catholic Enyclopaedia*, Vol. xi.

tributing the sacred elements. The fifteenth Canon of the Council of Arles (A.D. 314) runs : *De diaconibus quos cognovimus multis locis offerre, placuit minime fieri deberi.* The eighteenth Canon of the Council of Nicæa, Hefele translates from the Greek as follows :

> "It has come to the knowledge of the holy and great Synod that in certain places and cities deacons administer the Eucharist to priests, although it is contrary to the canons and to custom to have the Body of Christ distributed to those who offer the sacrifice, by those who cannot offer it. The Synod has also learned that some deacons receive the Eucharist even before the Bishop. This must all now cease ; the deacons should remain within the limits of their functions, and remember that they are the assistants of the bishops, and only come after the priests. They must receive the Eucharist according to the rule, after the priests—a bishop or a priest administering it to them. The deacons ought no longer to sit among the priests, for this is against rule and order. If any one refuses to obey after these rules have been promulgated, let him lose his diaconate."

It is quite true that St. Ignatius (of Antioch) in his *Epistle to the Trallians* (written probably between 110 and 117 A.D.) wrote : "Those too, who are deacons of the mysteries of Jesus Christ must in every way be pleasing unto all. For they are not deacons of meats and drinks, but are servants of the Church of God." Mr. Srawley, translating and editing these Ignatian epistles [1] remarks, in a footnote, that "mystery" "probably refers to their work as teachers, rather than to their assistance at the Eucharist. St. Paul similarly uses 'mystery' in the sense of a revealed truth. Cf. e.g. Romans xvi. 25." This point is important, because even if the supporters of the priesthood for women, could, as a preliminary, establish the equality of deacons and deaconesses, they would not

[1] *The Epistles of St. Ignatius,* Vol. i. p. 73.

apparently thereby have gained for women any right, according to primitive custom, to distribute the elements. This further weakens the never-too-good plea, of one of the "favourable thirty," who urged that " in the Early Church women deacons administered the chalice. In the mission field it might be of great use if deaconesses were permitted to do this, and perhaps administer the reserved Sacrament."

It is difficult to meet so vague a statement ; but it seems to be a reference to certain practices once current in parts of Syria and Asia, recorded by F. Thurston, S.J., in his article on *Deaconesses* in the Catholic Encyclopædia and which he describes as " abuses which ecclesiastical legislation was not long in suppressing."

The still more fundamental point remains : Did the Early Church recognize the " ordination " of deaconesses at all ? Deaconesses existed, that is admitted. *Had they Holy Orders ?*

The XIXth Canon of the Council of Nicæa appears to indicate that deaconesses are lay persons, and receive no ordination. The Council of Orange laid down decisively (A.D. 441) that the ordination of deaconesses was prohibited. Some people seem to think a prohibition points to a *custom* : but " prohibitions " strictly, are directed against claims which should not be made. Heresies and heretical propositions have disturbed the Church in every age : but heresy is one thing and a practice is another.

No one denies that deaconesses fulfilled charitable duties : the *Didascalia Apostolorum* further shows that at one time they were allowed to baptize (a privilege accorded, under certain circumstances, to all

Christians) and to instruct catechumens. The *Apostolic Constitutions*, a fourth-century treatise largely derived from the *Didascalia*, gives this instruction :

" I, Bartholomew, enjoin, O Bishop, thou shalt lay thy hands upon her with all the Presbytery, and the Deacons and the Deaconesses, and thou shalt say, ' Eternal God, the Father of our Lord Jesus Christ, the creator of man and woman, that didst fill with the spirit Mary and Deborah, and Anna and Huldah, that didst not disdain that Thy only begotten Son should be born of a woman ; Thou that in the tabernacle of witness and in the temple didst appoint women guardians of Thy holy gates. Do thou now look on this Thy handmaid, who is appointed into the office of a Deaconess, and grant unto her the Holy Spirit, and cleanse her from all pollutions of the flesh and of the spirit, that she may worthily accomplish her work committed unto her, to Thy glory and to the praise of Thy Christ."

Evidently the duty of guarding the Church doors, and shepherding such women of the congregation as might need it, belonged to the deaconess : but these same *Apostolic Constitutions* (viii. 27) expressly laid down that " the deaconess gives no blessing, she fulfils no function of priest or deacon."

Further, the undivided Church (from whose practice and discipline no Catholic can escape) in the fifth century " ordered " deacons differently from deaconesses. For a deacon, this petition is offered : " Fill him with spirit and power as Thou didst fill Stephen the Martyr and follower of the sufferings of Thy Christ." Also prayer is offered that the deacon " may be counted worthy of a higher standing," which is taken to be a reference to the priesthood.

Fr. Thurston, S.J., who is acknowledged to be a learned and fair controversialist, thus sums up the position · " The Church as a whole repudiated the idea that women could in any proper sense be recipients of the Sacrament of Orders."

Therefore, the *Ecclesia Anglicana*, which claims to belong to the Catholic Church (for when she bids her children declare " I believe in the Holy Catholic Church," she cannot mean them only to intend " I believe in the Province of Canterbury "), must meet any demand for Holy Orders for Women with an unyielding *non possumus*, or renounce her claim. What falling away in such a matter would mean, the following passage indicates :

" All schism is either between Patriarchal Churches, or provincial Churches, or diocesan Churches, or some of these respectively, or some of their respective parts. . . . Many schisms have arisen in the Church about rites and ceremonies, about precedency, about jurisdiction, about the rights and liberties of particular Churches, about matters of fact. Obstinacy in a small error is enough to make schism. St. Paul tells us of divisions and factions and schisms ' that were in the Church of Corinth, yet these were not about the essentials of religion, but about a right-handed error, even too much admiration of their pastors. The schism between the Roman and the Asiatic Churches, about the observation of Easter, was far enough from the heart of religion. How many bitter schisms have been in the Church of Rome itself, where two or three Popes at a time have challenged St. Peter's Chair, and involved all Europe in their schismatical contentions ! Yet there was no manner of dispute about Faith, or Sacraments, or Holy Orders, or the Hierarchy of the Church ; but merely about matter of fact, whose election to the Papacy was right ? "[1]

These grave words of Archbishop Bramhall entitle us to argue that any tampering with Holy Orders makes those who tamper schismatics : a Church which pretended to admit women to the Sacrament

[1] *Replication to the Bishop of Chalcedon* (1656) by John Bramhall, D.D., Archbishop of Armagh, Anglo-Catholic Library, Vol. ii. pp. 27, 28.

of Orders would thereby forfeit its Catholicity and lose the allegiance of the Faithful.

But if it be admitted that women cannot receive ·Holy Orders, and therefore are incapable of exercising priestly functions, there still remains the lesser question, may they preach or teach in church? In a book too little read by English Churchpeople, *The Church and the Ministry*, in a footnote on page 230, Dr. Gore wrote: " St. Paul recognizes a ministry of women in the Church, see Rom. xvi. 1. . . . But it is a ministry which is concerned with works of mercy, and, if with teaching also, only in private."[1] This last reference is to Apollos, a good man and learned, yet only " of John's Baptism." When he attempted to teach at Ephesus we learn that Aquila and Priscilla " took him unto them " (in the Greek προσελάβοντο αυτὸν, in the Vulgate, *assumpserunt eum*), " and expounded unto him the way of God more perfectly." None of these verbs imply that they interrupted and preached correctively to him in the Assembly. This kind of personal remonstrance, practised in all ages and countries by women on men, cannot by any dialectical skill be twisted into a justification for women preachers. It is and always has been a purely private discipline. Dr. Gore adds: " St. Paul clearly excludes women from public teaching." This particular Apostle is nowadays to some so little *persona grata* that it may be worth while to add that no other Apostle gave the least shadow of countenance to women preachers.

Still, " prophesying " remains: and even St. Paul apparently contemplated the exercise of that in public.

[1] Acts xviii. 26.

The meaning of the Greek προφητεύουσα, the Latin *prophetans* is disputed, but seems to mean " speaking as one inspired." This opens up a painful prospect, enhanced by the form of the resolution which Miss Maude Royden convoyed through the Council of the National Mission : " To urge upon the Bishops the importance of giving definite directions as to the best ways of using the services and *receiving the message* of women speakers, whether in church or elsewhere." It seems possible that some women may have deluded themselves into the idea that they are " inspired," and that like " Philip's four daughters " who have figured so largely in this controversy they have the power and right to prophesy.

Yet it may reasonably be asked if this charismatic prophesying be still among the Church's privileges ?

In her *Nineteenth Century* article, Miss Picton-Turbervill makes statements and propounds views ; e.g. (p. 525) :

" Revelation is progressive, and we see in the coming order the advent of a completeness hitherto, on account of artificial restrictions and traditions, unrealized in the Church, for throughout the ages one half of humanity has been called to guide in thought the Church of Christ . . . in the main, man has reserved to himself the power to express fully to the world his conception of the mind of God, and in the aggregate woman has been told that to the world at large she can have no such message to give."

This is not only not true ; it is nowhere near the truth. If only people would study the History of Scholarship and Education they would find that women have borne their part in learning and teaching and education all down the stream of time.

The early history of convents reveals other learned

women besides the Abbess of Thanet, who copied for St. Boniface the Epistles of St. Peter " in letters of gold," and his kinswoman Lioba, who addressed him in Latin hexameters. The Renaissance allowed absolute intellectual freedom to women, of which numbers amply availed themselves ; indeed no century in the life of Europe can be found when women were entirely shut out from letters. Miss Picton-Turbervill goes so far as to write (p. 525) :

" It is impossible not to spend some little time in wondering what power the Church would have to-day if the attitude of Christ had been truly followed ; if women had been taught to think for themselves, and their full development encouraged."

One cannot but deprecate in serious controversy a vague phrase like the " attitude of Christ." It may be made to cover so much more than the facts. Apart from that, her last sentence is utterly misleading. Have these aspirants to Holy Orders entirely forgotten the great abbesses, or the members of contemplative and educational Orders ? Have they overlooked the Saints ? St. Catharine of Siena, whose practical sense and political sagacity were as marked and as operative as her sanctity ; or St. Teresa who will ever remain a shining example of holiness, self-discipline, wisdom and brilliant capacity, the one woman " Doctor of the Church." If they will say these are not modern instances, let them consider the life and work of La Vicomtesse de Bonnault d'Houet, so well set forth by the Capuchin, Fr. Stanislas, or Miss Sellon, the foundress of the Society of the Holy Trinity and of the Company of the Love of Jesus, the latter, as Dr. Pusey called her, " the Restorer under

God of the religious life in the English Church." Moreover, have they forgotten those whom we call the Mystics ? Let them search any good Bibliography of Mystical Writings, and reckon up those contributed by women.

Another of the "favourable thirty" committed herself to the astonishing statement, "The Church has no use for educated women, so far as my experience goes." Her experience must be excessively limited in the regions of ecclesiastical history, holy literature and practical life. Of the spokeswoman of "the Coming Order," Mr. Athelstan Riley, in a counter article, wrote : " Miss Picton-Turbervill's excursion into Church history could hardly have been more unfortunate for the thesis she desires to maintain."[1] The following passage seems to show that her Biblical exegesis is scarcely happier :

" Suffice to say, that in His attitude no trace can be found of relegating woman to the place she now holds in the Church of to-day, nor is there a single note in all His teaching of either class or sex distinction. There is no suggestion in any words uttered by Christ that women were to be excluded from the highest ministry. To women was given the first great Easter message of new life and power ; given, let it be noted, that they might pass it on and instruct the other disciples. On that first great Easter Day we cannot fail to note that women too were in the upper room where all the disciples were gathered for fear of the Jews, when the great commission was given, and that therefore those wondrous words ' As My Father hath sent Me even so send I you ' (John xx. 21) were spoken to the believing women as well as the men. We are so familiar with the story of the Woman of Samaria that we lose its significance ; yet how revolutionary it is !"[2]

The twentieth chapter of St. John makes no mention

[1] *Nineteenth Century,* October, p. 839.
[2] *Ibid.,* September, p. 523.

of the holy women : the word used is " disciples." The parallel passage in St. Mark (which presumably applies to the same occasion) specifically mentions " the eleven." St. Luke, however, records that the two returning from Emmaus " found the eleven gathered together and them that were with them." Tradition may warrant such a description as Father Gallwey's (*Watches of the Passion*, vol. ii. pp. 677 and 678), e.g., " Contemplate the apostles, the disciples, the devout women gathered together with the doors closed " ; and again, " Our Lady is, perhaps, in an inner chamber, alone, or with John and Magdalen," but on page 690, there is no colour given for Miss Picton-Turbervill's suggestion : the commission is there understood, as the whole Church has ever understood it, to be to the Apostles alone :

"In this hour He gives to them the second great power of the priesthood. At the Last Supper He had already given to them the marvellous power given only to His priests : the power of consecrating and offering up the Everlasting Sacrifice. A few days later He will add the third power : *Go and preach the Gospel to every creature.*" [1]

Again, only one bent on making a special point would ever have thought of urging that the Holy Women who received the Easter message were to " instruct the other disciples " ; " pass it on " is a suitable epithet to apply to a " message " " instruct " is here the term of a special pleader. Miss Picton-Turbervill entirely disregards the conclusive fact that every Apostle chosen by our Lord was a man : while the reference to the Woman of Samaria is obscure indeed

[1] *The Watches of the Passion.* Fr. P. Gallwey, S.J. Vol. ii. p. 691.

what help she affords to women preachers or women priests it is hard to discover.

Finally, we shall be wise to remember that it is the vulgar error of our generation to have yielded to the temptation of doing most things with a noise, and a fuss, and an abundance of publicity and advertisement. Never more than now do we need to recollect Who said, " The Kingdom of God cometh not with observation," and to realize its vital, insistent truth.

But when all this has been urged, some facts should not be overlooked. If it be, as it clearly is, contrary to Catholic tradition and discipline that women should receive Holy Orders, contrary to the Church's age-long practice, that women should preach in church, yet it will be a disaster if the distaste excited by these pretensions provoke a reaction against women's lawful work for the Church. Under their extravagant pleas, doubtless lie some burning love for our Lord and His Church, some earnest active desire to use great gifts in His service. There are few things more painful, more sterilizing to most natures, than to be denied an outlet for real, legitimate power and capacity. The quaint phrase in the ancient prayer at Vespers, " O Holy Mary . . . make supplication for the devout female sex," is not only a moving appeal, but covers a profound truth. Women *are* the devout sex. The Church never has wasted them, and it is more than ever essential now that she should not waste nor hamper them unduly. Still, to-day, there is scope for women in religious orders. May they increasingly grow aware of and respond to vocations.

More and more, women are needed for *teaching* : not only in secular schools and Universities, but in Training

Colleges, in Sunday schools, still more in society. By this, drawing-room meetings are not meant, but rather private conversations between friends. Any woman who has cared to understand the Faith and has striven, with however little success, really to practise it, cannot avoid being the recipient of more questions than she can answer, from friends, acquaintance, and even casual strangers ; questions which will tax most of us to the utmost and far beyond.

As ever, the profession of writing is open to women · it need not all be technically theological. It is easy to believe that John Oliver Hobbes and Mrs. Wilfrid Ward, if one may venture on names, have rendered more service to religion with their pens than they could have done in the eminently expensive and wasteful business of platform-speaking, whose result is so seldom commensurate with the effort involved. There is still happily among us one woman-poet whom one could not picture willing to exchange her " singing-robe," with " the Paradisal air," for any privilege of pulpiteering. Moreover, there may be books yet to be written which the Mystics of past days have not rendered wholly superfluous. In theology proper, if women will but train themselves, or be trained, the printing-press, through the book, the journal, the review, will afford them plentiful opportunity.

It is quite possible that some organization both of chance and effort is required, and urgently required. In the things which matter most, we are a dilatory and wasteful nation. Much would be gained if all Churchwomen would relinquish pretensions which clash with the whole tradition of the Church, and combine and concentrate on the wide field of activity where women can render yeoman service to the Church. It will be distressing and disastrous indeed if women end in dividing into two camps, one failing through unlawful ambition, the other through retrograde reaction.

When Browning wrote :

> Be sure that God
> Ne'er dooms to waste the strength He deigns impart,

he hit on a truth of wide application. Yet, we have to remember that very seldom can any truth stand alone, it almost always needs the counterbalancing proposition ; and so along with Browning's dictum we may put Fr. Richard Benson's :

" Really God does not want such clever men to do His work. . . . God will sooner work by a simple peasant who gives all the glory to Him because he knows that it is His, than by one of those very clever men who think they are such, and a gain to any cause they join. . . . Our faith must not stand in the wisdom of men, but in the wisdom of God." [1]

The two pronouncements seem to complete each other.

When the Church called women " the devout female sex," she seized on their greatest, most specific strength. Yet, it must be remembered that devotion is easily spoilt by self-will and self-assertion ; that its bloom may soon be lost in a desperate fight to obtain unlawful power.

Besides, when all is said and done, what great complaint have women, since the highest created being is a woman ?—Holy Mary, Mother of GOD. Real devotion to her may surely spur us all on to use every GOD-given power, while curbing the destructive impulses of undisciplined desire, and checking aspira-

[1] *Letters* of Richard Meux Benson, No. cxix., p. 247.

THE PLACE OF WOMEN IN THE CHURCH

tions, which even if they do spring from eager love and genuine capacity, are still tinged with lawlessness, with self-will.

On the Feast of our Lady's Nativity, in 1912, at Vespers, the Dean of Ferté-Milon preached in the Cathedral of Soissons. In the stainless beauty of that unique place, his clear voice rang out in this clenching sentence, so French in its perfect simplicity · "La très Sainte-Vierge aima profondément l'humanité parce qu'elle aima profondément la Divinité." If women will copy that example, they can go forward in confidence and hope.

VI

The Medical Ministry of Women

By Mary Scharlieb, M.D., M.S.

THE ministry of women in the Christian Church has existed from the days of our Lord. The evangelists tell us of the women who followed Him from Galilee and who ministered to Him of their substance. A little later we find that the daughters of Philip the Evangelist were church workers, and that St. Paul commended to the Romans, "Phoebe, our sister, which is a servant of the church which is at Cenchrea," for " she hath been a succourer of many, and of myself also." He speaks of " Priscilla and her husband Aquila, my helpers in Christ Jesus ; who for my life laid down their own necks ; unto whom not only I give thanks, but also all the churches of the Gentiles." Another woman friend of St. Paul was " Mary, who bestowed much labour on us," and Amplias and " Stachys my beloved." Again he mentions " Tryphena and Tryphosa, who labour in the Lord," and the " beloved Persis which laboured much in the Lord."

From very early days there was apparently an order of deaconesses devoted to the temporal works of mercy, to whom perhaps Dorcas belonged, and there was a body of Christian widows who appear to have been supported by the funds of the Church, and who in return for this benefit brought up children, lodged strangers, relieved the afflicted, and diligently followed every good work.

From scattered records in very early Church history we find that devout Christian women and many noble Roman matrons gave freely of their time and of their substance in helping the work of the Church, and curiously enough that very rugged Saint, Jerome, seems to have possessed the gift of attracting and utilizing the services of women.

In the Middle Ages women's work was of great consequence both from the social and the religious points of view. The men were so much occupied in the defence of their country, and in teaching the arts of war to growing lads, that domestic comfort and well-being would have fared badly had it not been for the industrious and intelligent care that noble maids and matrons bestowed not only on fathers, brothers, and sons, but also on servants and poorer neighbours. In those days the women were the doctors, and possessed a good working knowledge of the treatment of ordinary complaints, and in particular of the accidents that were so common in those rough and war like times. From still older times some women attained to distinction in medical science and proficiency in the art of surgery, such for instance as Agnodice, the Greek woman physician, and Agnes of Salerno. In the Middle Ages religious instruction was imparted to children and to dependents either by monks and priests or by the mother of the family.

Thus women seem to have taken their full share in the educational, the religious, and the domestic work of the times, and not unfrequently they were called upon to take upon themselves the duties of châtelaine, to command the men-at-arms and to provide for the defence of the castle and its dependent village in the absence of the master who was frequently called away on his king's business or some private affray in his own interest.

At first sight it is not clear why the women who had been true helpmeets to their husbands and worthy handmaidens of the Church for many centuries should as time went on have lapsed into an inferior position and a lessened usefulness, but it is certain that during the centuries immediately preceding the modern movement for the emancipation and education of women they occupied a less honourable position and that their activities were circumscribed within narrower limits. The management of the house and the care of children were for a long time the only occupations assigned to women, and in a certain proportion of cases even these duties were not satisfactorily discharged. The women were poorly educated themselves, and were quite unable to teach their children more than the barest rudiments of learning; they ceased to read Latin and Greek as did the women of former generations, and having but little intercourse with continental nations, and despising or ignoring their literature, the women of each country became practically mono-lingual. Apparently the worst depths of ignorance and uselessness were reached by women about the end of the seventeenth century. The spacious times of Queen Elizabeth and the earlier better years of the House of Stuart were adorned by many strong and resolute women. During the Civil Wars the hearts and consciences of the women were touched and not unfrequently they displayed courage, prudence, and resource, but between the days of Lucy Hutchinson and those of Elizabeth Fry few names of really great women are recorded in our history.

Among the causes of this decadence of the women of England we may perhaps reckon the absence of learning and education amongst them, especially the decline of knowledge of Latin and Greek, which seem to have been comparatively common studies in the times immediately preceding the Reformation, but which fell into neglect when Latin at any rate was no longer needed as an aid to devotion. Another reason for the inferior condition and status of women is to be found in the general lowering of the moral standard of the nation, and the wellnigh universal dissolution of social responsibility. Men began to see in women only the instruments of their passions and their pleasures; they no longer considered them as honourable yoke-fellows and as heirs together of the grace of life; and women, like all classes of whom little is expected or required, gradually sank to the level that public opinion considered to be appropriate to them. This very great and regrettable decay of woman's character, education, usefulness and position, is well illustrated by the different manner in which she is celebrated by the authors of the periods. Contrast, for instance, the estimate formed of women by the Elizabethans, Sidney and Spenser, on the one hand, and Pope on the other. The latter said:

> " Some men to business, some to pleasure take,
> But every woman is at heart a rake."

And the very height of the condemnation of the women of his own time is to be found in Lord Chesterfield's letters.

During the seventeenth and eighteenth centuries few women were learned, and of the few who cultivated their mental faculties a large proportion were tainted with the vices of their period. It is therefore quite easy to understand that Puritan fathers associated learning with vice in women and consequently refused a liberal education to their daughters, and desired for them nothing but domestic ties, duties, and efficiency. The women of fashion seldom received a sound education, for success in life they needed nothing but good looks, wit, and smartness. In consequence of the sternness of the Puritan ideal, and equally in consequence of the lax morals of the fashionable world, sex, and sex only, ruled woman's destiny. To find a similar social condition at the present time we should have to look to Hindu and Mahommedan races. In them, as in our own decadent days, the woman is too frequently only a slave to promote the pleasures and amusements of her master, a domestic to provide his comforts, and a mate, the mere instrument by which he perpetuates his family. All idea of equality, all obligation of a father to educate his girls, and all sense of feminine responsibility, faded away. The ideal of marriage became debased, and the age at which marriage was contracted was lowered until royal and aristocratic girls usually married between twelve and fifteen, while seventeen was the upper limit of the age of marriage for girls in general. These unfortunate children, immature in body, undeveloped and untrained in mind and moral nature, were absolutely unfit to be mistresses of households and mothers of families. In consequence of their deficiencies the birth-rate for live children was low, and infantile mortality reached an inexcusable height. Even in families where many children were born, few were reared, and the many manifestations of tuberculosis, together with the ordinary infectious diseases of childhood, prevented the attainment of adult age in an undue percentage of children born alive.

Further consequences of the immaturity and ignorance of the wives were to be found in the general unfaithfulness of their husbands. The pretty, amusing child, married far too young, quickly lost her good looks and charm, she ceased to interest and amuse her husband, and there was, alas, no solid foundation for love and respect. What wonder that the man was unfaithful and that his wrong-doing frequently resulted in disease and disaster to himself, his wife and his children. The woman never matured. Having been set to a woman's tasks when she was a child exhausted by premature maternity, and all too frequently injured by her husband's sin, she was frequently an old woman at thirty, and still more frequently dragged on a useless existence, unable to manage her household and to guide or educate her children.

Even when women were useful and efficient members of society they do not appear to have had any share in the legislation of the country or in any kind of Church work. The laws were made by men, and generally speaking were made in the interests of men. A woman was not considered to be an individual. As soon as she married she ceased to possess property, she had no legal responsibility, and had no right to the guardianship of her children. Her husband was entitled to the possession of all her real property during their joint lives ; all her personal property, even the money she earned by her own toil, was his. A woman could not make a will without her husband's consent, and this consent even if given could be revoked any time until after probate. From this absence of civil rights two especially bad consequences followed : first, the dual standard of morality which still exists and which is at the bottom of much that is wrong and destructive in our social system ; and secondly, the relative want of education for girls. To take the second of these consequences first, we find that education of women in the eighteenth century amounted in the leisured classes to very superficial instruction in accomplishments ; a little French, a little music, a very little drawing, and a good deal of dancing and deportment was the curriculum for these young ladies. The lower middle class were more fortunate, for although their minds were not cultivated some elements of useful learning they did acquire. Like the German *hausfrau* of a few years ago, " cooking, children and church " were their province, and in some cases at any rate they were faithful to what light they had.

In the midst of this darkness there are some brilliant stars, e.g. Lady Mary Wortley Montague. She was endowed with a fine intellect and attained some amount of education. She was profoundly discontented with things as they were and was anxious to raise the social and educational status of woman. Mary Astell, nearly 200 years before the foundation of Girton and Newnham projected and advocated a college for

women, but she was much before her time, her project
came to nothing, and her name is scarcely known.
Curiously enough the two events that seem to have
brought some hope of betterment to women appeared
in the first instance to be wholly disastrous, for little
good could have been expected from the influence of
the French Revolution and the loss to England of a
large portion of her North American colonies, and yet
the general shock that was administered to the indo-
lent, pleasure-loving and self-satisfied society of those
days, and the unanswerable demonstration of the
necessity of liberty for free peoples, laid the foundation
of the release of women from a tyranny and neglect
that far exceeded the tyranny of any aristocracy,
or the tyranny of a dominant over a subject
nationality.

Hitherto women had been uneducated, imperfectly
educated, as in domestic arts only, or wrongly educated,
as in accomplishments and the arts of pleasing men, but
the stormwind that overthrew the great forest trees of
aristocracy and of national stability also shook the
briars and thorns of domestic and family tyranny,
and men began to realize that women had their rights.
Among those who thought most profoundly and wrote
most convincingly was Mary Wolstonecraft. Her
book *The Vindication of the Rights of Woman*, still
deserves to be read. She believed in the individuality
of woman and in her capacity for being trained and
developed so that she could be fit to perform a definite
share of the work of the world. Great as Mary Wolstonecraft undoubtedly was she was hardly judged
in her own days, principally because she was un-
orthodox, but partly also on account of an irregular

148

union. Quite probably had she lived in these days her supposed unorthodoxy would, have been found to be enlightened belief, and it is arguable that had she lived in freer and happier times she might have married a man of her own calibre and escaped the reproach her lapse incurred.

Early in the nineteenth century the great increase of industries and manufactures led to women abandoning the hand industries that they had hitherto followed in their own homes, and taking their place in the factories and workshops. The results of this economic change were both bad and good. Among the evil results were low wages, deterioration of body, manners, and morals, neglect of home and of children; but among the good results were growing self-reliance, and complete or partial economic independence, leading to the great advantage that marriage ceased to be the only profession for women. Little by little women found, somewhat to their own surprise, and greatly to the surprise of men, that they were capable of good work in nearly all the arts, trades, professions, and callings, of which men had hitherto had a monopoly. Anything like a perfect evolution of women's powers was hindered up to the middle of the nineteenth century by the persistent inferiority of their education. A girl's parents still did not desire that she should receive a really good education, nor would they give her such a training as would teach her how to think, and how to carry out her education after school days. They thought it useless because they did not believe that she had the faculties that would respond to good training, they also thought that serious education would spoil the girl's chances of marriage, and that it was a pity to waste money upon girls which might otherwise be spent on boys. However, about this time what we must really suppose to have been a Divine influence moved over the chaos and darkness of woman's lot. Almost suddenly, as it seems to us, little groups of enlightened men and women started many schools and colleges, having for their object the education of girls much on the same lines and aiming at the same standard as the education of boys. Thus Queen's College, Harley Street, was founded in 1843 to train women teachers ; Bedford College in 1849, the Ladies' College, Cheltenham in 1859, followed quickly by Miss Russ's North London Collegiate School for Girls, and by Girton and Newnham in 1871.

Thus the way was opened not only for better education and proper mental development of women, but also for their entrance into the professions and activities of the body politic. Among the warmest friends of women in those early days was John Stuart Mill. His book, *The Subjection of Woman*, is one of his claims to remembrance. He had no desire to exalt woman at the expense of man, but he demanded what we have not yet obtained, " equality of opportunity for equality of merit." He enunciated the doctrine, strange in those days, that no appointment should be closed to a woman simply because she was a woman.

In 1869 women became qualified to vote in municipal elections, a year later they were qualified to be members of the School Board, and in 1875 they could take their seat on Boards of Guardians. Admission to medical qualifications followed in 1876, and in 1907 women were first admitted to the membership of County

Councils and Borough Councils, and Mrs. Garrett Anderson, M.D., and Miss Dove were elected Mayor, the one of Aldburgh and the other of High Wycombe.

Having traced the gradual improvement in the education and in the status of women it is pertinent to inquire what use have the women made of their increased privileges and opportunities; how far have they shown their appreciation of the fact that rights and privileges bring with them obligations and responsibilities? It is quite easy to point here and there to women who have made no adequate return for the advantages purchased by the practical martyrdom of many men and women who sacrificed time, money, and reputation to secure for future generations the privileges they had missed themselves. To admit this is only to admit the imperfection of human nature, and the practical impossibility of all the members of any community proving themselves worthy; but on the whole it is evident, and is daily becoming more evident, that the improvement in the education and in the social status of woman, is bearing abundant fruit, and that the nation is profiting by the investment made in this matter.

In a short chapter such as this it is impossible to do justice to the great army of women whose lives are a practical thanksgiving for benefits received, but where justice cannot be done to individuals, or even to orders of individuals, it is still possible to mention representative bodies, and among the women whose work is repaying the debt due to those who fought their battle, and to the country which somewhat grudgingly acknowledged their victory, we may mention women scientists and doctors. The story of the medical women should by this time be pretty well known, but perhaps it will bear repetition in outline. The pioneer of modern medical education for women was Dr. Elizabeth Blackwell, of English birth but domiciled in the United States of America, who obtained the M.D. of Geneva in 1849, but it was not until fifteen years later that Miss Garrett, now Mrs. Garrett Anderson, found her way on to the British Register, having obtained the Licentiate of the Apothecaries' Society. It grieved these worthies to place her name on their roll, but inasmuch as she announced her intention of compounding medicine and selling drugs their charter did not permit them to refuse her, but they carefully banged, bolted, and barred the door behind her.

The next venture was made by Miss Jex-Blake and six other women who sought the degrees of the University of Edinburgh. With much difficulty they obtained permission to matriculate provided that they could find professors willing to instruct them in private. This was done with difficulty, as each professor required a guarantee of £100 for each course of lectures delivered, and finally when this was arranged the male medical students showed their disapproval by hooting, jeering, and even stoning the women.

The women students appealed to the law to enforce the rights granted by the Senate, but after much litigation and trouble they failed to carry their point and eventually left Edinburgh.

They were more fortunate in London, although each step had to be fought for, and three great difficulties were encountered. First, no examining body was willing to admit women students to a qualifying examination. This trouble was solved by the generous action of the King's and Queen's Colleges of Physicians in Ireland, who opened their doors ungrudgingly to the women.

Second, the difficulty of tuition was met by the kindness of certain medical men who were prepared to give lectures to the women students, and by the generosity of friends who provided the necessary accommodation in a charming old house in Henrietta Street, Brunswick Square. The third difficulty was perhaps the most formidable. The means of study had been provided, and access to a qualifying examination had been secured, but for the time it seemed as if lack of practical instruction in a recognized hospital would wreck the whole scheme.

There were twelve great general hospitals in London, but not one of them was willing to admit women students to its out-patient department and its wards. Finally, however, the Royal Free Hospital, Gray's Inn Road, with much reluctance, and in consideration of a subsidy, resolved to face the difficulty and to risk the disapprobation of its subscribers. The initial battle of the campaign was thus won, and a great further advance was made when the University of London threw open all its medical examinations, together with honours, prizes and medals, to the women.

All this is ancient history, dating back to the late seventies, and women have proved all over the world that they are able to profit by the advantages offered them. But even now, after forty years, we cannot say that medical women have obtained that " equality of opportunity " which John Stuart Mill asserted should reward equal merit. According to the results of University examinations, and according to the frequently expressed opinions of teachers and of professional colleagues, the women's merits are equal to those of the men, but the Royal Free Hospital remains the only British General Hospital in which women hold positions on the Senior Staff, and the majority of hospitals still exclude medical women from all participation in their post-graduate work.

Now, as to the work that medical women have been able to offer to the Church and to the nation in return for benefits received. The most direct service rendered by medical women has been given by those who have gone abroad as medical missionaries. Excellent work has been done by them in connexion with the chief missionary societies, such as the Society for the Propagation of the Gospel, the Church Missionary Society, the Wesleyan and the London Missions, indeed it would be difficult now to find a missionary society that has not a medical branch, and it is probably true to say that more medical women than men are thus employed. At the present time nearly all the societies are anxious to extend their medical work, and although their financial difficulties may be great the practical impossibility of obtaining properly qualified medical agents is much greater. All the great missionary societies have come to the conclusion that it is worse than useless to send out as medical missionaries men and women who are not fully qualified. Some years ago this plan was tried, but it resulted in general want of success, and in not unfrequent disaster. The reason for this is not far to seek. Medical missionaries, more especially in the case of women, frequently have to work in isolation, without proper assistance, and without the possibility of consultation with colleagues. In India, for example, where social customs forbid women patients to be seen by a male practitioner, it is frequently impossible for a young woman doctor to obtain assistance or advice from any senior practitioner either male or female. It is therefore necessary that women medical missionaries should enjoy a full curriculum and as much post-graduate experience as possible. In the mission field they are thrown on their own resources, and are forced to make momentous decisions as to treatment without the many aids which are enjoyed by doctors at home.

Medical missionaries, and more especially women medical missionaries, are of importance to the health and efficiency of their fellow workers, and undoubtedly there is less loss both through death and also through invaliding, in those missionary stations where medical help is always available.

Medical women are also serving the Church, indirectly it may be but quite efficiently, as medical officers in charge of the female side of asylums, prisons, Poor Law infirmaries, and schools. Their services as house physicians and house surgeons are invaluable in hospitals, and in wards of hospitals set apart for the treatment of women and children. Another large field for their usefulness is to be found in the Inspection of school children, as tuberculosis medical officers, and assistant medical officers of health. Some of their number enjoy well paid and dignified positions under the Board of Education and the Local Government Board. Another set of medical women are giving freely of their time and strength to Mothercraft Schools, and Infant Consultation Centres.

In addition to these purely professional works of mercy, medical women are finding a sphere of usefulness as lecturers on hygiene and in all the varieties of rescue and preventive work. There can be no doubt of the special fitness of medical women as officers of Rescue and Preventive Homes, and as officers in charge of the special departments for the treatment of diseases of women and children.

Nursing has always been regarded as woman's work, but up to the time of the Crimean War there was little special education of nurses, no standardization of their abilities, and in too many instances the nurse's only qualification for her important and onerous work was goodwill and need to earn a living. It was Florence Nightingale's great merit that she recognized the importance and dignity of a nurse's profession, and also the absolute unfitness of many nurses with whom she was brought in contact to discharge the duties laid upon them. Her social position and her personal gifts enabled her to break down the many annoying difficulties of official opposition and social inertia. From her time the training of nurses has steadily improved, they have become more and more a profession with traditions of honour and fitness, and with a constantly rising standard of professional education and skill. The Church was not slow to recognize the value of the services of nurses, and there are many associations intended to minister to their spiritual and social welfare, e.g. the Guild of St. Barnabas, which holds before its members the highest ideals of duty and of service.

The work of nurses, like the work of doctors, is by no means confined to the care of individual patients in private families, nor even to their work in hospitals and infirmaries in times of peace. They, too, like the doctors, have heard and answered the call of national necessity, and have followed the flag along the whole of our far-flung battle line. Nurses, too, are to be found in the service of all Christian missions, they have worked and they have died for the sake of the plague-stricken peoples of India, and quite as truly, although less dramatically, they have died in the service of their faith and their profession in malaria-haunted plains and in deadly climates all over the tropical world.

Another wing of the army of women in the service of the Church is to be found in the different religious orders which have been renewed in England during the last fifty or sixty years. The great services that religious orders of women might be able to bestow upon the Church was present in the minds of the fathers of the so-called " Oxford Movement," and in the *Life of Dr. Pusey* by Dr. Liddon we see how large a share this idea held in his hopes of the strengthening and advancement of the Anglican branch of the Holy Catholic Church. The fruit of all the effort and sacrifice that had been needed to secure better education and a more stable social position for women was seen in the ready response to the call for definite religious service in the middle of the nineteenth century. At the present time there are many orders of English sisters ; a few of them are devoted entirely, or practically entirely, to spiritual service, and may be fitly described as " Contemplative Orders." The public little knows the debt that is owing to these devoted women. They have secured to themselves leisure for adoration, thanksgiving, supplication and intercession, they have trained themselves to undergo spiritual exertion with the same patience and heroism that other people display in military or civil service. They are unhampered by family cares, and uninterrupted by social duties, and therefore they are able without distraction to be the Lord's remembrancers and to further in a quite special manner the religious life of the nation. On the other hand, many Orders of Sisters are engaged partly in spiritual but partly also in corporal works of mercy. Among them we find Nursing Sisterhoods, Teaching Sisterhoods, and those who devote themselves to rescue and preventive work. It would greatly surprise the public if it could realize the amount of hard work that is done by sisterhoods, and the large proportion of strong, business-like, and capable women among their members. Indeed efficiency and capacity appear to flourish within the convent walls quite as readily as do devotion and other spiritual graces.

Next to the Orders of Sisters there is an important body of women who while sharing to some extent in the methods and obligations of the Sisterhoods are yet more nearly associated with family and social life. The order of Deaconesses is, as we have seen, very ancient, although it may be difficult or impossible to trace a continuity between the deaconesses of the present time and those of Apostolic days. Many Sisters and many Deaconesses might also be described as women theologians, for they have made a specialty of theological and allied studies the better to qualify themselves as teachers of the young and as leaders of religious thought. Latterly there has been a stamp set upon their work by the diploma conferred by the Archbishops. These ladies do not form a separate Order but to some extent they supply a special need to Orders of Sisters and Deaconesses while they frequently serve the Church and the nation by producing literary work and also as teachers of various grades.

Rescue and Preventive Workers may be found in the ranks of the Sisters and of the Deaconesses, but many of them have not the advantage of belonging to any special professional class; they are simply good women, eager to serve God and to succour the distressed and afflicted. It wants a very definite gift to make a woman an efficient rescue worker. Personal purity and holiness will not suffice, common sense, tact, an insight into character are also needed, so too are business capacity and the essential grace of a sense of humour. There are relatively few women who possess the necessary characteristics, and fewer still who have received a suitable training for probably what is the most difficult work that a woman can undertake.

Within the limits of one short chapter it is not possible to mention, and still less to do justice to the many different ways in which women may serve God and their country, but the presentment of our subject would be entirely marred if one omitted to mention the great army of women teachers. They exist in many different grades, from the University lecturer to the Elementary School teacher, and their field of usefulness is both wide and important. Upon the adequacy and the moral strength of the Elementary School teacher depends, to a great extent, the value of the instruction provided for the great mass of the children of the land ; upon their religious knowledge, and equally on their religious fervour, depends the attitude that the child is likely to assume towards the more open and positive teaching that he receives in church and Sunday School.

The opportunities enjoyed, and the responsibilities devolving on Secondary School teachers are great in proportion to the more extended influence that their pupils are likely to acquire. Much is said about atmosphere and moral tone, but that the atmosphere and the moral tone shall be good depends on the purity, the frankness, and the courage of the headmistress and her colleagues. No more important body of women exists within the Church. Their teaching is not restricted, and their influence for good or evil is proportionately great, their responsibilities therefore are heavy, and their need for adequate training, for self-knowledge and self-discipline are great in proportion.

Of late years another body of workers has developed. In practically all large factories, in houses of business, and controlling the armies of young women employed by Government, there is an officer known as the Welfare Supervisor. She stands, as it were, between the employer and the employed, translating and explaining the rules and requirements of the one, representing and voicing the desires and necessities of the other party to the contract. Such a lady needs a good general education, a knowledge of the world, an intuitive insight into character, together with shrewdness, common sense, and a first-rate acquaintance with the business in hand. Upon the Welfare Supervisor devolves the care of the physical well-being and the comfort of the girls and women committed to her charge. She is responsible for their health, she must see that they are adequately fed and clothed, she has to supervise their housing and to arrange for their transport if unfortunately they live at a distance from their work. Matters of ventilation, lighting and warming are in her province, and so, too, are the essential arrangements of lavatory and cloakroom accommodation. What wonder then that her knowledge must be encyclopædic, and that she is supposed to possess the hands of Briareus and the temper of an angel. In many instances the Lady Supervisor becomes the trusted friend of the employés and the much valued and respected agent of the employer.

And so throughout all the domain of woman's work, from the highest to the humblest, there runs the wonderful opportunity and the heavy responsibility which belong to those whose work is done for the Commonwealth and upon whom the welfare of the present and the future depends. It would be idle to pretend that all women workers are consciously religious women, nor dare we assert that their work is done as " unto the Lord," but in spite of many failures and many shortcomings, in spite of mixed motives and in some cases of a superficial agnosticism, there is no reason to doubt that the great bulk of our women workers are actuated by a strong sense of duty, that their work is done under this high sanction, so that when the moment of supreme decision comes, and the woman worker has to choose between the easy and remunerative, and the difficult but right, she will, like the young men of the country, choose aright. Men who have studied the work of women say that among its char-

acteristics are painstaking accuracy and a most con-
scientious attention to details ; they say that it is seldom
marred by self-indulgence or by sloth, and many of
them confess that a woman colleague is always reliable,
and usually pleasant.   Some critics of woman's work
say that it is mechanical and imitative, unmarked by
originality and genius.   Probably the higher education
of woman is rather recent to permit of full fruition,
and the struggle for equal opportunity for equal merit
has not yet been won.   When it is there is reason to
hope that the fully emancipated and developed woman
will prove what she was designed to be by the Creator
when He said of Adam " I will make him an help meet
for him."

Women have another sphere of usefulness in the
Church : they are peculiarly well-fitted for the office
of teachers of religion, especially among women and
children.   Many women exercise this function without
other qualifications than fair general education,
religious enthusiasm, and a love of souls, but latterly
many women have wisely gone through special training
both in the science of theology and in the art of
teaching which makes their work easier and more
valuable.

In lecturing to adults, and in class teaching of children and adolescents, it is wise to give opportunities
for instruction by means of question and answer.
Nothing less than a profound knowledge of the subject
and a ready wit in framing answers can make this
valuable method available ; and therefore all women
who wish to serve the Church as lecturers and teachers
of divine truth should devote the necessary time and
trouble to study the subject and to make themselves

not only capable but also acceptable to those they wish to help.

Most educated women have the capacity for teaching, but this capacity needs cultivation, and the would-be teacher must know her subject, she must study method and manner of teaching, and she should be trained in the arts of speaking and of voice-production.

We see that women have great opportunities of service within the Church and that the clergy can find in their gifts valuable help in their sacred task. But there is one part of their work from which women must stand aside. The office of the Levite may be theirs but not that of the Priest. Throughout the long ages of revealed religion as depicted for us in Old Testament times we find no record of women being called of God to minister before the Altar. Prophetesses there were, and strong and wise women, but they were never priests. In the New Testament we find women closely associated with Church work, honoured and beloved for their discharge of their duties, but they never received the call to Holy Orders.

Times and manners have changed and the education and social status of woman have advanced and improved, but still there is in the order of the Christian Church and in the judgment of the women themselves something that appears to demonstrate the unseemliness and undesirableness of women sharing in public services in church.

It is not lack of intellectual ability, nor deficiency of zeal, nor is it a lesser measure of the love and grace of God ; but in this respect as in some others we feel that it is not a question of inferiority, but that it is a question of unlikeness of natures. To our minds it appears that women may be, and are, wise counsellors, efficient teachers, capable organizers and administrators in the Church, but we shrink from the idea that she should " seek the Priesthood also."

The Religious Life for Women

BY MRS. ROMANES

" I beseech you that ye walk worthy of the Vocation wherewith
ye are called."
Ecce Ancilla Domini. Fiat mihi secundum verbum tuum.

WE all recognize the great truth so fully set
forth by St. Paul in the 12th chapter of
I Corinthians, that there are many callings, many
offices in the Christian Church, and behind St. Paul we
have our blessed Lord Himself uttering those searching
words which were to prove too hard a saying for him
to whom they were said, " If thou wilt be perfect."

" If thou wilt be perfect " : our Lord seems to call
certain of His redeemed to consider soberly if they
cannot go beyond the ordinary life of Christians who
are in the Way. Sinners come and are welcomed and
told to go in peace and sin no more. Another is bidden
to return to his own house. Others live in their homes
and welcome Him there, as did the favoured family
at Bethany. And a certain number leave all and
follow Him, and it was to this that He invited the youth
who shrank back and went away sorrowfully.

165

Still our Lord calls certain elect souls and in low tones and in different ways repeats " If thou wilt be perfect." All down the ages men and women have heard that voice and have replied. And in our own portion of the Church we have come to recognize that what is technically called the Religious Life is a real part of all true Religious Life in the Church, and that any portion of the Church which did not produce men and women who sought for perfection would find her whole religious life stunted and poor.

So it was with the Church in England. When the spirit of God breathed on the dead dry bones of the ecclesiastical system, then came the desire for dedication to God. Little by little, the principles underlying this life of dedication were elucidated.

As Father Hughson says in his admirable book called *The Religious State*, we must make use

" of the experience of the Religious Life in the Roman Church. . . . Because we do not agree with Rome in certain theological and devotional matters is no reason why we should reject results of the experience she has had in the identical work we are seeking to do."

And when in the great revival of Church life, which we now look back on from a distance of nearly a century, the desire arose for dedication of life and of service, the various founders of the Religious Orders among us naturally studied what they could learn from the great religious Orders abroad. Dr. Neale in the judgment of the present writer grasped more thoroughly than any of the others the real principles which underlie the Religious Life. But Dr. Pusey, Canon Carter, Dean Butler and one or two others were real and great founders.

THE RELIGIOUS LIFE FOR WOMEN

The Religious Life for men followed later and we need not in this paper do more than mention that there are now three or four prominent Communities for men in our portion of the Church.

Naturally mistakes were made at first. People fancied the primary reason for embracing the Life of Religion was the call of God to work in His vineyard. Not very many years ago an ardent Church worker consulted a well-known High Churchman whether or not she should join a Community, as in her work the dress might be some protection. Her version of his reply was that he thought Communities were only for weak women who needed support. Of course he lived and learned, but this account of the state of mind in persons of perfectly good faith as regards the Religious Life shows how long it takes to get ideas into the ordinary Englishman's head, even when he is not biased by prejudice.

In spite of opposition, and all kinds of crude objections and restrictions, Communities for women came into being. No doubt at first the wish to work for God was the ruling idea. The need of consecrated women, who would give themselves to reclaiming the lost, nursing the sick, teaching the young was greatly felt. Also Mission work among the poorest was largely under taken. Most people have read the story of St. Saviour's Priory, which was an offshoot from St. Margaret's, East Grinstead.

As time went on mistakes were rectified, and little by little the right conception of the Religious state was established. The call to leave home and father and mother, and the hope of married life, is a call to perfection : it is the abandonment of earthly ties and earthly distractions in order to serve God. It is the *way* of *perfection for those who are called.* Just as the holy state of matrimony is a way of perfection for those who really use it as such. We are all in our different Vocations called to perfection by our Lord Christ. Certain people are called to a very special method and state for the attaining of that perfection which will only be consummated in Heaven.

Let me quote Father Hughson's words:

" The Religious Life is defined as a state of life, approved by the Church, tending towards the perfection of Charity by means of a rule observed under the perpetual vows of Poverty, Chastity and Obedience."

We see therefore that those who embrace the Religious Life live under a rule and bind themselves by vows. Just as in marriage we contend that unless a vow of faithfulness is made by the man and woman, the idea of permanence could rarely be attached to marriage, so in this holy state of Religion we must have an idea of permanence. We enter on our ordinary Christian life bound by vows which ensure to us a permanence in the way, so long as we persevere, and so those who enter on the life of Religion consecrate themselves by vows which " constitute moral stability." It is extraordinarily uplifting to consider that our Lord Himself calls certain souls to heroic surrender. If we will, we can surrender ourselves quite definitely to Him and make over all that the world holds precious. This must be quite clearly understood. To enter on what is called the Religious Life does not mean that one wants to work for God. One can often do excellent work for God and yet live an ordinary and blessed life in one's home.　Again to quote Father Hughson :

> "When the young man went away sorrowful unable to rise up to the high and extraordinary Vocation that our Lord had offered him, in reply to three questions He says to His disciples, ' Every one that hath forsaken houses, or brethren or sisters, or father or mother or wife, or children, or lands, for My name's sake shall receive an hundred fold and shall inherit everlasting life.'　Here we have the call to Holy Chastity, the forsaking of the joys of home . . . for My sake and the Gospel's leaving the earthly obedience of father and mother, to follow Him and this ' for the Kingdom of God's sake.' "

Not indeed that our Lord does not call many to heroic sacrifice outside the definite and special forsaking of all.　We know :

> "Meek souls there are, who little dream
> Their daily strife an Angel's theme,
> Or that the rod they take so calm
> Will prove in Heaven a martyr's palm."

Yet all this does not militate against the reality of the call to some to quit the bliss of home and earthly joys to follow Christ.　There is some difference of opinion as to the propriety of irrevocable vows, and in some Communities these vows are renewed from year to year.　But no one who is entering on the Religious Life could look forward to any possibility of release, any wish to escape, ány more than pure and ardent lovers would wish to have a loophole of escape held out to them when they were pronouncing their marriage vows.　Most of the Religious in Anglican Communities pronounce what are known as Solemn Vows.　It must be remembered that these can be nullified.

What are meant by Vows of Poverty, Chastity and Obedience ?　Poverty really means that the Community follows out the ideal of the Church at Jerusalem. " Neither said any of them that aught of the things which he had was his own, but they had all things in common." Of course a Community requires many things for the use of the members, but the members lay no claim to any possession. They have their own habits, their own books of devotion, beyond this nothing is their own. In the case of money inherited by a member of a religious Community, she can hand it over to her Community, or to her relations. She does not keep it for her own use and enjoyment.

But why, we hear an impatient Anglican exclaim, why this absurd rule ? It is the virtue of detachment which the true Religious seeks to cultivate. She ceases to desire to possess the good things of this world ; she ceases to care even about trifles. The true Religious understands the poor, and goes among them as one of themselves. " Unshackled by the love of private wealth," St. Augustine says of those who are free from all affection for it. It is perhaps the most difficult of the vows, for it is such a temptation to every Order to value the rich and great of this world, and we know. how easily the world can enter the cloister.

The Vow of Chastity compels the Religious to abandon the hope of husband or wife and children, but it goes far deeper than that. Chastity does not preclude marriage ; a holy married life is a chaste life, but the Religious dedicates her body and soul to God, so that she may wait upon the Lord without distraction and in consequence many amusements and pleasures are renounced by her, which are lawful, even desirable, for Christians living in the world. We should feel that a Religious would be absolutely out of place in a theatre, a large concert-room or even a crowded lecture-room. So too we should not like to see a Religious reading certain novels which it is quite necessary for many Christians to read if they are called to face modern problems. This question as to theatre-going and reading is a question of Vocation. It is positively necessary for many priests and teachers to know what is being written and thought in the world.

The Religious Vocation is different, and for the sake of avoiding distraction much idle reading, much conversation, self-indulgence even in such small things as lounging or using arm chairs when one is well and many other matters, are forbidden. It all seems small, but experience has proved how needful such rules are. So too, the Religious is taught moderation in food, and avoidance of immoderate friendships. Of course there are holy friendships in all Vocations, but anything which tends to *silliness* is rightly checked. This explains the care that is taken about Sisters' Rests. Perhaps I may quote Father Benson : [1]

" If Sisters have no immediate friends to whom they should go on a visit, they ought to feel rather thankful that there is no call to leave the roof of their Society. They should remember how many people there are in worldly life who never leave their place of ordinary sojourn. A poor person cannot go to the seaside. Why should we, who have taken the vows of Religious Poverty ? Sometimes a Sister needing change might go to a branch house situated in the sort of climate that is most desirable. But going out to stay with secular friends or in lodgings is most undesirable. We ought never as Religious to be going unnecessarily where the restraint of the Rule will not be felt. We never ought to desire a holiday as an escape from the Rule. We *may* need *rest*. Sometimes a change

---

[1] In *Fundamentals of the Religious State.*

for awhile to another house may be a refreshment. But to go outside the restraint of the Rule must always be undesirable. It only tends to make such restraint irksome. The more we keep our cell, the more we shall love it. It may be right to visit parents or immediate relatives ; and sometimes an old friend, living in a quiet retired way, who is like a mother to one, may be approved by the Superior. But Sisters should nèver go to friends living in the world, so as to respond to social environment, unless it be to visit their actual, immediate family.''

Following on this comes the vow of Obedience. Perhaps this is the vow which most repels the outsider. Even good people have been known to exclaim that it is an impossible thing to give up one's own will. Yet in all Christian life it is just this which is always being asked of us. Our Lord set us the example of resignation of His will, and every follower of His has to learn this most difficult lesson : the surrender of the will. It takes years to begin to learn very often. Sometimes it seems as if it were only imperfectly learned in old age. Very good Christians are often most backward in this surrender of the will. In the Religious state, the vow of Obedience enables those who make it to learn this hard lesson more quickly. We repeat this is not for all. A bishop, a general, a professional man, the head of a school or a household, nay even the young man or woman cannot put their wills under the control of another. We see lamentable instances of people in the world who have allowed themselves to be dominated by some friend, perhaps one in an inferior worldly position, and who have spoilt their own and other people's lives by this foolish delegation of their rightful authority. But to those who sooner or later hear a call to the life of Religion, the vow of Obedience is a real aid. It is not obedience to a tyrannical

Superior, but to a Rule which has been carefully drawn up, though of course the Rule enjoins that the Superior will direct the Community and that her orders will be obeyed. We must notice, however, that obedience to the Rule and to the directions of a Superior does not mean that the Religious surrenders her conscience. It merely means obedience to commands, prompt, unquestioning. For instance, a Sister may be working in a branch house and may be suddenly recalled, and she yields without murmuring or disputing. Another may be sent abroad and she may feel strongly disinclined for foreign work, and nearly broken hearted with the parting, but she goes cheerfully, nay joyfully. At the same time, in view of modern conditions it is to be hoped that no Superiors will send Sisters to work for which they are manifestly unsuited. Anything like arbitrary exercise of authority is to be deprecated. But the vow of Obedience is an integral part of the Religious Life, and all experience has taught that the best and most truly Religious is the one who is loyally obedient to the Rule.

It is perhaps needless to say how high an ideal is held up to Superiors by every authority on the Religious Life. Tenderness, firmness, no manifestation of anger, no unreasonable commands, a great regard for a due sense of proportion, that is to say not exacting small matters with as much exactness as great things, because the Superior's own personal wishes are concerned. And much more. We only quote these to show that to a Religious the rule of a Community is not an Office for which to long, but rather to fear.

But deep beyond all vows, all Rules, is the inner life of each Religious. The response to God, 'the personal Love to Him Who has caused the desire for perfection because Christ desires perfection, because their sanctification is the Will of God. Father Congreve, in his lovely book *The Parable of the Ten Virgins*, has spoken fully and beautifully on the Life of Religion :

• "These vows then bind you, not to do more work for Christ (perhaps your life was already well filled with honest and charitable work) but they bind you never to do anything apart from Christ, never to do anything like a machine, of weary necessity, hopelessly or with pride and self-confidence. Jesus Christ's ' Religion,' the life of His consecration (that is of His love to the Father) is to come into all the drudgery of your charitable service : the marking of registers, the perpetual repetition and drill of classes.

"Your vow is Jesus Christ's vow as the Religious, the dedicated Man, and is offered as His was, ' *through the Eternal Spirit*,' and with all the merits of His sacrifice ; this vow then obliges you to bring Christ into all you do or bear.

"*Christ's* Poverty, not the idler's sordid poverty, not a sad and hateful poverty of necessity, but the poverty of Jesus Christ and of the Saints with God, who rejoice to have nothing but God.

"*Christ's* Chastity, not the chastity of stone or of iron, of a nature without feeling ; never a life without love ; but every faculty of loving lifted up, consecrated, given first to God, that it may come back from God to you, holding you up to Him, and so becoming a joyous force in you of freedom and strength with which to raise your children to Him.

"*Christ's* Obedience, never the obedience of machinery, of a system wound up to go of itself : but always the perfectly free, intelligent, affectionate obedience of Jesus Christ ; ' Lo, I come to do Thy will, O my God ; I delight to do it.' Is not this what we who make these vows mean by ' True Religion ' ? "

And he also says :

"Just as a wife on her wedding day ceases to be free, so as a Religious I cease for ever to claim anything in the world for myself : time, money, independence, I give it all to Christ, that it may be His, and that He Himself may take the place of all that I let go for His sake.

"By choosing this state of Religion I settle for ever many

questions that absorb most lives out in the world, and enter into the liberty wherewith Christ sets free those whom He wills to 'attend upon Him without distraction.'

" And I am choosing a state which not only sets me free from many needless distracting interests, but commits me to a positive single and definite aim, the highest imaginable, and binds me more closely and for ever to Christ. And, my Sisters, I am sure that all the happiness of your future life in Religion depends upon the clearness with which you realize *that positive and interior side of your Profession.*

" It would be easy, for example, to make a life narrower by shutting it up within four walls, or emptier by separating it from society ; but the cramping and emptying of the human soul was never the object of Religion. On the contrary, true Religion is that which binds the Christian soul to the fellowship of the Lord Jesus Christ in Heaven, making it free of all that is God's, as it makes it possess and be possessed of God. It is the discipline which makes human life participate in infinity, since it associates, not some acts, but all that the Religious does every day, with God, bringing the greatness and blessedness of God into the smallest details of life."

Now let us consider some of the duties of a Religious. The Life of Religion is divided into the Active and the Contemplative, but at present we are speaking of the Active Life. The primary duty of a Religious is the recitation of the Divine Office, the *Opus Dei* as it used to be called. For the chief work of a Religious is prayer, and the Office has gradually grown. In fact, as is well known, the Offices of Morning and Evening Prayer in the English Church were taken from the Offices for the Hours in the Breviary with additions and alterations. In our own portion of the Church the Day Hours of the Church of England is the book used in most Communities, and one Community at least recites Morning and Evening Prayer in addition. The Day Hours contain the Offices for Lauds, Prime, Terce, Sext, Nones, Vespers and Compline. Perhaps it is needless to say how reverently and devoutly such Offices are said and how deep a meaning is given to each verse and hymn and chapter. The constant recital of the Office teaches not only those who are bound by rule to recite it, but the faithful in the world, how great a reality is the Communion of Saints.

Everywhere, from the whole round world at all hours the Holy Mysteries are celebrated and the Divine Office is said or sung. The prayers of the Religious strengthen the rest of the Church. Besides the recitation of the office each member of a Community has a work of Intercession and of Mental Prayer and is helping on the whole Church in the great work of Prayer.

But in Active Orders there are of course great diversities of work. Education, the care of penitents, Parish work, Mission work in parishes, recovery of inebriates, hospital work, the care of girls discharged from prison, Church embroidery : these are a few, not by any means all, of the work carried on at home and abroad. Two Communities devote themselves entirely to work in the Mission Field. Others have Branch Houses in foreign lands. But all Religious Life has this in common : to seek for the Perfection of Love to God and to effect the stability of this desire by the threefold vow of Poverty, Chastity and Obedience. The Glory of God is the only aim of a Religious and of a Community. Again to quote Father Hughson ·

" All communities are bound to seek the glory of God by means of the perfection of their members. All are bound to seek this end by labouring for and tending towards perfection. All live under the perpetual vows of poverty, chastity and obedience, the exact mode of their life being determined by a Rule according to which all their members promise to shape their lives."

But the active Life of Work is not the only form of the Religious Life. In our own Communion the desire has arisen for the Contemplative life, and there are several Communities of women who devote themselves to the Life of Prayer. Their manual work usually consists in the necessary labour a house entails on those who live in it. Our Lord seems to call just a few to this most wonderful of Vocations. A Contemplative Order is naturally more shut in from the world, and possibly more austere than are the Active Communities. Of course, there are special dangers attending both, and indeed it has struck an outsider more than once that there is a danger in a Community allowing itself to undertake too many works. A Religious in an Active Community should have breathing spaces in her day over and above the formal recreation and the prescribed time for prayer. In those breathing spaces a few elect souls would find themselves responding to the Vocation to Contemplative Prayer. There is no reason why a true mystic or contemplative should not be also intensely practical.

There seems no reason why in our own portion of the Church there should not be many diversities and varieties, and the revival of something like the hermit life : the life of prayer led by women not distinctly Religious but desirous of giving themselves to a life of which prayer should be the chief occupation.

No one who has not stayed in a Religious House can really understand the blessedness of the life of a Sister. A Retreat in a Religious House is infinitely more edifying than anywhere else, for all the surroundings, the peace of God which rests on the inmates, the kindness and gentleness which surrounds the Retreatants, help to deepen the impression made.

We have not tried to describe the various Communities ; a very good account of Wantage is given by Father Fitzgerald in a little penny manual, *The Religious Life for Women*. It should be read if only because of the story of the foundation of the Order of the Servants of the Poor.

We must pray that more Vocations to this Life, of which one, early called away from her Community to the larger service beyond, wrote to a friend : " I long for you to be able to enter on this blessed life." Of this dear Sister a friend wrote, " Her life was so full of happiness that any day she might have said ' Ma vie est un Paradis anticipé.' "

As Bishop Gore has said

" Voluntary sacrifice on a great scale constituted and set there in the Church as the glory of a great life, as a city set on a hill that all men shall see it, stirs the imagination and makes men see what the Christian life means. . . .

" Now, whether among men or among women I desire to make, I desire to ask your most fervent prayer, that this great restoration, which we owe to those of the generation which has passed away from us, may not be, through any slackness or lack of courage, or love of licence, or undue individuality of temper, dwarfed and rendered nugatory by our failure to respond to a definite and permanent vocation."

VIII

Younger Women and the Church

By Miss E. K. Sanders

THE sense of Waste had no small part in the general impression of disaster during the first year of the Great War, and, while regret for waste in money and material may be left to the economist, the waste of human power, of trained intellect and of skilled craftsmanship misused and squandered, is rightly a theme for general lamentation. In another part of the life of the community the same danger in another form is threatening ; it is one that concerns the Church, that the Church has power to avert, but when the time of crisis comes it will be too late to begin to consider how to use it, and the attempt made then will only increase confusion.

Some idea of the situation that lies ahead can be drawn from a glance backward. Before War began, scattered among country houses and parsonages, in seaside villas and the residential quarters of provincial towns, as well as in the endless streets and squares of London and its suburbs, there dwelt tens of thousands of women under thirty, whose time was divided between social and home duties and various forms of outdoor exercise. In most instances probably the record of a week would include some time devoted to service outside the demands of home, but this was often a concession to a growing custom, it was not an essential part of life. To-day, in hospitals, in bureaux of inquiry, in munition factories, and in the many other centres of war activity, these same women work through the long hours of a working day and accept all forms of drudgery and discomfort without protest. When peace comes the grip of the great need that holds them now will loosen, but the energy and courage that prompted them to yield themselves to it will remain. No one, surely, who reflects upon the force implied by the voluntary work of women in these last years can fail to deprecate the possibility of its waste when war is over, but waste or misuse will be inevitable unless the difficulty is faced and provided for in time.

It is as an assistance in dealing with the problem of the future of these ardent workers that a report on *Younger Women and the Church of England* has been published. It was compiled by a Committee of Churchwomen and is a summary of evidence given in the replies to questions circulated among girls of the leisured class. At a moment when the nation has been forced to realize the value of the individual capacities of women, and the environment of woman's life and labour has undergone a revolutionary change, it is well that the all-important subject of her position in the Church should have been given prominence. In these days the tendency to drift away from the Church in the younger generation of well-educated women is a very strong one, but the tendency is due, in part at least, to an unrealized sense of waste. The girl of to-day is eager in thought and in labour, and the Church has made little provision to meet and guide her eagerness. The Report on the Younger Women depicts the situation vividly, the questions and their answers fall into four divisions and each has both spiritual and practical value, as will be seen from the following extracts.

I. The object in view was to discover if the Spirit of Service was the real motive power of activity, and if that spirit is sufficiently vigorous to survive the War. The replies show generally that " a spirit of service has been roused and the only chance of keeping it alive will be to sanctify it, to turn the strong war motive into the motive of the love of God based on a strong personal faith ; in some the spirit is sleeping, in others it is awaking, but will sleep again after the war unless a spiritual call arouses it to renewed vigour.

There is a wide gulf between the spirit of restless activity and the spirit of real service ; both are present to-day, and both are showing themselves more and more in their real colours as the war lengthens out. One paper sums up the situation by saying :

There are, generally speaking, three kinds of girls engaged in the numerous activities of to-day : those who have realized that Christianity implies service for others ; those in whom patriotism has kindled a desire to serve their country ; those who do things because they want to be in the running or because their usual occupations are taken away.

" The writers hold that there are many girls throughout the country to whom real patriotism and love of humanity have appealed enormously. The call for their service has been clearer and more insistent than ever before, and they have responded nobly, proving thereby what can be given to the country by girls caught by the joy of service."

THE PLACE OF WOMEN IN THE CHURCH

As ground of hope for the future we find such suggestions as these :

" We must supply the only sufficient motive : the love of God, by transferring enthusiasm from England to the Kingdom of God. Our aim should be to bring all girls to the knowledge of the love of God and the Higher Patriotism which makes as real and more real a claim on our service ! They all know that the great need to-day is ' to deepen the spiritual life of England,' making the great motive the love of God, or, as one of them sums it up : 'I suppose that a love of our Lord and a wish to save souls for Him, however feeble and poor our attempts are, are the only real incentives to do Church work.' "

II. The questions were framed to reveal the position of the Younger Women towards Conventional Standards in Religion, and the answers suggest that the spirit of revolt is prevalent.

" Many of the papers say that ' the Church seems to accept barriers and does not try to break them down,' and the feeling of fellowship and brotherhood which is so strong to-day in other circles makes them wonder at the seeming exclusiveness of the Church. Also it is said that ' its teaching is so unlike Christ Who established no mere code of morals to which all must blindly adhere, but founded a universal religion in all its simplicity and freedom ; ' and ' that people who return now to the simplicity of the Gospel and who try to live in the spirit of the Sermon on the Mount are looked on as cranks, and we sit down contented with the second-best.' It is obvious that such girls hesitate to cling to convention if it is only the husk which holds no grain, and therefore often give up adherence to principles not understood by them. ' The Church to them seems to have nothing to do with the big movements or difficulties in the world, and the members of it with whom they come in contact seem, far too frequently, to be blind to the needs of others.' "

III. The objection among girls to what is called Church Work is the subject of definite inquiry, and it must be acknowledged that many of these answers are lacking in depth. But, passing over the superficial reasons that are given, we arrive at one which

embodies an important truth · " The status of the
Church worker is too low." " Work is very often
given to those who have no qualifications for it. . . .
For almost any other kind of work training would be
demanded, and would be available."

It is obvious that no work can have a high standard
unless efficiency is demanded of the workers, and
without a high standard enthusiasm disappears and
work becomes drudgery. There is close connexion
between this third division of questions and the fourth
which is concerned with the instruction and help
offered by the clergy, and one of the comments elicited
applies to both sections :

" Religion as clothed in the garb of the Church of England
appears dull and unheroic, and the inner life of joy is
obscured by what is conventional and stereotyped.

" It is held that to awaken and capture enthusiasm there
must be the sense of a great cause, and a conception of the
Church as the Body of Christ, which claims the loyalty of
its members and their readiness for higher service and adventure. The heroic demand is constantly made in national
life ; girls do not feel that this is the case in the ordinary
course of Church service and sermons."

The element of superficial criticism in all generaliza-
tion does not deprive these opinions of their weight
and importance, and it is not only the Younger Women
but a vast host of voluntary workers of all ages
who are represented in the statement of them. The
whole subject demands serious consideration. Looking
ahead to the probabilities of the future in time of
peace, there can be no doubt that the country will still
have need of personal service and that very many who
responded to the call of war will be ready to offer it,
but in value and in permanence their offering will
depend on the spirit that engenders it.

The majority of educated women have within them, potentially, the sense of Vocation. To those who use the term in its narrow sense this may seem a bold assertion, but the failure to recognize the call of God in the life that circumstances have forced upon her is the root of restlessness in many women; and, for those who have the opportunity of choice in the employment of their energies, an awakening to the very simple truth that God is the Object of all worthy service would transform drudgery into enjoyment. We are told in the Report on them that our Younger Women are longing for a call on " all the ardour, adventure and romance that they know they are capable of expressing." No call will really satisfy that longing save that of their vocation : the call of God to the individual. This idea is embodied in one of the most striking paragraphs of the Report :

" We are of opinion that the Church needs to capture, even before the end of the War, the enthusiasm and ardour of the girls who are so ably serving humanity and the State, and to give them a real motive for further service. High demands should be made on them, not on their hearts only, but on their brains and awakened thought; practical common sense should be appealed to. They need to serve God now, in hospital, canteen, munition factory, so that whatever is demanded of them later on will be but a continuation of their present service."

The picture is an inspiring one ; the idea of war-time effort being merged smoothly in the peaceful service of the State, because both were equally an offering to God, appeals to the reason and the imagination ; but, when we bring it into relation (i) with the existing conditions of voluntary labour ; (ii) with the position of the Church towards the voluntary worker, the realization of the idea appears, to say the least, hard of attainment. So long as the Church maintains the definition of the limits of Church work as they are accepted at the present time, she cannot hope to capture the enthusiasm and ardour of the vast host of those who now give willing service to the State. In the wide field of social service that is now under State-control many an eager worker will find the place for which her gifts have fitted her (her true vocation), but, though she may be a faithful Churchwoman, she will find no recognition of her service as being service to the Church.

This question of the limits of Church work has been too long neglected ; it is of infinite importance not only to women-workers but to the Church herself. If the work in the poorer quarters of the great cities, which is now regarded as purely secular, was claimed by women who would be supported through its disappointments by their privilege as Catholics, and could turn from the turmoil of committees to prayer and silence, the spiritual indifference and irreligion now so disastrously prevalent among the objects of their care would be continually challenged. Warm friendships often grow up between visitor and visited, even when the reason of their first introduction was one of those " inquiries " sometimes resented as intrusive ; and the woman who knows the value of her own inheritance may have many opportunities of helping others to their share in it. Nevertheless, the secular worker from another region, though she be the most convinced Churchwoman, must be prepared for the indifference, and often for the scarcely veiled hostility, of the priest to whose parish her labours call her. A variety of reasons may be accountable for this lamentable situation, one of the most potent, probably, being the difficulty of adjusting parochial interests to the rapid changes in State organization, while the tendency to self-assertion which is apt to be connected with the enthusiasm of the voluntary worker should not be overlooked. Whatever the reasons for it may be the situation is a false one, and the failure it implies goes deeper even than the failure of mutual charity. If work, undertaken by a Communicant in the true spirit of service, cannot be recognized as work for the furtherance of Christ's kingdom and therefore Church work, there is something radically wrong in the position of the Church's representatives towards the present generation and its needs.

" The status of the Church worker is too low," is the cry of the Younger Women. Is it not true that the standard of work which the Church is setting is too low also ? Would it indeed be possible for the standard that is to inspire the worker of the future to be set too high ? Imagination is the most indispensable of gifts for those who would work among their fellows, but its possessor is not likely to respond to a call for " the second-best." The highest ideals, the most searching claims, are those which find the worthiest response. We are needing in this moment of transition to be awakened to the realization of the Supernatural. There is nothing else that will satisfy : and if this could be vividly awakened so that constant personal experience took the place of vague intellectual belief, the barriers between the worker and the Church must collapse.

Three hundred years ago, in Paris, two or three persons met together to discuss the failure of the

Church in dealing with the evils of the time. From that meeting there sprang, by a process of very rapid growth, a Society which, for thirty years, exercised an enormous influence throughout the kingdom. Its aims were, first and foremost : to promote and safeguard the teaching of the Catholic faith ; and then to provide for the needs of the poor, contributing and applying various forms of relief ; to protect the weak in all cases of oppression ; and under all conditions to endeavour to raise the standard of social and of business life. It was a secret society, the ordinary world had no knowledge of its existence, and for thirty years it used its silent power. At the end of that time it became known to Cardinal Mazarin and it was suppressed, but other societies had sprung up to carry on its message, and the immense need which had called it into being was fulfilled. There is a clear connexion between that incident of long past history and the difficulties of to-day. The founders of the Society intended it to perform tasks which seemed impossible and which could only be accomplished by a large number of devoted members ; with this in view they set its standard very high and made the conditions of membership very exacting. They were justified by the result. But it was not merely to the instincts of charity and justice they appealed : their external rule was " to do as much good and prevent as much evil as came within their reach," but their inward motive was to be the honour of our Lord in the Blessed Sacrament. The absolute secrecy in which their service was enveloped was supposed to be adopted in imitation of His hidden Presence among men. The Society named itself the Company of the Blessed

Sacrament; it was continually active and there is no record of disaffection among its lay-members.

The lesson is obvious. The experience of Frenchmen of another period is applicable to the Englishwomen of to-day. To elicit devoted service mind and imagination must be fired to the highest effort of which they are capable. If the spiritual faculties are once awakened their response will be in ratio to the demands made upon them. The parallel does not bear pressing, there is a wide divergence between the opinions of twentieth-century England and of the France of Louis Treize, and oaths of secrecy seem to us to-day to savour of the melodramatic and the absurd. Yet it is conceivable that among the many guilds and associations already existing there is room for yet another, simple in outward form but rooted in the hidden life of every one of its members, whose object should be to emphasize the unity between social work and a spiritual religion, whose members should be outwardly engaged in some form of service to the State, but should be bound by a secret pledge to constant consecration of their service. Then, whether in London they journeyed from west to east, or in the provinces came in from the country to the town, one result of their membership, practical as well as spiritual in effect, should be that it secured from the priest into whose parish duty called them, a tacit recognition of their status, actual although hidden, as fellow workers with himself.

The haphazard methods which are a part of our national heritage are not in favour of deliberate adjustments of this nature. Yet, for lack of them, work that in the hands of Churchwomen might be used for the glory of God lapses to a far lower level, and workers whose labours would be strengthened and uplifted by a sense of community with others as servants of the Church are left in isolation. And there is no good reason why immense and ever-widening fields of labour should not receive a hidden consecration. To some minds, even in these days, the place of women appears to be in a sphere of hidden influence, and it may well be that by the quiet doing of secular tasks, which in themselves have little glamour for the religious mind, women are destined to fulfil a part of their mission in the Church.

In actual fact the power which at this moment lies within the reach of Churchwomen is limitless, while the waste of it has long been a melancholy spectacle. In every part of England and in all the social grades are the people who miss all that the Catholic Faith could give them for lack of knowledge of it. Many of them will not listen to the deliberate presentation of it and are reached only by the method adopted by the Companions of the Blessed Sacrament, whose vast influence depended on the secrecy of their aim and the completeness of their self-dedication. When we consider the zeal and enthusiasm of women in voluntary work, it becomes clear that, if as an object they could set the glory of God in place of the accomplishment of an individual purpose, and could make the extension of Christ's Kingdom their hidden intention in all that varied intercourse with others which makes up the life of modern women, there would cease to be ground for controversy over their place and value in the Church.

It is a strange anomaly that in the midst of our

neglected opportunities any among us should arise to demand a new field of service for themselves and for their sisters. It is a tragedy that at the moment when the Church in England sent out her special call on the loyal and loving service of her children there should have been Englishwomen whose response was an assault on the sacredness of her teaching and traditions. Yet the claim to the ministry of preaching (we cannot touch the further and more intolerable pretension) involves a confession of failure; for a woman's rightful place in the Church is so important that, if she realized and fulfilled it, it would suffice her; and so it may be that even by such devious ways as this we are being led to repentance and amendment.

It must not be forgotten, however, that if, after the manner of the Companions of the Blessed Sacrament, there was a special and recognized consecration for secular workers, they would be pledged to the constant renewal and vitalizing of their sense of consecration. The life of Christian service cannot be lived in a perpetual hurry; as we are reminded in a recent well-known treatise [1] " thought is the necessary preliminary to prayer," and thought, with the prayer resulting from it, claims a possibility of silence. In the midst of the excitement of these present times and of the clamour of war-workers, there is nothing more desirable for the women of England than that they should learn to use and to demand some measure of silence for themselves. If it should be that the future holds in store for them new possibilities for the highest employment of their powers, it will hold also a demand for personal consecration more searching

[1] Rev. W. T. Carey on Prayer.

than they have ever known. And neither freedom, nor recognition, nor leadership will have power to raise the next generation of women above the failure and dissatisfaction of their predecessors, unless they will realize that their true life cannot progress without a definite offering of time in which all the world is shut away, and they can seek to know God and to know themselves.

Appendix

WOMEN AND THE PRIESTHOOD

This is a print of the Papers on Women and the Priesthood referred to in the published correspondence between the Archbishop of Canterbury and Mr. Athelstan Riley. No alterations have been made except the deletion of names, otherwise the matter is printed just as it was received.

July 26, 1916.

DEAR MADAM,

Your name has been suggested to me as that of a Church-woman who might possibly be sympathetic towards an attempt which I am making to organize an informal Conference to discuss the question of the ordination of women to the priesthood. I have written to about 150 people, and have received favourable replies from between thirty and forty. Miss Maude ———, Dr. Jane ———, and Miss Elizabeth ——— have consented, among others, to read papers. The Conference will probably be held on September 18 in London. It is hoped that in coming together for prayer and discussion we may be shown more clearly what is the will of God in this matter.

Our feeling is that priesthood is a human office, not at all a sexual one, and that since women are human beings it is unreasonable to refuse them an opportunity of holding it merely because they are women. I know at least one woman who feels that she has the vocation ; and this woman would have made, so far as one can see, an almost ideal priest. The weight of custom seems to us to be quenching the spirit of God. The loss to the Church appears to us lamentable.

APPENDIX

I enclose a summary of the answers which I have received.
I shall be very glad to hear from you if you are interested.
Yours faithfully,
(Signed)   Mrs.——

DEAR MADAM,

I had hoped to have completed long before this the enclosed classification and summary of the answers to my letter referring to the ordination of women to the priesthood. Circumstances, however, have combined to make the delay inevitable. I think that the response has been, on the whole, encouraging, and I hope that it may be possible to hold the proposed Conference in the coming autumn. I think that there is no doubt as to London being the most convenient centre.

I will now try to find a date which will suit those who have promised to read papers. As soon as this has been settled I will send you a provisional Agenda, with particulars as to place and date of the Conference.

Meanwhile, I shall be very glad to receive any comments that you may care to make on the summary of the answers, and also to hear your opinion on the following questions:

(1) Should women exclusively be invited to attend the Conference?

(2) Should Churchpeople only be invited?

I think myself that there is a good deal to be said for confining this preliminary Conference to Churchpeople on the ground that our aim at so early a stage should be to find as wide as possible a basis of common agreement, which aim can obviously be more easily obtained if those of us who meet together may assume that we are already agreed as to certain fundamentals. (If this preliminary Conference leaves us with a determination to persist in the work which we have begun, it will, I think, be very helpful to hear, on a subsequent occasion, the views of those who, while they are in agreement with us as to the need for the ministry of women, are, for one reason or another, outside the Church of England.)

If, however, the opposite point of view is that of a majority of those interested, then men or women who are not Churchpeople will, of course, be welcomed. I have no wish to press unduly my own opinion.

I have not felt at liberty to mention in the enclosed papers the names of sympathizers, but it would be convenient to do so in future, and, unless I hear to the contrary, I shall assume that you will have no objection to your name being included in a list to be enclosed with the provisional Agenda. (It would perhaps be well to enter, besides the names on such a list the numbers by which they are designated in the accompanying summary. This would enable any one interested to identify the letter of any writer. The number would, of course, be omitted in the case of any one who preferred her letter to remain anonymous.)

The following list of books may perhaps prove useful to those who wish to study the question previous to the Conference :—

1. *The Ministry of Deaconesses* (Cecilia Robinson).
2. *The Ministry of Grace* (Bishop Wordsworth).
3. *The Diaconate of Women* (Howson).
4. *Der Dienst der Frau in dem ersten Jahrhunderten de Christlichen Kirche* (Zscharnack).
5. *Priesthood and Sacrifice* (edited by Sanday).
6. *Ministerial Priesthood* (Moberly).
7. *The Church and the Ministry* (Gore).
8. *The Christian Ministry* (T. M. Lindsay).
9. *History of the Christian Church* (Schaff).
10. *Histoire ancienne de l'église* (Duchesne).

Yours faithfully,
(Signature cut out).

SUMMARY OF ANSWERS TO CIRCULAR LETTER

Class A

UNFAVOURABLE.

1. Is very strongly opposed to the putting forward of the claim, thinking it premature and calculated to alienate many who are now sympathetic towards the Suffrage movement. To enfranchised women other openings would come naturally. Women should take their place as an active part of the laity. Freedom to enter the ministry would have no effect on " Freethinking women."

2. Thinks the limitation not an accidental but an essential part of the Catholic Faith.

3. Says that Priesthood is a vocation and an absolutely arbitrary act of God. Only some men are called, and if it is

a hardship for a woman not to be called, it is an even greater hardship for the men who are not called, for women have their own great vocation. But it is no hardship. We are all ordained priests at our Confirmation and receive then the power to offer the Sacrifice of the Body and Blood of Christ. Ordained or official priests must be men because they must be ready to celebrate Holy Communion at any moment. Women cannot because of their potential motherhood. The Church is wise to keep the sexes apart in connexion with the most holy things because of the weakness of human nature and the appalling scandals which might arise. Finally, only an Œcumenical Council could authorize such a change, and an Œcumenical Council is out of the question for hundreds of years.

4. Objects that " there was no woman among the Apostles."

5. Says " Our Lord never contemplated it ; it would do much harm to the Church."

6. Says " the first principle of Catholicism is submission to authority. I have never coveted priesthood for myself nor have I ever met any woman whom I could for one moment have tolerated in such an office.

7. Says " the time is not ripe. We had better work for the increase of the order of deaconesses and concentrate our energies upon Church Councils."

8. Says " from time immemorial the emotional side of a woman's nature has been zealously and artificially cultivated and chiefly through the medium of religion. Therefore it would be as well not to place a woman yet in a position where too much fervour is needed with a purely emotional basis. Balance and judgment are more needed which the sterner (?) professions offer. Priesthood is one of the badly paid professions of men : open rather the well paid walks of life to women. . . . . To be really in earnest a woman must study the doctrines of the Church. Could she take this position on a basis of common sense, or would it be merely a doctrine of " Faith " and emotion ? The Church does not want the weakness of some women but the stronger thinkers. And would she get them ? I think *not*."

9. Says " the time is not ripe. . . It would hinder suffragism. Work is needed in regard to Church Councils."

10. Says " the Priesthood was intended by Our Lord for men alone."

The remaining seven give no reasons for their opposition.

APPENDIX

INTERESTED BUT NOT CONVINCED.

1. " The order of deaconesses furnishes ample scope for the energies of those who are able to consecrate their lives entirely to the service of the Church. What we want far more is an accredited order of *lay*women to whom the religious education of children and of older girls, including the preparation for Confirmation, might be entrusted, without their being made to feel that they are doing such work under the supervision of an inexperienced curate."

2. " I feel that the idea of removing the sex barrier to the priesthood is enormously revolutionary. At the same time, as an enthusiastic believer in the Women's Movement, I cannot shut my eyes to the idea that that is one of the logical outcomes of it."

3. " I have a prejudice or conviction in favour of a celibate clergy. Some such feeling as this in favour of a reform of existing conditions prevents me from wishing to consider in its practical aspects the admission of women to the priesthood. From an ideal standpoint I am in sympathy with the aims of your letter, but the practical difficulties just now obscure for me the ideal standpoint."

4. " I see no logical reason against it ; but I do see very grave practical objections to a mixed priesthood of men and women in the present state of society."

5. " Our Lord was not a woman, and therefore it is not necessary for a woman to be everything that a man may be. His Mother was a woman, and motherhood is the supreme vocation of women : possibly the priesthood is the supreme vocation of man. There was no woman Apostle. . . . 2,000 years of history count for something. . . . . Surely there are reasons behind these things ? "

6. " I think people who leave the Church on account of this sex limitation cannot have a very deep love or understanding of the Church, for where else can they go ? If any step at all should be taken, surely it would first be to apply for women to be lay preachers."

7. " I cannot answer any other questions in the affirmative except C."

8. " I am afraid there is too much prejudice against women entering the ministry at present for the movement to succeed,

and it may retard the enfranchisement question. If only women were recognized as citizens, I think their entering into fuller professional life would follow in time and more naturally. The Clergy, too, are upholding a better standard of good living and self-denial than any other class of men, that (*sic*) I am afraid popular feeling would be very strong against women wanting to share their duties at present."

9. " My sentiments are against it ; but my reason makes me think it ought to be."

10. " I should much like to attend a Conference, for my own ideas on the subject are very hazy."

11. " I should like to attend a Conference."

12. " I do not know of any inherent bar that should exclude women from the priesthood for all time, but I am decidedly averse to any movement to that end at the present time, for the following reasons among others :

" (i.) Such a movement could only be justified if it came in response to a felt need. I do not think that need is at present felt. It must be felt by the Church at large and not only by the women who may desire the privilege ;

" (ii.) It would be, in my mind, an obstacle in the way of reunion with the Eastern Church (not to say the Roman), of which there is at least a vision ;

" (iii.) It would hinder the progress of the deaconess movement within the Church if it were thought that the diaconate of women was to be a stepping-stone to the priesthood. We have not yet overcome the prejudice of many, clergy and others, to the ordination of women to the diaconate. I am certain that if the priesthood for women were openly talked of it would raise an opposition to the ordination of women which would put back the deaconess movement many years, and imperil what we already have. The practical suggestion I would make is that everything possible should be done to strengthen the diaconate of women by influencing women of education and ability to become deaconesses, and by securing wider recognition of their ministry, which might be made more distinctive, e.g. in the early Church women deacons administered the Chalice. In the Mission Field it might be of very real use if deaconesses were permitted to do this, and perhaps administer the reserved Sacrament."

APPENDIX

CLASS C

FAVOURABLE, BUT WILL TAKE NO ACTION.

The fifteen who make up this class feel that they must refrain from action until the Parliamentary vote is won. One writer adds : " I am by no means certain that we should really gain in influence or help the Church by attempting to become ' clergy.' My own impression is that the most hopeful religions movements of the present day are those which are mainly lay."

CLASS D

FAVOURABLE, BUT NOT CHURCHWOMEN.

The eleven members of this class are either Agnostics, Quakers, Romans, or Nonconformists.

CLASS E

FAVOURABLE.

1. " I believe that any feeling I have against it is merely due to unreasonable prejudice against anything so revolutionary."

2. " I think the more the secession of valuable women from the Church is brought home to the leaders the better. . . . My own ideas as to the admission of women to offices of deacon and priest are perfectly clear. I would have them neither deacon nor priest, but ordained to hold a position in the Church which would be a modification of the office of deacon and priest, and which could best be described as that of a deaconess. They would be qualified to hold services and to preach, but because it is necessary that the Church hold fast to the doctrine of the Apostolic succession passing through a male priesthood, it is not fitting that the deaconesses should administer any of the sacraments. This is the thing to which in my opinion sex is a bar. I am perfectly convinced that the introduction of women into the Church and its services publicly in this capacity would do untold good."

3. " It is an ideal which will have to be dealt with very carefully ; it would be quite as possible to alienate Church-people by urging such an ideal in a proud unchristian spirit as it is now by ignoring women's spiritual equality with men."

APPENDIX

4. " I am in complete sympathy and agreement."

5. " I am most decidedly in favour of your object, but I feel that it would be wiser to wait a little longer before forming any society."

6. " I wholly agree that the sex bar should be removed, and the sooner the better ; otherwise I think there will be no salvation for the Church or the country either."

7 and 8. Answer the questions in the affirmative without comment.

9. " My feeling is that the admission of women would be of incalculable service to the Church. Some women speakers and preachers have a wonderful influence over men, as men have over women. Is it not possible that among other good results, the disproportions between women and men worshippers in our churches might be rectified ? I am only doubtful whether this is the tactful moment to begin to agitate. The clergy are coming forward warmly, and often with the disapproval of their parishioners, to champion us in our fight for the vote. Until their support is more widely and strongly established would it be wise to introduce a new demand which might frighten some of them from the Women's Movement altogether ? There would, however, be no harm in preliminary study and conferences."

10. " I do not on the whole think that the time has come for the formation of a society to press this. A ' secret ' society cannot do much good and a society which was pressed publicly would, I think, do a great deal of harm at the present juncture. The only kind of organization which I think would be of use would be one which would promote the study of the position of women in the Church, and of further possibilities, especially in regard to missionary work. The past and present position of deaconesses would of course be a foremost subject of study. It seems to me that progress in the matter can only come on the lines of evolution, and that the surest path of progress is probably along the lines of a development of the diaconate among women. Here the historical basis is so sure and the ground already won so secure that it would not only be the line of least resistance, but the experience gained be of the greatest possible value."

11. " I am entirely with you in your desire to see women priests. But I am a little inclined to think we should get the vote first. . . . I am quite sure that the influence of women would make an enormous difference to the life of the Church."

12. " It is such a tremendous fact that our Lord on each

occasion of the most vital importance to our Christian faith chose a woman to be the messenger. Therefore we seem to have His sanction. On the other hand, I have a feeling that the time is not ripe ; that at present we should shock many earnest-minded women, more than we should win over. . . . One stumbling block to me is that until the Catholic Church is once more united and we can have our restored Council of the whole undivided Christendom, I don't see where we can get valid orders. . . . I do deplore and recognize that we women are getting dissatisfied with many things in the Church, and if one could see one's way to stop, as you say, the leakage, I should wish to help. But first of all, surely we must get our rights as laity, and at present so far as Church government goes we are outsiders. . . . We Anglicans are a branch of the Catholic Church, and not a sect to do what pleases ourselves, apart from the whole undivided Church, whose Œcumenical Councils were binding on all. If Anglicans had an ordained women priesthood they would be eligible to be Bishops and to ordain in their turn both men and women. Would our orders be considered Apostolic and valid without the sanction of an Œcumenical Council of the undivided Church ? . . . The first woman Bishop would be a marked break in the continuity. I am honestly puzzled as to what effect it would have. The Eastern Church is so much nearer to us than Rome ; would they accept the validity of our orders under these conditions ? "

13. " My feeling is that the time is not ripe for making any kind of claim. The situation is so tense, and the matters involved of so sacred a nature, that to advance any claims at present would be to invite a violent opposition and add one more entanglement to the confused thinking of the public. But I think the time is ripe for study of this question, that we may know exactly what it is we are aiming at."

14. " I am entirely in sympathy with your scheme."

15. " I should like to see priestesses and women bishops in due course ; but it seems to me that the first thing to do is to make sure of the diaconate. Since we have working in the English Church a large number of episcopally-ordained deaconesses, ought not the new movement to originate with them, or at least, if possible, with their co-operation ? · This would give the movement a much sounder basis than it would have if it were founded on a few isolated experiments in training women for the Holy Orders *de novo*. I think that our ordained deaconesses should ascertain whether they have

been admitted to the diaconate or not. If there is any doubt about this, they should ask to be re-ordained with the form regularly used for the ordering of deacons. In any case the form used for men and women should surely be the same in future. Then the training of deaconesses should be so modified as to fit them to discharge all the duties of the diaconate, including such preparation as will put them in a position to ask for the priest's orders when the time comes. But obviously if these are our aims, the first thing to be done is to secure the co-operation of the diocesan deaconesses, and specially the head deaconesses who have charge of the training. If *they* could be induced to approach the Bishops, they would, I think, be much more likely to get a hearing than any number of unordained women. I hope very much that you will *from the first* secure the co-operation not only of Churchwomen, but also of Churchmen, specially of some priests if possible. The Conference will, it seems to me, be very much more effective and influential if not confined to one sex."

16A and 16B. "As you suggest, there is a strong current setting away from the Church and clericalism in which most, or at any rate a great many, of the thoughtful and progressive women may be found now. It is true that the Church is not now what it would be if the saner and more vital influences of womanhood were directing it. But as it stands at present there is little in it or in its philosophy or modes of operation to attract us. At the same time I believe women have first to meet men on their own plane and demonstrate to them their capacity to ' play the game ' in the masculine fashion before they can get the men to accept the changes their womenhood would initiate."

17. "I am quite in favour of women being admitted to the priesthood because I think women have gifts for that work which would supplement and inspire the work of men. As long as women are admitted as deaconesses it seems absurd that the higher office should be denied them. . . . I am not sure whether this step will bring back ' freethinking ' women or even serve to make others less bitter. I think the question might very well be linked up with the Spiritual Militancy League. . . . It seems such a pity to scatter our forces. . . . Union is more wanted at this time than anything else, especially among the women's part of our movement. I think we want also to be more loyal to our Church. It will be by living in the Church and fighting prejudice that we shall win."

18. "I am deeply interested in your proposals. But I

should be anxious to go exceedingly slowly in the matter. . . .
I should like the subject to be studied very carefully before
any society to take action is formed. . . . I do think it is
time some of us made a beginning about this."

19. " I most warmly approve of all your suggestions."

20. " I think your suggestions are excellent, and I do
sincerely feel that unless something is done the Catholic
Church will lose its hold for ever upon women."

21. " I am greatly in sympathy with your suggestion."

22. " Your letter appeals to me very strongly. It expresses thoughts and convictions which have become increasingly definite and persistent during the last few years
with me ; but I have so seldom found any one to share them
that I have been inclined to despair of the possibility of any
definite movement for the present."

23. " Your letter interests me extremely. The position
of women in the Church is one which I feel very keenly. It
is not merely that there is no opportunity for taking part in the
ministry, but women do not in any complete sense seem to
form part of the laity. The Church has no use for educated
women, at any rate so far as my experience has gone. . . .
It would certainly have seemed to me that, having regard to
the strong clerical opposition which such a proposal must
arouse, it might be better to try first to secure recognition as
members of the laity. Until it is realized that women should
be represented on Diocesan Conferences, etc., one can hardly
hope to be represented in the priesthood."

24. " I certainly agree with you that we should not keep
silent on such a matter, but I feel that all our energies should
first be given to the winning of the vote. . . . The struggle
for entrance into the priesthood will be hard and prolonged.
It will be well for us to enter into that fight armed with the
weapon of the vote. In the meantime, we can well discuss
the subject."

25. " I am indeed in sympathy. . . . I feel the Church
has lost a great deal by limiting the priesthood to one sex. I
feel that it has a deteriorating effect both on men and women.
It tends to increase pride and arrogance on the part of men
and false humility on the part of women."

26. " Certainly I am in favour of the admission of women
to the priesthood. It comes under the general principles
that women should be freed from all artificial restrictions and
free to serve God and their generation according to the gifts He
bestows on each. . . . But I do not think that the time will

be ripe for this momentous change until two generations after the vote has been won and after the Church has been disestablished. This change is to my mind not one to be quarrelled over. I would rather wait till opinion has changed very much, as it will."

27. "I am much interested in your letter and am in sympathy with your scheme."

28. "The really important thing seems to me that it should be a movement from *within* the Church. I have been thinking a great deal about vocation, and that seems to me the key-note of it."

29. "I am sure there are many women who would make excellent priests provided they could get the necessary training. It is absurd that women who are allotted the high-priestly intercessory office should not be officially recognized as members of the priesthood. You have my sincerest sympathy."

30. "I am very glad you are thinking of stirring about in the matter of the removal of the sex-bar to the priesthood. I think your idea is an excellent one."

(59 to whom the letter was sent returned no answer.)

Printed for ROBERT SCOTT, *Publisher,* PATERNOSTER ROW, LONDON, *by* BUTLER & TANNER, FROME

EDITED BY

THE REV. WM. C. PIERCY, M.A.

Dean and Chaplain of Whitelands College.

Each Volume, Demy 8vo, Cloth, Red Burnished Top, 5s. net.

THE GREAT SCHISM BETWEEN THE EAST AND WEST.
By the Rev. F. J. FOAKES-JACKSON, D.D.

THE CATHOLIC CONCEPTION OF THE CHURCH.
By the Rev. W. J. SPARROW SIMPSON, D.D.

THE PRESENT RELATIONS OF SCIENCE AND RELIGION.
By the Rev. Professor T. G. BONNEY, D.Sc.

ARCHÆOLOGY OF THE OLD TESTAMENT.
By Professor EDOUARD NAVILLE, D.C.L.

MYSTICISM IN CHRISTIANITY.
By the Rev. W. K. FLEMING, M.A., B.D.

COMMON OBJECTIONS TO CHRISTIANITY.
By the Rev. C. L. DRAWBRIDGE, M.A.

RELIGION IN AN AGE OF DOUBT.
By the Rev. C. J. SHEBBEARE, M.A.

THE RULE OF WORK AND WORSHIP.
By the Rev. R. L. OTTLEY, D.D.

THE RULE OF LIFE AND LOVE.
By the Rev. R. L. OTTLEY, D.D.

THE RULE OF FAITH AND HOPE.
By the Rev. R. L. OTTLEY, D.D.

MARRIAGE IN CHURCH AND STATE.
By the Rev. T. A. LACEY, M.A.

CHRISTIANITY AND OTHER FAITHS.
By the Rev. W. ST. CLAIR TISDALL, D.D.

THE BUILDING UP OF THE OLD TESTAMENT.
By the Rev. Canon R. B. GIRDLESTONE, M.A.

THE CHURCHES IN BRITAIN. *Vols. I and II.*
By the Rev. ALFRED PLUMMER, D.D.

CHARACTER AND RELIGION.
By the Rev. The Hon. EDWARD LYTTELTON, M.A.

THE CREEDS : Their History, Nature and Use.
By the Rev. HAROLD SMITH, M.A.

THE CHRISTOLOGY OF ST. PAUL (Hulsean Prize Essay).
By the Rev. S. NOWELL ROSTRON, M.A.

MISSIONARY METHODS, ST. PAUL'S OR OURS ?
By the Rev. ROLAND ALLEN, M.A.

"The 'Library of Historic Theology' is a project of great promise. Several volumes by eminent writers have already appeared and the issue of such a series amply demonstrates that there is no decline in the interest felt all through the ages in theological literature."— *Homiletic Review.*

Further important announcements will be made in due course ; full particulars may be obtained from the Publisher, Robert Scott, Paternoster Row, London, E.C.

LONDON : ROBERT SCOTT, PATERNOSTER ROW, E.C.

Lightning Source UK Ltd.
Milton Keynes UK
UKOW06f0939191116
288021UK00024B/748/P